Heroes, Antiheroes and Dolts

Heroes, Antiheroes and Dolts

Portrayals of Masculinity in American Popular Films, 1921–1999

Ashton D. Trice *and* Samuel A. Holland

McFarland & Company, Inc., Publishers
Jefferson, North Carolina, and London

Library of Congress Cataloguing-in-Publication Data

Trice, Ashton D., 1958–
    Heroes, antiheroes, and dolts : masculinity in American popular films,
1921–1999 / Ashton D. Trice and Samuel A. Holland.
        p.   cm.
    Includes bibliographical references and index.
    ISBN 0-7864-1097-3 (softcover : 50# alkaline paper) ∞
    1. Men in motion pictures.   2. Heroes in motion pictures.
3. Motion pictures — United States — History.   I. Holland, Samuel A.
II. Title.
PN1995.9.M46   T75   2001
791.43'652041— dc21   2001044064

British Library cataloguing data are available

Manufactured in the United States of America

*McFarland & Company, Inc., Publishers
    Box 611, Jefferson, North Carolina 28640
    www.mcfarlandpub.com*

Contents

Part IV — Superheroes and Dolts   165

Preface

by Ashton D. Trice

I like movies. I like big budget Hollywood movies — musicals, special effects films, Biblical epics, Disney animation, social dramas, comedies. *E.T.* and *Dumbo* never fail to provoke a sad reaction, and I can still, after a dozen viewings, get a jolt or two out of *Jaws*. I can watch *Bringing Up Baby* twice in one day and still find every scene funny. I like the current spate of low-budget independent films. *Clerks* and *Living in Oblivion* make me laugh out loud, and I can go back again and again to serious independent films like *Matewan*, *Swoon*, and *Box of Moonlight*. I like foreign films, particularly those of Truffaut and Kurosawa — the *Wild Child* and *Ikiru* are two of my favorite films, and I almost always show them in my freshman course in human development. The first movie I remember seeing as a child — which continues to be one of my favorite films — was *Rear Window*. I have copies of all of Hitchcock's sound films, and I watch them again and again, particularly *Blackmail*, *The 39 Steps*, *The Lady Vanishes*, *Vertigo*, *Psycho*, *The Birds*, *Marnie*, and *Frenzy*. My other favorite film is Fellini's *8½*, but picking a favorite Fellini film is difficult. On different days I might pick *Il Bidone*, *La Strada*, *La Dolce Vita*, *Roma*, or *La Barca Va*.

My ambition when I was a college freshman was to be a composer for the movies. In college I worked on two experimental films which were distributed by Film Maker's Cooperative, from which, over two decades, I received almost 40 dollars in royalties. I was the vice-president of the college's film board during my junior year, during which we showed *Citizen Kane*, *The Red Desert*, and *La Dolce Vita*, as well as Jack Smith's *Flaming Creatures* and Kenneth Anger's *Scorpio Rising*. Because of the last two shows, I wasn't invited back the following year to the film board. After graduation I composed a couple of scores for PBS. Then I became a teacher. And then a psychologist.

Ten years ago a colleague of mine at Mary Baldwin College asked me to make a presentation at a state humanities conference on the topic of men in film. She was the program chair and was trying to get an interesting mix of perspectives. I asked a friend, Professor John Wells from the sociology department, to join me in an analysis of films, because he taught a course in Men's Studies which focused on the representation of male role behavior in contemporary films. We looked at the 16 most popular films in the decades of the 1940s, 1950s, 1960s, and 1970s in four categories — Westerns, war films, romantic comedies, and social dramas. The original version of that paper is lost, due to many mutilations on our computers, but that paper was the origin of this book.

John and I conducted a series of analyses of popular films over the next five years which resulted in ten papers at regional and national Popular Culture conferences in the men's studies and film sections. We tossed around the idea of a book, but it never materialized, partially because the analytical tools of the disciplines of psychology (mine) and sociology (his) are fundamentally different, and because we both had competing interests in our personal and professional lives at the time. Eventually, I decided that another problem Professor Wells and I had was that we were both from the same generational cohort: we saw things from the same historical context, although from different disciplinary takes. We had grown up watching the films of the 1940s on television. We had seen *The Godfather* in our early twenties, and were nearing 30 when *Star Wars* came out. The teen-pics of the past decade we viewed through the eyes of middle-aged men. If I were to ever write this book, it would have to be with someone from a younger generation. Some of the ideas in this book are attributable to discussions (sometimes arguments) that John and I had. In addition, the comments from audience members and reviewers of those papers shaped the ideas in this book.

In the summer of 1998, I had an opportunity to teach a course in "Images of Masculinity in Popular American Films" at the American University in Bulgaria. The 20 Bulgarian, Macedonian, and Romanian students in this class helped me look at a dozen American films from a very different perspective. Martin Andronov and Nicki Pentchev in particular helped me focus on aspects of the films that were peculiarly American. During the next year and a half I looked at about 300 films which were derived from Sackett's (1996) list of the five most popular films of each year from 1938 onward.

In the fall of 1999 I asked a student of mine, Sam Holland, to help me put the ideas I had about these films in order. Sam's major qualifications were that he had a sharp eye, had seen a lot of movies, and was in his early twenties. For ten months, Sam and I looked at a smaller group of films I had selected for this book and discussed them. His perspective on films often conflicted with mine, but because we both came from the disciplinary perspective of psychology, we also often saw things in the same way. While I did much of the initial writing, Sam provided essential commentary on what I had written.

It is perhaps useful to say how Sam and I see this book. It could be viewed as a book of film history, film criticism, or men's studies. But our primary focus was on these films and their representation of masculinity from a popular culture perspective. We want to ask why these films were popular and what their popularity says about what it has meant at various times to be male. Although guided by a few ideas, such as Pleck and Pleck's (1980) social history of masculinity and Sandra Bem's and Carole Gilligan's sex role theories, we have tried to be empirical rather than theory-driven. We wanted to let the films speak for themselves without a certain perspective being imposed on them.

It is also fair to say, upfront, that as psychologists, we have not used psychoanalytic tools in discussing these films, except in the cases where the filmmakers, such as Hitchcock, themselves were using Freudian theory to tell stories. The vast majority of psychologists have rejected Freudian and neo–Freudian analyses for the last five decades. We honor Freud because he asked many of the right questions. We reject him because most of his answers were wrong. We realize that this rejection of psychoanalytical perspectives will put us at odds with traditional film criticism, but as we point out throughout the book, there are many others who are becoming dissatisfied with this perspective.

I also want to acknowledge an enormous debt to my long-time friend and media writer Donna McCrohan Rosenthal, who answered many technical questions about writing a film book, as well as answering questions about specific films, and who commented on several chapters in the book. We have exchanged many dozens of e-mails about this book over the last year and a half. If I remember correctly, Donna and I first had a conversation around 1961, on the bus home from eighth grade, and it was about Valentino. She tried to slip one of Valentino's poems into the high school literary magazine I edited in 1964. We have been correspondents over the ensuing 30-some years, and my first publication was a small piece in her book *The Honeymooners' Companion,* a nice gesture to a first year graduate student who needed money. Donna threw a few other welcome writing assignments my way during my student days. Donna's commentary on these chapters made me realize that had I selected a female co-author rather than Sam, this book might well be quite different, but a male perspective on masculinity in American movies was what we intended.

I have also had many long and productive conversations with my father, a retired psychologist, about these films, particularly those of the 1930s and 1940s. His insights as a person who watched these films when they first appeared have been particularly helpful.

Our primary hope is that this book will spark readers to watch some of these films which they have never seen before, and to enjoy them with an understanding of the times in which they were created. As we look back on the 20th century, certainly one of the jewels of our culture is Hollywood cinema. Films like *The Best Years of Our Lives, Casablanca, The Son of the Sheik, Who's Afraid of Virginia Woolf?, Battleground,* and *The Lion King* should help us understand who we are and where we have been.

Any mistakes are the authors'. The perspective is only one of many that can be taken on looking at films and masculinity.

Introduction

In this book, we will examine changes in the representation of men and masculinity in popular movies from 1921 through 1999. Before beginning this effort directly, it may be of use to answer four questions related to the book's contents: Why study only popular films? Why limit our examination to the American audience? Why study men and masculinity? and Why study change?

Why Study Popular Films?

By "popular" we mean those films which had the highest box office at the time of their release.[1] Films which draw large audiences may not always please the critics (although many did when released and continue to do so), but they are of special interest to students of popular culture for two reasons.

First, the movie industry is a social institution which mirrors prevalent images of our culture. The mass appeal of a film is of special importance: a film's popularity attests to its being a mirror into which the audiences of its day liked to gaze. An analysis of a popular film, or better, a cluster of films, gives us clues about how large numbers of people liked to see themselves at a particular time. In the present context, it will help us understand what it meant to be male at a particular time.

Second, film influences how we see ourselves and conduct our lives. Film influences us in small and large ways. *The Son of the Sheik* (1926) is credited with making the wristwatch replace the pocket watch for men, and when Gable took off his shirt in *It Happened One Night* (1934) revealing only his chest, the undershirt industry took a tumble. Today's students who grew up on *Star Wars* (1977) will probably never tuck in their shirts. In addition to

1

fashion, film influences our language (*Bill and Ted's Excellent Adventure* [1989] introduced a half dozen moronic expressions into everyday speech) and our social customs (*Father of the Bride* [1950] defined home weddings for several generations), and may even change the way in which we view important cultural prohibitions, such as interracial marriage (*Sayonara* [1957] and *Guess Who's Coming to Dinner* [1967] clearly argued for tolerance on this issue). The most popular films have the potential to effect the greatest societal change because of their direct influence on the largest numbers of people.

We are faced with the problem of how movies can function both as a mirror to society and as an agent of social change. Hollywood has certainly tried to accomplish both of these feats. It is not difficult to understand the industry's motivation of achieving popularity. Producers, distributors, and studio executives, if not writers and directors, want to attract large audiences, and from the beginning, business strategies aimed at popularity have intruded on the artistic tactics of filmmaking. "Sneak previews" that test the market, and the changes that sometimes result from these tests, offer conspicuous examples of how Hollywood struggles to find the right mirror.

Efforts have also been directed toward influencing audience behavior. Most of these efforts recently have been aimed at inducing the audience to buy spin-off and "placed" products: the recipe for the Bond martini was changed from equal parts of gin, vodka, and vermouth in the Ian Fleming novels to vodka and vermouth — shaken, not stirred — when Smirnoff backed the early films. George Lucas early on envisioned the *Star Wars* engine as a means of selling T-shirts and toys. But it is also clear that studios have tried to influence the social and political behavior of their audiences, particularly in the 1940s and 1950s. Individual directors and screenwriters have had and continue to have similar motivations about a very wide range of social and political issues.

As we wrote this book, the restriction of looking only at popular films sometimes proved frustrating. Some films that we wanted to discuss fell short of the mark on box office. It was difficult at the start of writing this book to imagine talking about the postwar 1940s without *It's a Wonderful Life* (1946), the 1950s without *Rebel Without a Cause* (1955), or the 1960s without *Dr. Strangelove* (1964) or *A Hard Day's Night* (1964). But we have found that we have a wealth of information without these films.

Why Limit Our Attention to the American Audience?

We will be concerned in this book only with films which were popular with American audiences. Mostly these were Hollywood films, although some British films and an occasional European film made the cut. We are interested in the relationship between the representation of men in movies and the culture of the time in which they were made — how they reflected cultural values, and how they changed them. By concentrating on one culture, the relationship between the images and the times will be more obvious. Moreover, our reading of authors outside of American culture on American films often finds them out of touch with our understanding of those movies. We are not simply talking about something as peculiar as the French admiration for Jerry Lewis or the fact that baseball films don't export well. In a later chapter we will discuss Umberto Eco's commentary on *Casablanca* (1943). Eco is certainly a critic to be reckoned with, but much of what he says about this film seems oddly wrong. His statements that the film is badly acted and that the dialogue is unbelievable make one wonder whether he knows the film in an English-language or Italian-language version. One of us recently caught *Casablanca* on Italian television, and the dialogue was hilarious ("I am watching you, little goat" does not have quite the same meaning as, "Here's looking at you, kid") and the choice of voice actors seemed completely misguided. Likewise, seeing films such as *Pulp Fiction* (1994) and *The Matrix* (1999) in Italian theaters was distinctly different from seeing the same films at home. No one laughed once throughout *Pulp Fiction*, which was not perceived by any of our Italian friends as a comedy. After viewing *The Matrix*, our Italian friends wanted to try to work out its sociological and political meaning. At home, in America, discussions were mostly about the cool effects.

If one needs more convincing, we recommend the excellent new book by James Chapman (2000), *License to Thrill*, about the Bond film series. This study places the individual films in their British contexts, which are often quite different from the American ones. In our chapter on the Bond films we are interested in such issues as the Cuban missile crisis; Chapman is interested in issues such as the loss of empire, the welfare state, and even specific events, such as the theft of major paintings from British museums which find their way into SPECTRE headquarters.

Why Study Men?

Our search of our university library for books on gender studies of films produced 72 titles. Seventy-one were about women in the movies; one, W.R. Robinson's 1969 edited volume *Man and the Movies*, was about men, though only occasionally about "the male." Many of the contributions are about "the human." One reason for undertaking our book is to address the imbalance of gender-film studies.

Some, but by no means all, feminists have strenuously objected to "men's studies" because they assert that prior to the emergence of "women's studies," all academic studies were of men. In our discipline, psychology, there *were* more studies of men than women prior to 1970. This is true largely because many psychological studies are of students in psychology 101 courses, and prior to 1970, there were more male college students than women. Studies of school children and clinical populations were more balanced. Now the majority of subjects in psychological research are women because of the preponderance of women in introductory psychology classes.

In other areas such as art, music, and pre–nineteenth century literature, where most of the practitioners were men, most analyses were given to male artists. Yet there have been few studies, prior to the beginning of gender studies in the 1970s and 1980s, of these artists *qua* men. One finds, for example, in art historical studies, some attention to the impact of the sexual orientation of (presumed) gay artists such as Donatello, Michelangelo, and Caravaggio on their work, but there is little attention to the obvious heterosexuality of painters such as Fra Lippo Lippi or Orazio Gentileschi. Likewise in music or literature, attention to maleness is given only to male composers and writers whose sexuality deviate beyond the norm. No one comments on Bach's maleness.

In film criticism, too, one finds much more commentary about deviation than maleness. While Hitchcock's films are occasionally discussed in terms of his assumed repressed homoeroticism or his presumed hatred of women and considerably more attention has been given to Ed Wood's transvestitism than his film *oeuvre* deserves (Grey, 1994), little attention has been paid to John Ford or Howard Hawks as men.[2]

In this book, we will be rarely interested in the sex, sexual orientation, or sexual quirks of the writers or directors or actors who made the films; instead we will concentrate on the characters on the screen. Whatever the facts and quirks of Edith M. Hull (novelist), George Medford (director) or Valentino (star), when we view *The Shiek* (1921) it is Ahmed Ben Hassan who is on the screen — pop-eyed would-be rapist, morose lover, or leader of a warrior tribe — and it is that image to which the audience responded and which is our basic unit of analysis.

There are, of course, excellent books about the representation of men in the movies, to which we will be referring throughout this book. But these books typically are about individual actors or directors, specific genres — particularly those considered male genres, such as westerns or war films — or limited periods of time. There is nothing comparable in scope to Molly Haskell's (1967/1987) pioneering book on the representation of women in the movies, *From Reverence to Rape,* for men. We want to look across genres and over a long period of time, primarily from 1939 to 1999, because our interest is in *change.* What will be different in our approach from Haskell's work is that rather than trying to be encyclopedic, we will concentrate on representative, popular films.

Preparing for this book, we viewed the five most popular films of each year, from 1939 through 1999. Rather than writing a few sentences about each of more than 300 films, we decided to select about a fifth of them on which to make detailed commentary.

Why Study Change?

Many studies of women in film (although certainly not all) appear to take the position that the representation of women — and by extension, men — has remained the same over the last century of filmmaking. We believe, however, that there have been at least three distinctly different clusters of the representation of men in film. Prior to World War II, men were most often represented within the context of a family, corresponding to what Pleck and Pleck (1980) refer to as "the Companionate/Providing" society.[3] In their study of American social history, the Plecks find that the role as romantic companion and family provider were the primary male roles from 1920 until 1965. Although we might immediately think of a film such as *Gone with the Wind* (1939) as a Civil War picture, the war itself is barely represented. Rather, it is about love and marriage and the loss of family. As we will see, even during the war years of 1942–1945, this image of the male as embedded in family was the most conspicuous in the most popular films. Films such as *Mrs. Miniver* (1942) and *Yankee Doodle Dandy* (1942) are basically films about how families work: true battle films never rose that high in popularity.

While the Plecks see the Companionate/Providing society as extending until 1965, we believe that there is a new perspective on men following the war, in which the masculine roles of companion and provider came to be questioned, and the ordinary man (and woman) began to be concerned with issues beyond their immediate family. The popular social dramas of the 1950s and 1960s did not portray the family as a safe refuge for anyone, and there were concerns that the fabric of American society was coming unraveled. One need only think about films like *Cat on a Hot Tin Roof* (1958) or *Peyton Place* (1957) to note a change in the depiction of the American family. Prior to World War II, most Americans lived their whole lives in the region of the country in which they were born. They accepted the social norms and customs of those places. But exposure to others from distinctly different American backgrounds, as well as Europeans and Asians, brought about questioning of many of those norms, including views on racial and religious segregation, women's roles, and social class barriers. The blockbuster *Giant* (1956) shows a difficult but loving family dealing with segregation, independent women, and the sudden rise of poor, working class men into the social and political elite after the discovery of oil.

After the war, there were two major migrations — one geographic, as more people entered corporate America and were moved about the country because of their jobs, and the other economic, as large numbers of individuals, because of educational and financial benefits afforded to veterans, entered the middle class. Many of these migrants felt out of place and uncomfortable with their new situations. It became more acceptable for couples to divorce. People became more comfortable discussing extramarital affairs, delinquent children, and personal problems. Literature and film gave rise to a new principal character, the antihero, the man or woman overwhelmed by his or her situation.

The third period begins sometime after 1970. Although placing the transition somewhat earlier, the Plecks ascribe this transition to social movements, such as civil rights, the anti-war movement, and feminism. Perhaps the pivotal film events are *Butch Cassidy and the Sundance Kid* (1969) and *Star Wars* (1977). *Butch Cassidy* established the tradition of the popular buddy film. Here, we are almost relieved when Etta Place (Katharine Ross) exits and leaves Butch (Paul Newman) free to complete his wayward life with Sundance (Robert Redford). Eight years later, in *Star Wars,* Luke Skywalker (Mark Hamill), Han Solo (Harrison Ford), Obi-Wan Kenobi (Alec Guinness), and the male androids R2-D2 and C-3PO team up to rescue Princess Leia (Carrie Fisher); the plot reminds us of the way that the Scarecrow, Tinman, and Cowardly Lion team up to save Dorothy in *The Wizard of Oz* (1939), but the Princess is much less a central character than Dorothy. Luke's attraction for her turns out to be fraternal, and the relationship between the Princess and Han will never go anywhere serious. The film is concerned with male relationships to other males.

Very recently there is a hint of a return to a positive view of romantic relationships. This trend will be discussed in the last chapter of this book.

Plan of the Book

We will begin our analysis in earnest with the five most popular films of 1939, because it was only at that time that reliable box office figures began to exist, and because we want to have a basis for comparing the changes which occurred in the representation of men during and after World War II. We will then move on to the films made during World War II and those made about the war subsequently. We will consider the fad of biblical epics in the 1950s, James Bond and Disney films, the *Star Wars* films, and recent films in which men are portrayed as idiots.

Regrettably, starting in 1939 seriously truncates American film history. There were 40 years of silent filmmaking and a decade of sound films prior to 1939. It is estimated that over 75 percent of these early films are lost, entirely or in part, and it is very difficult to estimate viewership prior to the late 1930s. Nevertheless, it would be remiss to totally ignore these early five decades, so we will begin our analysis with a nod to the greatest silent male star, Rudolph Valentino.

PART I

In the Beginning

The purpose of these first two chapters is to provide a baseline against which to compare later films. For most of the first four decades of filmmaking, we have little to go on. As few thought of the movies as an art form that might be appreciated in the future, little regard was paid toward preserving the original prints, so most of these films have vanished; many which remain can be viewed only in partial or damaged versions. And we have little or no evidence with regard to popularity until the very late 1940s.

Yet it would clearly be a serious omission to disregard these years completely, so we have included two chapters focusing on them. The first is on the films of Rudolph Valentino, perhaps the first male movie star, and certainly the longest lived male movie star. People who have never sat through an entire Valentino film may have some notion of who he was and the kinds of roles he played. That notion may not be correct, however. We will discuss three of his most important films, *The Four Horsemen of the Apocalypse* (1921), his first starring role, *The Sheik* (1921), his most enduring screen image, and *The Son of the Sheik* (1926), his last role and — for better or worse — the film which showed studios that sequels made money. In this chapter we will try to arrive at an answer to the question: Why was Valentino so popular?

In the second chapter, we will look at the five most popular films of 1939, the so-called "watershed" year of Hollywood filmmaking. These include *Gone with the Wind*, certainly not a film about men, but including some complex male characters; *The Wizard of Oz*, a film that may be more about masculinity than one would suspect at first glance; *Jesse James*, a Western with a fatalistic theme and a lawman who sees everything as morally ambiguous; *The Hunchback of Notre Dame*, a film about sound and silence, truth and illusion; and *Mr. Smith Goes to Washington*, a film that started out its life as a screwball comedy of jumbled sex roles and evolved over time into a drama about integrity.

One — Valentino, the First Star?

Rudolph Valentino may have been the first male movie "star."[1] If he was, although there is little consensus about anything in the age of silent films, he is an appropriate point for beginning a study of the representation of men and masculinity in popular American movies. He is the one male actor of the silent age who remains an icon of masculinity. He appears to be one of the first male actors whose presence in a film could guarantee box office success, whether the films were critically well received or not, and in his brief six years as a leading man between 1921 and his death in 1926, he appeared in more than a dozen feature films which included several mega-hits: *The Four Horsemen of the Apocalypse* (1921), *The Uncharted Seas* (1921), *Camille* (1921), *The Sheik* (1921), *Blood and Sand* (1922), *Monsieur Beaucaire* (1924), *A Sainted Devil* (1924), *Cobra* (1925), and *The Son of the Sheik* (1926). He published a best-selling fitness book in 1923, and that same year a book of poetry, entitled *Day Dreams*.

In 1924, a survey of high school students indicated that their favorite film, for both boys and girls, was The *Four Horsemen of the Apocalypse*, and among girls, their second favorite film was *The Sheik* (Koszarski, 1990). There is evidence that Valentino's posthumous release, *The Son of the Sheik* was the most widely seen film of the decade. It is of interest to ask: Why was Valentino so popular?

As elsewhere in this book, we will concentrate on a few films. Here we will examine three of Valentino's films, *The Four Horsemen of the Apocalypse*, *The Sheik*, and *The Son of the Sheik*. These films were selected because they are known to have been very popular and are currently available in inexpensive, restored versions.

Valentino was also one of the first film actors whose personal life was a matter of popular interest. He was born Alfonzo Raffaelo di Valentina d'Antonguolla in Castellaneta, Italy, in 1895, and came to the United States by way of Paris in 1913. In New York he made his living as a dance hall dancer and then as a dancer in the theater. The following year he was working in East Coast films. Two years later he moved to the West Coast to become a full-time film actor. Beginning in 1918 he found small roles in a number of films.

Valentino's personal life often came dangerously close to overwhelming his image as the world's greatest lover. His first marriage was not consummated because his wife left him on their wedding night for a female lover, and his second marriage was to the domineering acting coach Natacha Rambova, who took control of his career and placed him in a number of roles which played dangerously with his virile image: in *Monsieur Beaucaire* he spent most of his screen time hideously and effeminately made up (although he does strip to the waist in a central scene), and this role lead to the so-called "pink powder puff" scandal — a series of innuendoes that Valentino's heavy make-up carried over to his personal life[2]; he is dominated in lovemaking in *Blood and Sand*; and he is viciously whipped and tortured in *Son of the Sheik*. Valentino's subservience to Rambova was hinted at in the press, and his sporting of a slave bracelet lead to speculation about his "masculinity." Yet the innuendoes did little to prevent his box office draw. He died suddenly in 1926 before the release of *Son of the Sheik*. His funeral was one of the pop culture events of the century, with thousands of women weeping outside the funeral home, and the vamp screen goddess Pola Negri hurling herself on his coffin, vowing eternal devotion.

The Four Horsemen of the Apocalypse

Valentino's first starring role was as Julio in Rex Ingram's *The Four Horsemen of the Apocalypse*, a film which has been described as a "canny arrangement of grand emotional episodes, which highlighted Valentino in scenes of aggressive sexuality, seduction, rejection, and reconciliation" (Koszarski, 1990, p. 301). *The Four Horsemen* was regarded at the time as a fine film, one which still bears viewing for Valentino's performance. But it is not a film which one could universally recommend to today's viewers: there are two unbelievable coincidences on which the plot hinges, and there are a lot of bad special effects, based very loosely on the Book of Revelation, which may have given the film a kind of meaningful symbolism at the time, but which now seem pretentious. The fiery beast of the Apocalypse now looks like something from a 1950s Japanese sci-fi movie, and the four horsemen themselves remind us more of a KISS concert (heavy make-up, fire-breathing, tongue wagging) than the Biblical end of time. (More likely it is KISS that is imitating the

Four Horsemen, but the association will be the other way for most present-day viewers.)

The plot structure, although set in South America and Europe, seems very familiar: the members of an aristocratic plantation family find themselves on opposite sides of a great conflict. Here, rather than being the American Civil War, we have the third generation of an Argentinean family on opposite sides of World War I. One major difference occurs between this film and the typical Civil War stories of the period: there is no hesitation in which side has the moral prerogative. While the French may have their faults (Julio's father is a stereotypical French miser), the Germans are thoroughly unlikable and evil. Twelve years before Hitler's assent to power, they are obsessed with being a master-race, disdainful of all cultures but their own, regimented, amoral followers of vicious leaders, and potential murders and rapists all.

Julio is the spoiled grandson of an old bandit who has become the largest landowner in Argentina. The grandfather has two daughters. The older, Julio's mother, has married a Frenchman, while the younger has married a bespectacled German and produced three bespectacled blond sons, whom the grandfather dislikes. The grandfather has lead Julio into the wild life of heavy smoking, heavy drinking, and tango dancing, which Julio can do adroitly, simultaneously. Now that the film can be seen at its original speed rather than in the speeded up versions often seen in clips, Valentino's dancing ability is clear, and his tango in an early sequence very appealingly combines incipient violence with enormous grace and strength.

When the grandfather dies, everyone is startled that he has not left everything to Julio. Rather, he has divided his fortune equally between his two daughters. The German immediately announces he is going back to civilization (the Fatherland), and Julio's mother suggests that perhaps her children, too, should become aware of their roots by moving to Paris. There Julio takes up painting, presumably because he likes the models. Dad's penurious ways put a crimp on his style (although Julio has an enormous studio, a servant, and a very likable pet monkey who answers the door and reads the evening paper). Eventually he falls in love with the young wife of one of his father's cronies. At first he merely takes her dancing, but they start meeting in his studio for at least heavy petting. She's young; her husband is old; the marriage was arranged. Perhaps there was sympathy with their situation. But we are only on the cusp of the age of the flapper, so when their affair is discovered, almost simultaneously with the outbreak of the war, her husband divorces her, and Julio's father can barely look at him. She begins nurse's training, and Julio begins to feel the strain of being an outsider in a land where right and wrong have suddenly become very clear: he is not French, so there is no imperative for him to fight, but fighting on the side of the French is clearly the right thing to do, and thus his do-nothing position becomes morally ambivalent. As he walks through the streets of Paris in his aristocratic clothes, he is out of synch with all the men in uniform.

In the first of the major coincidences, Julio tracks down his sweetheart at Lourdes where she is working as a Red Cross nurse, moments after she has been assigned to her ex-husband, who has been blinded in battle. Her ex does not recognize her, but seeing him in his helpless condition has left her unwilling to continue her affair with Julio. Julio, despondent, decides to enlist.

This scene, improbable as it may seem, is also unsettling because it is based on a message about masculinity that is at odds with more recent popular films about war: it is the connection with women which normally makes men brave. The husband, boyfriend, or son will fight for the sake of the women in his life. But in this scene, we discover that both the ex-husband and Julio find their heroism when their bonds with the women they love have been broken. Then, they have nothing to lose. All of the women in this film try to prevent the men they love from risking their lives: Julio's mother does not want him to volunteer; his sister Chi-Chi is happy that her fiancé Rene will remain in Paris as a "sugar soldier"; and one Parisian woman is so distraught when her boyfriend goes off to the front that she hurls herself from the top of a building. Of course, this is a film made immediately *after* a war, when the audience was dealing with the aftermath of war. Many men did not return, and many, like Rene, would return mutilated. This is no propagandistic film, espousing the virtues of war, but a film dealing with its realities.

There is a long and interesting sequence in the movie which occurs when Julio's father goes to his castle in the country which is commandeered by the Germans as their headquarters. The Germans plunder his prize possessions, drink his wine, prance about in drag, and generally behave like loutish Huns. One of the occupiers is his nephew, who has no sympathy for his uncle. When the butler shoots an officer (Wallace Beery) who is about to rape a young female servant, Dad protests, and his nephew locks him in the cellar for daring to criticize Germans. The next morning as he is reluctantly digging his own grave, the French liberate his castle.

Four years pass, and we are told that Julio has become a war hero. Valentino now looks lean and tired, and his face is dirty and unshaven. His father comes to visit him near the trenches, finally reconciling with him over his extravagant ways as an art student and as a seducer of his friend's wife. He's even brought along the fetching little monkey, who has his own little uniform, little helmet, and little backpack.

The second coincidence is the climax of the film, in which Julio and his cousin meet on No Man's Land; despite his father's warning not to be sentimental in war, he hesitates before shooting his cousin — but, no matter — they are both blown to bits by a mortar shell.

While this coincidence is strange enough, there is more. Framing this sequence are two scenes where Julio's girl is ministering to her former husband. Immediately before Julio is killed, she has decided that she has had enough of her dependent ward, and she writes him a letter (although he is blind) telling him that she is going back to Julio. After Julio's death, as she is about to leave, Julio's ghost appears at the door, and she comes back into the room, and, understanding that Julio is dead, she burns the letter.

In the final scene, Julio's family is standing in a huge, crowded graveyard on a steep hill. Chi-Chi, mom, and dad are saying good-bye to Julio. Rene stands nearby, his face scarred and missing an arm. Off to one side is Julio's strange upstairs neighbor from his art student days, the one who unleashed the images of the four horsemen by showing Julio Albrecht Dürer's engravings of the Book of Revelation. "Did you know my son?" Dad asks the neighbor. Gesturing grandly to the whole cemetery, the neighbor says, "I knew them all." We then see the four horsemen riding away, and the final written image tells us presciently that they might be back.

Despite all the metaphysical hooey and the contrived plot,[3] it is not hard to understand why *The Four Horsemen of the Apocalypse* made Valentino a star. He may no longer be our image of a sex symbol, but at times he photographed extremely well, and he moved with an easy grace that might remind us of current movie stars who began as dancers, such as Patrick Swayze or Jean-Claude Van Damme. What Valentino did well was portraying conflict. He is particularly effective in showing the man who is ashamed of having branded the woman he loves as an adulteress, of being a stranger in a strange land, of being cut off from his family.

We believe that there are also fairly clear standards of what it meant to be masculine in this film. While women may flinch at their men going away to war, when faced with a serious threat such as the Germans, a real man must fight. Real men can also love women passionately, but there are boundaries which must not be crossed. The husband who is too blind to see either that his wife needs attention or that others will give her what she needs, becomes literally blinded. Julio's affair with a married woman leads to only unhappiness for all involved.

The Sheik

Although *The Sheik* is a fairly straightforward action film, retelling the "beauty and the beast" story, it is a problematical film for many modern viewers. First, it portrays Arabs in a negative way, through a confused and inaccurate blend of Arab, Turkish, and Moorish images. Second, it appears to portray women as servile and masochistic.[4]

Its opening sequences focus on Lady Diana Mayo (Agnes Ayres), who is a trial to her family because of her headstrong and independent ways. She is planning a lengthy trip through the desert. In the evening of her arrival at Biskra, she wants to go to the casino, but the casino has been rented for the night by Sheik Ahmed Ben Hassan (Valentino), who is arranging a sale of potential wives to his men. Lady Mayo is annoyed that she will be excluded from the casino by the Sheik, whom she believes to be a savage desert bandit. She is informed that Ahmed is not a bandit, but a ruler of a group of honest Arabs. Moreover, she is told he is not savage: he has a Parisian education! She pays a dancer to give her an Arab costume so that she can enter the casino. There she is appalled by the treatment of women, and she is discovered and ejected unceremoniously. If this were the end of it, then we might view the film as a clear-cut reflection of the successful Suffrage Movement, which resulted in giving women the vote the previous year. But this is not the end of it.

The next morning, Ahmed enters Lady Di's room through the open balcony and leers at her while she sleeps. His exit wakens her, and she hears him serenading her with the tune "Beautiful Dreamer." But on the first leg of her desert journey, she becomes his captive. Captivity itself is not such a humiliation as is his insistence that she wear Arab costume. Ahmed attempts feebly to take her by force, but her resistance and horror prevent him from consummating the act. He allows her to return to European dress. Eventually, he also allows her some freedom, and while under the supervision of his French butler, she attempts an escape, but Ahmed finds her almost immediately. Slowly, they come to a *rapprochement*, and even mutual respect. During this period, Ahmed's friend, physician and novelist Raoul de Saint Hubert (Adolphe Menjou), arrives and supplies Lady Diana with information about Ahmed. He says that Ahmed has a great soul, and perhaps through the love of the right woman, he can get in touch with that part of him. She Orientalizes her costume, while simultaneously Ahmed begins to treat her as an English lady. Then, on another outing with the butler, after doodling a note of her love for Ahmed in the sand, she is attacked by real Arab bandits. Knowing what is in store for her in this camp, she asks the butler to shoot her, but before he can pull the trigger, he is shot, and she is abducted. Ahmed comes upon her message, miraculously preserved in the sand, and he musters all his troops to save her.

The leader of the bandits (Walter Long) has again put her in full Arab gear and is preparing to rape her, when simultaneously his wife attacks him with a knife, and Ahmed and his men breach the walls of the bandits' city. Lady Mayo's virtue remains intact, but Ahmed is severely wounded. Back at his own camp, Ahmed is comatose; his men wait to see whether he weathers his physical crisis; and Saint Hubert provides Western medicine. In one of the most outlandish moments of the film, Saint Hubert tells Lady Mayo that Ahmed is not really an Arab, but the son of English and Spanish parents who was raised as the son of the previous sheik. Now that race is out of the way, she can commit herself to Ahmed, and he opens his eyes and their love seems to be cemented. In an odd coda to the film, Saint Hubert goes out and tells Ahmed's men that time will tell whether he recovers, leaving some ambiguity to whether this is a happy ending or not.[5]

Reviewers were not enthusiastic. The central part of the short review in the *New York Times* (November 7, 1921) went as follows:

> ...the photoplay tells the story of an unusually spiritless English girl who is abducted by an exceedingly gentle desert sheik, but will not admit that she loves him until she is captured by a really tough Arab and realizes how perfectly safe she is with her tamer admirer. Somehow, this doesn't seem to be exactly the idea of Mrs. Hull's novel ... but never mind; here's the picture tale of a nice sheik and his agreeable English girl. And you won't be offended by having a white girl marry an Arab, either.... These romantic Arabian movies, you know, never have the courage of their romantics [20:1].

With regard to the negative image of Arabs, it is important to note that the book and film came out two and four years, respectively, after the end of World War I, in which Turkey was a member of the Axis (and this film cannot differentiate between Turks and Arabs). And while the most negative aspect of the portrayal of Arabs in this film is their treatment of women as chattel, it is worth remembering that women had become voting citizens in the United States only a year *after* the novel and a year before the movie. Moreover, some of the negative situations portrayed in the film, such as the sale of women, are historically accurate, although others, such as the drinking and gambling by Arab men in the casino, are not. Those are Western vices.

As for the film's portrayal of women, Molly Haskell (1987) comments sagely on the role of women in the films of the 1920s:

> For the most part, Victorian values prevailed in silent films and even as the "It" girl, who, with her inventor, the British novelist Elinor Glyn, became a naturalized Hollywood citizen, was not as naughty as she seemed, but rather a disturber of the peace, redeemable by marriage [p. 45].

Finally, what we are interested in is the portrayal of men and masculinity. Ahmed *learns* in this film. He learns that women are not chattel; he learns that there are things that are worth risking one's life for. And because he is a good learner, he is saved.

Six years later he has learned some of these lessons well, but not others.

The Son of the Sheik

Son of the Sheik established a pattern for movie sequels: the characters and plot are largely the same, but the special effects are better. Now we are dealing with the old sheik's son, and like father, like son. Ahmed Jr. (Valentino) has slipped away from his father's citadel, strictly against orders, and encounters a band of ethnically mixed entertainers/thieves. He is particularly captivated by the daughter of the French leader of the troupe, Yasmin (Vilma Banky), a dancer, whose act seems to be an over-the-top Charleston, which drives men wild. Young Ahmed and Yasmin are mutually attracted, and when she tells him of her poverty, he offers her money. She declines his offer, explaining that the men in her group would merely gamble it away. She tells him that she often walks in the evening alone in the ruins, and he gives her a ring to remember him by. She is overheard, and when he shows up, and after they bill and coo for a good while, he is captured and held for ransom. The problem with the abduction scheme is that they do not know who he is, and they must torture him to find out his identity. They truss him up by his arms, whip his bare chest, and pluck hair out of his abdomen and armpits. To demoralize him they tell him (falsely) that Yasmin has often lured other men into the same predicament.

Left guarded only by a loony dwarf, he is soon rescued by his men, and he abducts Yasmin and takes her back to his tent. He is less tentative than his dad had been, but he stops at actual rape. Anyway, despite their individual rage, he at being duped, and she at being abducted, they each still find the other attractive.

Meanwhile, back home, the senior Ahmed, also portrayed by Valentino in convincing make-up, hears the good news that junior's intended bride will be arriving from Europe soon and the bad news that he has skipped town. Agnes Ayres reprises her role as a matronly Lady Diana, who knows her son better than his father does. Dad is angry enough about his son's disobedience to go after him in a rage. Once in his son's tent, father confronts son, while one of young Ahmed's men tries to contain Yasmin's screams. Young Ahmed denies everything, but eventually objects are hurled in from the next room of the tent, and dad discovers what is going on. He demands that Yasmin be released. She had taken off Ahmed's ring, but she is unable to retrieve it before being sent home on the back of a donkey, in humiliation.

While Ahmed is recuperating from his beating, the troupe of entertainers/thieves arrives in town, and discovering that one of the men, Ghabah (Montague Love), has wicked, unwanted, and interracial intentions on Yasmin, young Ahmed enters and pays for a private dance with the ring he had given Yasmin. A fight breaks out and even dad joins in on the fun. With a nice bit of trick riding, young Ahmed stops and kills Ghabah as he flees with Yasmin. Dad notices the similarities between his son and himself, and sanctions the union between Yasmin and young Ahmed.

While this is another bit of fluff, there are several nice touches in this film. Gone are Valentino's bug-eyed leers — his acting is quite good, particularly in differentiating the older and younger Ahmed. The effects where Valentino portrays both Ahmeds, particularly in the fighting scenes, are really quite convincing, and probably a major reason for the popularity of the film. Despite decades of exposure to the technology of George Lucas' special effects wizards, we wonder: How did they do that?

So, we are still left with the question of why was Valentino so popular? The traditional wisdom is that he portrayed a new, exotic character, *the Latin lover.* The traditional explanation is that as women in the 1920s were becoming politically liberated through Suffrage and given more social freedom to do things such as to go to bars and restaurants unescorted, they became attracted to virile and even potentially dangerous men who were distinctly different from the men who would have been seen as desirable a generation earlier.

In these films and others, Valentino was certainly exotic. In *Four Horsemen,* except for the final trench scenes, he is dressed up in wild gaucho costumes or evening dress. His sheik costumes are straight out of the Ballet Russe staging of *Scheherazade.* He is handsome and athletic, and he does provoke an intense fascination for women. He is dangerous toward women — but only to a point. He may abduct them, but then he seduces them as willing partners with an almost adolescent intensity of emotion. He is the fantasy man who still exists today in romance novels. These fantasy men are often very different from the women who love them in terms of ethnicity and social class — potentially wild men like the moody gypsy Heathcliff in *Wuthering Heights.* But the love of a "civilized" woman transforms him into something between the savage and the bloodless WASP. Valentino's continuing fascination as a wild, sexual man who can also be counted on to exert a modicum of caution and discretion can be seen in the product named after his most enduring screen image — the Sheik condom.

We think that there is another reason for Valentino's popularity: his age. He was extremely young for a leading man at the time, 25 during the making of *Four Horsemen* and still only 30 during the making of *Son of the Sheik.* The typical older age of leading men reflected the actual age differences in husbands and wives during this period, when marriages were seen as economic institutions. Potential husbands had to have a track record in being able to support a family, and marriages were still commonly arranged or, minimally, approved of by the older generation. Today critics squawk if a fortyish male actor is paired with a twentyish female actor. The young wife and the older husband in *Four Horsemen* would not have appeared all that strange to the audience of 1921. But we are in a transition. The old husband's problem in *Four Horsemen* is not really his age but that he is not sensitive to her needs, and his young wife now has expectations that her husband will be more than a provider — he should be a romantic companion to her. Couples would be expected to find each other, now that women have the social freedom to meet men on their own. So each of these films represent a kind of fantasy hope that, while crossing the desert or dancing in a tango hall, a young woman might meet such a man, an agemate and perhaps, when tamed, a soulmate.

Two — 1939

We first see Rhett Butler (Clark Gable) in *Gone with the Wind* (1939) lounging on the lower curve of the banister of the grand staircase at Twelve Oaks plantation, looking up at Scarlett O'Hara (Vivien Leigh) as she ascends the stairs. Before we see him, Scarlett asks her friend Kathleen: "Who's that? ... that man looking at us, smiling ... the nasty, dark one."

After an establishing shot from Scarlett's perspective, the camera closes in as Rhett turns and leans against the finial post, smiling and staring back intently and directly at Scarlett as her friend provides a brief biography:

"My dear, don't you know? That's Rhett Butler. He's from Charleston. He has the most terrible reputation." Scarlett interrupts and says that he looks as if he knows what she looks like without her shimmy. Her friend continues: "My dear, he isn't received. He's had to spend most of his time up North because his folks in Charleston won't even speak to him. He was expelled from West Point, he was so fast. And then there's that business about that girl he wouldn't marry. He took her out buggy riding in the late afternoon without a chaperone. And then, and then he refused to marry her." The two women exchange giggles and whispers, and Kathleen comments: "No, but she was ruined just the same." Because of this information, we know that Rhett is going to be the more interesting of the two principal male characters. We also know this because it is Gable. By 1939 Gable had established himself as a virile rogue in dozens of romantic comedies and action films.[1]

We have just seen Ashley Wilkes (Leslie Howard) for the first time earlier in the scene. Scarlett believes that he will abandon his engagement to his cousin Melanie (Olivia de Havilland) when she tells him that she loves him. We also see him for the first time from Scarlett's point of view, as he ambles

19

casually down the same staircase toward her. He looks very blonde and very bland, and certainly not like a man greeting the woman he loves. What Scarlett says — that Rhett is "dark and nasty" and that Ashley is in love with her — is not at all what the audience sees.

Ashley cannot tell Scarlett directly about his love for Melanie. He can only hint about news he hopes will make her happy (that he and Melanie are to be married), and he pulls Scarlett and Melanie together and suggests that they should become great friends. His evasive chatter is in sharp distinction to Rhett's direct stare. Again, we suspect a good deal about this character because it is being played by Leslie Howard who had established his screen persona as the introspective romantic in *The Petrified Forest* (1936) and as the alternatively virile/effete hero of *The Scarlet Pimpernel* (1936).

1939

Nineteen thirty-nine is often called the "watershed year" in American filmmaking. It has this reputation not only because of the dozen or so enduring classics which were released,[2] but because 1939 was a high point in the motion picture business. The Hollywood studios produced over 400 feature films, and the average American saw 150 of them. Sound, color photography, and special effects had progressed to the point where directors could show whatever they wanted, and film acting had developed a more natural and less theatrical style, so that six decades later we can still view these films with pleasure.

We will describe male concerns in the five most popular films of that year, *Gone with the Wind, The Wizard of Oz, The Hunchback of Notre Dame, Jesse James,* and *Mr. Smith Goes to Washington.* We will be interested in the portrayal of the male characters as a base for which further studies can be contrasted. Particularly, we are interested in the idea that "World War II changed everything," and by spending some time on these five films produced right at the threshold of the war, we can see whether this commonplace slogan has legs.

Gone with the Wind

Gone with the Wind, based on Margaret Mitchell's 1936 best-seller, was the highest grossing movie of the year. Sackett (1996) estimates first release theatrical rentals over $77,000,000, considerably more than the second most popular film, *The Wizard of Oz,* which earned $4,500,000. But this figure is misleading because *Gone with the Wind* remained in first release for years, while *The Wizard of Oz* had a usual three month release.

The film is the episodic story of a planter's daughter from the first days of the Civil War through the first decade of Reconstruction. Scarlett's immediate world is full of women — a strong mother, two sisters and several sisters-in-law, two important house slaves, Mammy and Prissy, a daughter, and principally the ever present, ever patient Melanie Hamilton Wilkes, but her interests and actions are largely in the world of men, because her interests and actions are largely about money and land.

But what we are primarily interested in is the portrayal of the male characters and, by extension, seeing what vision of masculinity this film holds out for us. As our friend, media critic Donna McCrohan Rosenthal reminded us (personal communication, 1999), this film *is about Scarlett*. We do not want to repeat some of the blunders of various forms of deconstructionist criticism by transforming this picture into a film about Rhett and Ashley. It isn't. But Rhett and Ashley are well crafted, multi-dimensional characters, and we believe that they *can* tell us a good deal about the masculine values of 1939.

After the first scene on the staircase at Twelve Oaks, Rhett and Ashley are further contrasted in the two scenes which follow. In the first, Ashley and Rhett are having cigars and brandy with the other men while the women are napping upstairs. There is general excitement about the chance for Southern gentlemen to whip the Yankee rabble. Ashley is asked for his opinion. He says that if Georgia fights, he will, too, but like his father, he hopes that the North will allow the state to go quietly. When asked whether he does not want an opportunity to prove Southern gentlemen can always beat Yankees, he responds, "Most of the miseries of the world were caused by wars."

Mr. O'Hara then asks Rhett what he thinks, and he responds, "I think it's hard winning a war with words.... All we have is cotton, and slaves, and arrogance."

Rhett's comments provoke outrage and even a challenge to a duel by Melanie's young brother Charles, but Rhett excuses himself and asks permission to look around the plantation. When Charles suggests that Rhett's retreat reflects cowardice, cowardice which could be expected because Rhett is no gentleman, Ashley corrects him, telling him that Rhett is an expert shot and doesn't want to take advantage of him. Ashley then leaves, saying, "Mr. Butler's our guest. I think I'll just show him around." It is perhaps worth noting that Ashley, who is a thoroughly 19th century figure, is connected with his family — he is serving as host in his parent's house, while Rhett, a more 20th century hero, has been abandoned by his family because he has abandoned their values. (We will note later how often there is a mixing of types from the period represented and the period for which the film is intended.)

In the next scene Scarlett has been waiting for Ashley in the library. Here she confesses her love for him. Ashley is "too much the gentleman" to tell her the blunt truth: that he does not love her in the romantic way he loves Melanie. Instead, to let her down easily he says that he *does* love her, and all he can say of Melanie is that he and she are "of the same blood." Scarlett tries to cajole an amorous response from him, but when she pushes too far, he retreats. In fury, she throws a vase against the wall, provoking Rhett to sit up from the sofa on which he has been lying, unobserved. Scarlett is shocked that he had eavesdropped on her conversation and that he then teases her about what she said. Scarlett informs Rhett he is not a gentleman. Rhett agrees but promises that her guilty secret is safe with him.

Despite these and other deliberate contrasts throughout the film, Rhett and Ashley are not antagonists. They are, after all, on the same losing side of this war. While Rhett often holds Ashley in mild contempt, at other times they get along, most notably after Ashley is wounded participating in a Klan raid and Rhett covers his trail by taking him to Belle Watling's house of ill repute. Ashley and Rhett are in competition only in Scarlett's distorted perspective. (One way of viewing the Scarlett main plot of this film is that her perspective gradually becomes the perspective of the camera. She moves from childish egocentrism to an ability to understand the reality of the situation.)

Gone with the Wind, like many successful films we will discuss, deals with the issue of the difficulty of adapting to changing times. As *the* art form of the 20th century when rapid social change is the norm, it is not surprising that this is a perennial movie theme. Certainly this is the key issue in the most enduring of Chaplin's films, such as *The Gold Rush* (1925), *City Lights* (1931), and *Modern Times* (1936), and is the context for the problematic second half of *Birth of a Nation* (1915). The *Star Wars* films are also concerned with this issue: do Jedi values work in a post–Jedi society? Ashley looks back for rules to govern his behavior to a time of stability when there were workable conventions for every occasion. But the title of the film suggests the trouble with this approach is that such a time is "gone with the wind." His paralysis is due to the fact that his ideals provide no guidance in the new situations he finds himself in. Rhett, like Scarlett, makes up things pragmatically as he goes along. This pragmatism has two consequences. First, Rhett's conduct is often seen as outrageous by those who have not come to understand that there is a new world order — by the old rules, he is *not* a gentleman, as Scarlett frequently reminds him. More importantly for the romantic aspects of the plot, as both he and Scarlett are each making up the rules as they go, they are often out of synch with each other.

Rhett's disdain for the old rules is seen in high relief in the Monster Bazaar scene. He is introduced as a hero of the war. Yet, he is neither a soldier nor a planter, but a for-profit blockade runner — fundamentally a Yankee capitalist. He purchases a dance with Scarlett, even though this would be strictly forbidden under the code of mourning. (He will later propose to Scarlett in the downstairs room of her home which is still set up for the funeral of her second husband.) Yet, when it suits the occasions, there is chivalry about him. He does keep silent about Scarlett's meeting with Ashley, and after the Bazaar he purchases Melanie's wedding ring back after she has donated it to "the Cause." There is much about him that is similar to the kinds of characters that Valentino brought to the screen two decades earlier.

Hugs and Kisses

When Ashley returns to Atlanta for Christmas on furlough, he must deal with having the two women who love him under one roof. Again he fails to clarify his feelings for Melanie to Scarlett and allows himself to be drawn into her embrace. In distinct contrast to her furtive embrace with Ashley in the claustrophobic space under the staircase in his house in Atlanta, is the powerful scene with Rhett nine months later on the bridge at the fork to Tara. Rhett has led Scarlett, Melanie and her baby, and Prissy through the film's most spectacular special effect — the burning of Atlanta. There their figures seen only as shadows are dwarfed by the conflagration in which they find themselves. At the bridge, in extreme close up, against the flat, red sky of a sound stage, Rhett speaks the unadorned truth: "But there is one thing I do know, and that is that I love you, Scarlett. Despite you and me and the whole silly world going to pieces around us, I love you. Because we're alike. Bad lots, both of us, selfish and shrewd. But able to look things in the eye and able to call them by their right names."

By now, Rhett is more than selfish and shrewd. He has just given up a day of idle pleasure at Belle's to risk his life spiriting Scarlett and Melanie out of Atlanta, and he has just announced his intention to join the army because his conscience has finally caught up with him.

The beginning of the second half is the most compelling section of the film as the women begin to scratch a living out of the remnants of Tara and the men begin to recover from their physical and psychological war wounds. Prior to their third embrace, Scarlett and Ashley console and rally each other after a hard day of farming. Scarlett suggests that they run away together. "There's nothing to keep us here," she says.

Ashley looks startled. "Nothing?" he says. "Nothing but honor."

We can only speculate why he still cannot tell Scarlett that he loves his wife, and we are at a loss to understand Scarlett's infatuation with him. After talking about honor, he kisses her. This is a strange kind of honor, but both of them come immediately to their senses.

Scarlett soon engineers the complete emasculation of Ashley by giving him half ownership in her second husband's business, even after he states as directly as he states anything in the film that unless he makes something of himself on his own, he will have no self respect. Melanie suggests that they owe Scarlett a great deal, and Ashley caves in to her immediately. Then, in scene after scene, Scarlett compromises his idealism — by using convict labor, by forcing him to do business with the people who stole his plantation from him — leaving him with nothing for which he has any use. After the Klan action, he is wounded and helpless. Her second husband is dead.

With her second husband out of the way, Scarlett and Rhett are free to marry. On the honeymoon he comes to realize that Scarlett has demons which motivate her behavior, and he compensates for them. He builds a town house and restores Tara. In order that their daughter Bonnie will have social standing, he conforms to the demands of society for the first time. But in the sex-role understanding of 1939, it takes a "good woman" to tame a wild man, and when having a second child interferes with returning to an appropriate waistline, Scarlett cuts Rhett off sexually. Rhett (perhaps) misinterprets this action as Scarlett's continued love for Ashley, and he returns to his bachelor habits.

The most problematic scene in the film to contemporary viewers occurs after Rhett has forced Scarlett to attend a party for Ashley. Earlier in the day, she has been discovered yet again in Ashley's arms. Unlike the three previous embraces between them, which are romantic, this is one of compassionate friendship. But Ashley's sister India has seen them hugging, and the ugly rumor is abroad. Rhett dresses Scarlett in a flashy red dress and forces her to wear rouge. He leaves her at the front door to face the disapproval of Atlanta society alone. Melanie receives her, completely aware of the gossip and also completely secure of her husband's fidelity.

Rhett apparently visits Belle Watling's while the party is going on. Later, Scarlett awakens and comes downstairs for a drink. Rhett is drunk. Aware of what didn't happen at Ashley's party, he is angry that Scarlett has survived the social embarrassment he had planned for her. Scarlett says that she can explain. But Rhett is also angry that his wife cannot get another man out of her thoughts. He threatens to crush her skull like a walnut to get Ashley out of her mind. She tries to leave, but he wants to have it out with her. He tells her, "The comic figure in all this is the long-suffering Mr. Wilkes. He can't be mentally faithful to his wife and won't be unfaithful to her technically. Why can't he make up his mind?"

Rhett can of course make up his mind. He wants Scarlett, and he picks her up and sweeps her up the staircase. The next morning Scarlett is happy, conforming to the idea that what most uptight, off-sex career women need is a good boffing. Rhett is apologetic, but within moments they are at off-purposes, and Rhett says that he will be taking Bonnie to England. Uncharacteristically of them as individuals, but characteristic of them as partners, neither speaks his or her true mind.

Rhett does threaten Scarlett with physical violence in this scene. Scarlett likewise threatens him back, but is this scene one of marital rape? It is probable that the author and the audience of 1939 were disposed to view this

Rhett proposes to Scarlett in the room where her second husband's funeral has just taken place. Since both are modern folks, they have no hard and fast rules to guide their behavior, and they must make things up as they go along. Here Rhett seems to be trying to understand what lies beneath Scarlett's show of grieving widowhood.

scene positively, and that they looked at it in terms of romantic rather than sexual politics.[3] "No" didn't mean "yes," but it might mean "ask again." While Scarlett O'Hara might be an icon of the iron fisted woman entrepreneur, in the romantic arena she ascribed to the role of the flirt. This scene perhaps should not be viewed sociologically as a statement about all men and women, but rather psychologically about two specific individuals: Rhett knows Scarlett, and knows she is obstinate to a fault. She has not cut Rhett off because she no longer loves him, but because of her obsession with her figure. If viewed as a specific action in a specific context between specific people, Rhett's actions can be viewed more tolerantly. Moreover, another recurring theme of this film is the contrast between action, directness, and honest revelation against a code of reflective, indirect, and polite discourse. Because Rhett and Scarlett are modern creatures awash in a landscape which they understand is new but which they each imperfectly comprehend, they have only fragmentary means of communication. Resorting to the most basic forms of connection is their only recourse. We appreciate feminist perspectives on this scene, but perhaps the most important comment to make at this juncture is that this scene shows us clearly how much we have changed since 1939. The audience of 1939 probably viewed Scarlett's withholding of sex as wrong: she does love Rhett. They would have also viewed Rhett's actions as indiscreet, but marginally permissible because his intent was to rekindle their romantic involvement. Romance and functional marriage were ideals of the time, which superseded a woman's wish to preserve her pre-pregnancy waist. Today, with less emphasis on the role of romance, family, and compromise in relationships and more emphasis on absolute individual prerogative, this scene has become an ugly act of violence.

Rhett's apologetic and evasive conduct the next morning suggests that he understands he overstepped the boundaries of civility. His decision to take Bonnie to England might, on the other hand, suggest that in the light of day he still cannot tolerate a wife who cannot get another man out of her mind. Likewise his doting fatherhood seems moderated by Scarlett's treatment. When he has taken Bonnie to England, he dismisses a nanny because she has let Bonnie cry in the dark — surely the sign of an involved, if not excessively permissive, father. But he is wearing evening clothes as he comforts his daughter. He is not letting his paternal duties compromise his male inclinations. But he returns to Atlanta because he understands that Bonnie needs her mother. Like most men in films, he is confused by his role as father.

In the final scene of the movie, in which Melanie dies, we have a last direct contrast between Rhett and Ashley. Ashley is literally prostrate with grief. He cannot imagine a life without Melanie, and because he cannot imagine it, he does not know what to do. Rhett does not know what his life will be like, either, but he has had enough of Scarlett's infatuation with Ashley, and he decides to return home, "where I belong." While the end of the film is ambivalent — we know that Rhett does give a damn about Scarlett, although we suspect that if they reunite they will not live happily ever after — the film is clear about the relative merit of the man of action versus the man of contemplation. Action works in the modern world. The world in which imagination and the contemplation of timeless beauty are viable manly qualities is gone with the wind. And yet the film does not merely present stereotypes of the man of action and the man of contemplation: these are complex and flawed men. However much we may like Rhett, he is a cad toward the woman he truly loves. However stymied Ashley is by his outmoded and slavery-dependent ideals, he is fundamentally a man of principle.

From a male perspective, Rhett is the hero of the film. He undergoes a complete, humanizing transformation. The first half of the film is about Rhett's gradual acceptance of responsibility. Like Rick Blaine in *Casablanca* (1942), Rhett moves from being an outlaw, to cynical outsider, to conspirator, to hero. This is one of the great myths of masculinity which we will see repeated over and over in popular films. The second half of the film represents a cracked version of another repeated theme, the domestication of the male. Outlaw or hero, a man needs a good woman and, preferably, children to complete his civilization. Unfortunately, Rhett's woman isn't up to the job — not yet, although at the film's very end there are indications that she might be about to change. If it takes a redemptive transformation for a character to be a hero, Ashley is not one. He is fundamentally the same at the film's end as he was when we first saw him bounding down the stairs of Twelve Oaks. Only his status has changed from planter to manufacturer, from bachelor to widower.

The Wizard of Oz

Like *Gone with the Wind*, *The Wizard of Oz* is about a young woman gaining control of her situation through alliances with male characters (and a good witch). Along with *Gone with the Wind*, *101 Dalmatians*, *Star Wars*, *Titanic*, and *E.T.: The Extra-Terrestrial*, *The Wizard of Oz* is a film which has been seen by a majority of Americans and a substantial proportion of all people living on earth. Perhaps more than any other film, *The Wizard of Oz* is a central "text" of contemporary American culture. There are lines and tunes and visual images from this film which pervade life in America every day, from greeting cards and TV ads to casual conversation.

The antagonists in the film are female: Dorothy Gale (Judy Garland) has been swept away from her Kansas home in a tornado. Her house lands on the Wicked Witch of the East, provoking in her sister, the Wicked Witch of the West (Margaret Hamilton) a murderous hatred. Advised by the newly liberated Munchkins to seek assistance in getting home by going to see the Wizard in the Emerald City, Dorothy finds help on the way from three male characters who join her expedition in order to get something they lack from the Wizard: the Scarecrow (Ray Bolger), who is looking for a brain; the Tin Man (Jack Haley), who is looking for a heart; and the Cowardly Lion (Bert Lahr), who is looking for courage. Fortunately, Dorothy is also protected by mysterious ruby slippers, because the "men" in her life are incapable of intelligent action until very late in the film.

Both the book and the movie of *The Wizard of Oz* are allegory, although the allegorical content in movie and book are quite different. Some have found the book's origins in Bunyan's *Pilgrim's Progress* (Franson, 1995), while others have seen in the three male characters a commentary on the political situation in 1900 when L. Frank Baum published the novel: know nothing farmers, heartless union workers, and a government out of touch with the social and political problems of the times (Littlefield, 1964). Like most works of children's literature of the time (both 1900 and 1939), there is a strong moral. "There's no place like home" becomes the motto of the film, but it is a shallow motto: Dorothy's home has not been portrayed favorably. She is an orphan being raised by an aunt and uncle who ignore her and are incapable of dealing with the simple conflict between Miss Gulch and the mischievous Toto. Dorothy has in fact run away from home and is only reluctantly returning when the tornado strikes. When we look at the male characters in the film, the moral of the story becomes clearer. Whatever qualities the Scarecrow, Tin Man, and Lion possess, they are each less than intelligent, less than compassionate, and less than brave. Only when they come together to rescue Dorothy from the clutches of the Wicked Witch do they each express each of these characteristics. They have all of these attributes, they just don't know it. They must learn where their internal strengths are, and they do this by helping Dorothy.

Whatever the allegorical significance there is to the film it is overwhelmed by the performances of Garland, Bolger, Haley, and Lahr. If the moral of the story is that a real man combines reason, caring, and action (for only together can Dorothy's helpers overcome the power of the Wicked Witch), the three male characterizations are so distinctive that we have difficulty viewing them as really incomplete. Ironically, of course, the Scarecrow is the smartest of them all; the Tin Man is the most emotional, and the Cowardly Lion is no coward at all.

The Wizard of Oz must be considered as part of two traditional film genres, the musical and the children's movie. Both genres simplify character development, the first because with a dozen music numbers, there is little time for character development, the second because the intended audience is presumed to prefer characters drawn in broad strokes.

Two traditions exist in the American stage and film musical. The first is operatic — characters express their emotions through song and dance; the second, more common for musicals of this period, is about people who actually sing and dance, in musicals such as *Going My Way* (1942) and *Yankee Doodle Dandy* (1945). *The Wizard of Oz* belongs to the first of these traditions (and its operatic format, out of synch with the taste of the time, may account for the film's lukewarm reception — it was only later, when the audiences of the 1950s acquired a taste for big, operatic musical films, that the film gained the status of "a classic" and earned back its original investment). Even in the grim black and white world of Kansas, Dorothy gives expression to her hopes and dreams by singing "Over the Rainbow."

As Dorothy meets each of her male companions, he sings about his foibles (e.g., "If I only had a brain..."). These are men well along in the process of becoming whole: they know — or they think they know — what it is that will make them complete and how they will then behave.

Dorothy and her three male companions arrive at the Emerald City only to find yet another obstacle in their way.

In Oz, Dorothy doesn't sing much. Interestingly, neither do the Witches or the Wizard: the solo "arias" are left up to the three male characters. It is their interior longings and plans which the audience comes to know. The operatic part of the film, therefore, becomes less about Dorothy getting back to Kansas than about men integrating qualities to become whole, finished individuals. Perhaps it is because of this change in emphasis from Baum's book, that the scriptwriters felt they needed the dreadful "it was all a dream" ending. The mutual love between Dorothy and the Scarecrow, Tin Man, and Lion and the fineness of their complete selves would be too much of a loss, if they were not "really" waiting for her back home in Kansas.[4]

As a children's film, the *Wizard of Oz* follows several tried and true conventions. In one, a child is separated from his/her home, imprisoned by a malevolent adult, and rescued by a seemingly weak — but completely good agent. This basic plot can be found in films as diverse as *Pinocchio* (1940), *The Rescuers* (1977), and *The Lion King* (1994). The child is usually partially to blame for the predicament, often through running away from home. Likewise, the imprisonment of the child is often truly frightening. In the Wizard *of Oz,* the Wicked Witch says outright that she wants to kill Dorothy. The Scarecrow is unstuffed and the Tin Man is dismembered.

The *Wizard of Oz* also draws from the more literary fantasy tradition, in which a child falls into a magical "green world," as in *The Neverending Story* (1984), *Alice in Wonderland* (1951), *Peter Pan* (1953) and *The Secret Garden* (versions in 1949, 1993 and 1994). At first, the green world is beautiful and charming, as when Dorothy meets the Munchkins, but eventually the sinister nature of this other world makes the child long for a return to her real home. Dorothy realizes that the world "over the rainbow" also has wicked witches in it. The child usually has to accomplish a task — often a rather violent one — which is the key to her return.

It is important to remember that in the 1930s, families went to see children's films, so there had to be layers of understanding to the film. It seems reasonable to read the Dorothy-gets-home plot as the juvenile one and the maturing of the Scarecrow, Tin Man, and Lion plot — the focus of the operatic sections — as the adult one.

The Wizard of Oz is a one of a kind film — complex and flawed — a film which can be appreciated in diverse ways over the life span, but it is not too difficult to understand why it took a long time for audiences to understand it.

The Hunchback of Notre Dame

Very loosely based on an 1831 novel by Victor Hugo, *The Hunchback of Notre Dame* is also a film with a female lead in a world of men (the third in this chapter). The film follows the interrelations of seven men brought together by their love for the gypsy girl Esmeralda (Maureen O'Hara). These men are the poet Gringoire (Edmond O'Brien), whom Esmeralda marries in order to save him from the beggars' noose; the archbishop (Walter Hampden), who grants Esmeralda sanctuary in the cathedral when her crime is merely that of being a gypsy; Frollo (Cedric Hardwicke), the archbishop's brother and chief justice, who condemns Esmeralda to death for a murder he himself has committed, in order to free himself of his obsessive love for her; Phoebus (Alan Marshal), an army officer, Esmeralda's sweetheart (but in the book, her rapist, however), who is murdered by Frollo when he finds him kissing Esmeralda; Clopin (Thomas Mitchell), the king of beggars, who leads the storming of the Cathedral to rescue Esmeralda once her innocence is clear; King Louis XI (Harry Davenport), who is struggling to move himself and his country from the medieval into the modern world — another example of the theme of changing times — who first condemns Esmeralda to death in a trial by ordeal and then pardons her when presented rational evidence of her innocence; and Quasimodo (Charles Laughton), the deaf bell-ringer of the cathedral who snatches Esmeralda from the gallows but who is left watching her leave with Gringoire in the final shot of the film, crying pathetically to the gargoyle he is clutching, "Why was I not made of stone like thee?"

Like Hugo's novel, the film is set in 15th century Paris. The filmmakers frame the film politically with an opening scroll which invites the audience to view the film as the triumph of freedom of thought over superstition and prejudice. At a deliberate, surface level, the film is about racial prejudice. This message is particularly made at three points in the film. The opening scene shows gypsies being barred from the gates of Paris. Later, Esmeralda tells the archbishop inside the cathedral that gypsies are forced to steal because laws ban them from earning an honest livelihood. At the end of the film, the laws against gypsies are repealed as the swell of beggars, clerics, soldiers, and middle class artisans unite and leave Notre Dame square in triumph. But the film's attempts to deal with prejudice are unconvincing. There is little display of intolerance: every man in the film is infatuated with Esmeralda, despite her racial status. Phoebus' attentions are charming, not the attempted rape that occurs in the novel because he believes he has the right to force his way upon her. While she cannot officially be within the walls of Paris, she dances at the public Fool's Day celebration and is hired to perform at a society soiree. The fairy tale ending where everyone lives together happily ever after occurs because she is found innocent of murder, not because anyone has really changed his mind about gypsies.

Viewing the film as a statement about social class may be more rewarding. Little time is devoted to gypsies, but a great deal of time is devoted to the beggars. While the film has a liberal veneer (if we would communicate better we would understand each other better and live in peace), the film has a deeply conservative core. In this, the film owes something to Hugo. Grant (1945) describes Hugo's politics before the events of 1848 and the writing of *Les Misérables* as a "union of conservatism and humanitarianism, resulting in a moderate, tepid liberalism," (p. 145). The beggars have organized under the "kingship" of Clopin. They are rabble under the sway of a powerful trade union organizer. In one of the most dramatic moments in the film, Gringoire stumbles into the beggars' territory. Here, the blind see and the lame walk, but only because the blind are not blind — only have dead eyes painted on their eyelids — and the lame are not lame; they have merely hidden a sound leg within their rags. Director William Dieterle uses his best Expressionist techniques as we see that the beggars are all fakes. There may have been messages here to the audiences of 1939 about the unionization of American heavy industry workers: the leaders are in it for their own aggrandizement, and the plight of the worker is a sham.

Hope for the future is to be found in the film among the bourgeoisie. Such a message would be convincing to the young Hugo. The bourgeoisie artisans surround the Cathedral because they know that injustice is about to take place if Esmeralda is hanged. They believe in the law, and they respect the sanctity of religion. They hear Gringoire's logic and accept it. They know that corrupt officials and the mindless proletariat rabble will only upset the order of things.

The diversity of male characters in American film in 1939 can be seen by contrasting the fundamental messages about masculinity in this film with those of *Gone with the Wind*. As discussed above, the active life was seen triumphant over the contemplative life in *GWTW*. But Gringoire, the poet and pamphleteer, is the clear hero of this film as his approach is the one which saves the day, and at the end of the film he gets the girl. But he is not a man of action — he specifically cautions against premature action. He is a man of words and intellect who only reluctantly takes action at the end of the movie. (Of course the hope that reason and words would prevail against tyranny was a message which not only resonated in 1939 American film audiences: it was foreign policy.)

Throughout this book we will often look hard at those movies which seem "dated," and those aspects of films which do not hold up. When we see a film or an event or a character that seem odd or unbelievable, we may at first want to dismiss the film. But because we are looking at films which were very popular when released, we need to try to imagine what the audience at the time perceived when they saw the film. Often this tells us something important about changes in cultural assumptions and understandings. Frollo is a character whose psychology no longer rings true. The screenwriters did not entirely liberate him from the religious obsession of Hugo's character, who believes that his feelings for Esmeralda must be the result of witchcraft. Yet he has also taken on aspects of a Freudian obsessive-compulsive, a man as twisted psychologically by his attempts to repress his libido as Quasimodo is physically. Cedric Hardwicke's performance is creepy enough, unless we actually give his character much thought. Then he becomes merely a plot engine. Since the plot has been seriously changed, his motivation becomes chaotic. In Hugo's novel, Frollo attacks Phoebus as he is about to rape Esmeralda, and Phoebus is not actually murdered, as he is in the film. Frollo does have his good point: he has been the protector of Quasimodo. Yet, he does not step forward to save Quasimodo from the lash. In an inversion of the traditional theme of man redeemed by the love of a good woman, we have a very 20th century counterpoint of the good man corrupted by lust.

Quasimodo is the third important male character in the film. The 1923 silent film of Hugo's novel established Quasimodo as the central character of the story — Hugo's book is called *Notre Dame de Paris,* not *The Hunchback.* Certainly, he is the most visually interesting character as he skips up and down the tower, rocks on the bells in his madness, or swings down to save Esmeralda from the noose. The visual medium of the movies propels him to be the focal point. But it is not his physical deformities which define him in this film: it is his deafness.

The film's only Academy Award nominations were for best score and best sound recording. Trailers for the film emphasize the care to which the producers went to use the actual bells of the cathedral of Notre Dame in the soundtrack. Such care to the sound of the film underscore the importance of sound to the filmmakers. Visually interesting as this film is in sequences like the transformations of the beggars, its use of music and ambient sound were revolutionary. The audience is treated to a rich aural experience and then forced to consider a silent world, a world in which the title character's job is ironically to make sound.

Deafness becomes the major metaphor in this film. This is exploited comically when Quasimodo is arraigned in front of a deaf magistrate, but this foreshadows the more serious trial of Esmeralda when the judges "cannot hear" the truth. Because Quasimodo literally cannot hear, he often misunderstands situations. He does not completely understand he is being "made a fool of" when he is crowned "King of Fools." He does not understand why Esmeralda runs away from him. Nor does he understand that Frollo is no longer his protector. He can understand only the most basic human actions, as when Esmeralda gives him water after his flogging. Like *Gone with the Wind,* the film is often about misunderstandings. In *Gone with the Wind,* Rhett and Scarlett never find the right way of communicating with each other. More literally, in *The Hunchback,* the characters cannot hear each other.

Jesse James

Jesse James opens with a title that identifies the villain of the film as the transcontinental railroad which is about to disrupt the life of small farmers in Missouri. This situation is exemplified as the action begins, with two scenes in which Barshee (Brian Donlevy), the agent of the railroad, and his henchmen swindle land first from an illiterate farmer and then from a widow and her young son, the first by threatening state condemnation, the second by beating up the adolescent when he suggests his mother see a lawyer. The third farm Barshee visits is the Jameses'. The mother (Jane Darwell) resists and is backed up with gunfire and punches by her sons, Frank (Henry Fonda) and Jesse (Tyrone Power). Later that evening Barshee returns with a warrant for Frank and Jesse's arrest while local farmers, called together for collective action by the James brothers, permit their escape. Barshee is convinced that Frank and Jesse are inside, and he throws a bomb into the house, killing Mrs. James.

Against the combined power of a ruthless railroad and a complying government, Jesse has no recourse but to become an outlaw. He kills Barshee in a shoot-out in a bar. Immediately a price is put on his head by the railroad. (Throughout the picture bounty notices chronicle the depth of the James Gang's involvement in crime by ever increasing rewards; except for the duel with Barshee and one spectacular night train robbery sequence, when we see Jesse's silhouette creeping on monkey-arms over the top of the cars in which passengers sit securely in warm yellow light, we do not see him involved in criminal activity.)

Of course, historically, this is all nonsense. The members of the James Gang were Confederate guerrillas during the Civil War, who continued their disruptive tactics, first with banks and then with trains, because they hated and mistrusted the Reconstruction government of Missouri. Mrs. James was injured in 1871 by a Pinkerton bomb, but not killed. Popular press accounts, mostly in papers controlled by former Confederate editors and dime novels, did present Jesse James as a hero (Slotkin, 1992).

As Jesse is not presented often in his role as outlaw, the dramatic core of the film has to be elsewhere. The film is essentially about Jesse's relation to his wife, Zee (Nancy Kelly). Zee understands the impetus for Jesse's criminal career, but she also understands the need to stop it before he changes from an outraged citizen, seeking justice by taking the law into his own hands, to a craven brute who has no respect for any kind of law. Her first attempt to stop his downfall is when she forces him to either marry her or never see her again. She understands that her love is his only hope for redemption. He marries her in a cornball scene in which the preacher whose Sunday sermon they interrupt to perform the marriage turns out to be an enemy of the railroad, too. When the railroad forced him off his land, he had to give up "honest work" to go back to preaching.

Jesse soon joins Zee in a house she has fixed up including a "God bless our home" plaque which she has made and hung over the mantel. Immediately a farm family passes by and asks for directions, and Jesse decides they must move on, because he is not certain that they are farmers. On the surface, this may seem paranoid, but when the Pinkerton agent does arrive, he is disguised as a drummer.

At the middle of the film is a curious sequence in which the honest Marshall, Will Wright (Randolph Scott), arranges a plea bargain between Jesse and the government, allegedly endorsed by the president of the railroad. Jesse at first resists because he believes he will go crazy in jail, but eventually he agrees, to please Zee. The president of the railroad arrives and rescinds the agreement which from the start was a ruse. Again, the railroad/big business is seen as corrupt.

The demands of the profession of outlaw drive a wedge between Jesse and Zee. Soon after the arrival of their son, Zee realizes that she will never be able to redeem Jesse, and she returns home to her eccentric uncle and the benevolent protection of Will Wright. Deprived of the humanizing influence of wife and son, Jesse dives into outlawry for many years, becoming more and more ruthless, reckless, and cynical. Years later, broken psychologically and injured physically, he returns home and recovers his health and his soul, but he is shot by a former gang member hours before he and Zee are to leave to start a new life.

Jesse James deals with many of the masculine themes we have encountered in the previous three films: action *vs.* thought; the untamed world of men together *vs.* the civilized world of the family; a world turned upside down in terms of values. But this film is a tragedy of sorts, because Jesse fails to blend compassion with intelligence and courage and ultimately fails to construct a successful integration of masculine qualities.

Although this film and its sequel, *The Return of Frank James* (1940), appear often on cable stations, there is something very old fashioned and unconvincing about it. The acting is highly artificial, beginning with the prodigious amount of tobacco-spitting Henry Fonda accomplishes in his first scene, and climaxed by the bizarre "swearing" sequences by Zee's uncle, a confederate officer turned newspaper editor, as he dictates a series of editorials, calling for the execution of lawyers, railroad presidents, and anyone who inconveniences him. Apparently these swearing scenes were well received, because they were repeated in the sequel.

Likewise, the movie drives and drives its sex-role message home in a way that today we might find way too obvious. Zee suggests that if Jesse doesn't stop robbing he will become "a wolf." He scuttles over the train like a chimpanzee. He becomes an animal, addicted to robbery and killing, because he rejects connection with his woman. The other films we are discussing all make the same point, but make it much more subtly.

What we find fascinating about this film is the Will Wright character and his relationship to both Zee and Jesse. Will is in love with Zee, and one rainy night he encounters Jesse for the first time in the living quarters behind the newspaper office. His men are out hunting for the James Gang, but he accepts Zee's story that Jesse is Mr. Howard. He talks obliquely to Jesse before he leaves about his duties as a law officer, and that in the proper setting he would have to go after Jesse James, despite his affection for Zee. He hides across the street from the newspaper office and watches Zee and Jesse kiss — and then lets him escape. Later in the film, he brokers the deal between the railroad and Jesse (historically accurate), to allow Jesse to serve a short term for robbery, but when the railroad reneges on the deal, he allows the president of the railroad to deputize some of the James Gang, permitting Jesse's escape. Faithful, it is Will who is present at the birth of Jesse's son, not Jesse, and we assume, it will be Will who will be around for Zee and the kid after Jesse is shot.

It is not surprising that a character named "Will Wright," the representative of the law, might represent the moral center of a western, but it is perhaps unexpected that this character is a moral relativist. He sees the crimes of the railroad and the crimes of the James Gang as essentially canceling out each other. This lawman is, however, not a dispassionate observer. He is the also-ran suitor of the wife of the accused. He loves Zee and stands by her, but he is a gentleman, and appears never to take advantage of the situation.

Mr. Smith Goes to Washington

The fifth most popular film of 1939, Frank Capra's *Mr. Smith Goes to Washington*, was the highest grossing comedy of the year. That this film is a comedy comes as a surprise to many who know the film only from the clips of Jefferson Smith (Jimmy Stewart) staring at the major monuments in Washington or from the famous filibuster sequence. In fact, our local Blockbuster, classifies this film as a "drama" rather than as a comedy. Perhaps this is because much of the comedy in the film does not translate over the decades, although the patriotic and moral aspects of the film do.

The film begins with the announcement that the senior senator from Wisconsin has died, and we are quickly treated to a series of back room political scenes in which pressure is put on the governor (Guy Kibbee) to appoint the right short-term replacement. The political boss Jim Taylor (Edward Arnold), the head of a newspaper syndicate, and corrupted senator Joseph Paine (Claude Rains) demand that a party man be appointed who will look the other way as a pork barrel dam project goes through the Senate. (Taylor has bought up the land on which the dam will be built and stands to make a bundle.) Local officials, tired of the politics of Jim Taylor, want a reform candidate. The governor likes neither position and favors someone uncontroversial to fill out the term. In a hilarious scene, an unlikely source — the governor's large brood of children — suggests a compromise candidate, naturalist and leader of the Boy Rangers, Jeff Smith. What makes this scene so funny is that the children are completely aware of their father's political problems, and they are casual as they talk about him being in Jim Taylor's pocket, to their father's dismay.

Because our trust in politicians has been so tarnished, much of the political humor in this film has not withstood the test of time, but then the Washington premiere audience, apparently ahead of the rest of the country in terms of its cynicism, loathed the film. (In his self-aggrandizing autobiography, *The Name Above the Title,* Capra [1971] views his difficulties with this film as deriving mostly from his portrayal of the Washington press corps as cynical and boozy. But there were other more serious objections. Ambassador Joseph Kennedy, former head of RKO Pictures, warned that the movie would support fascist claims that democracy was corrupt. Despite efforts on the part of the government to suppress the film, studio boss Harry Cohn rose to the occasion, and it was distributed widely both nationally and abroad. Particularly in France, it was a popular offering in movie houses immediately before the fall to the Germans.)

Much of the humor derives from the fact that Smith really is a dolt, although Capra (1971) says that "Our Jefferson Smith would be a young Abe Lincoln, tailored to the rail-splitter's simplicity, compassion, ideals, humor, and unswerving moral courage under pressure" (p. 260). This is, of course, an earlier version of Lincoln, before we have come to regard him as an astute politician who freed the slaves only when it was politically expedient. But this young Abe brings pigeons to Washington in order to communicate with his "ma." He is told as soon as he arrives at Washington's Union Station, "You'll have to get yourself out of low gear, Senator." But he wanders away from his duties to stare teary-eyed at the Lincoln Memorial, listening to a child read the Gettysburg Address. He so often seems to be in a Forrest Gump–like daze that one doubts his basic intelligence. Unfortunately, in a press conference arranged by his chief aide in order for him to be humiliated, he mentions a plan to build a Boy Ranger camp for urban boys to get a taste of nature. The camp will be built on the land which has been designated for the dam project, setting up a showdown with the Taylor machine. When he presses on this project, Taylor arranges to have him accused of corruption to silence him. But he does not seem to understand the seriousness of the charges, and he forges ahead.

Usually what men gain from their relationships with women in the films of this period is compassion. What Smith gains from his female aide and love interest, Saunders (Jean Arthur), is political savvy. The reversal of sex role behavior has been the stock and trade of comedy from Aristophanes on, so the compassionate man learning from the hard-headed woman is basis for much of the humor in this film. This basis for humor is also dated. Smart, logical, money-oriented women are not an anomaly in current cinema or society. And so clips of this film often appear to present the story as an intense investigation of a decent man at odds with a corrupt political establishment. It was really supposed to be a screwball comedy, and outside of the beltway, it was received as such.

As Taylor uses his newspapers to slander Smith, Saunders teaches Smith about the senate's custom of filibuster. To block the spending bill which will fund the dam project, Smith reads the important documents of our government and rambles on about his life. He tires and falters, but he continues on, confused and sweating, in one of the emblematic moments of our film culture. He ends surrounded by letters of support for his position, like the dumping of letters to Santa Claus in *Miracle on 34th Street* (1947). Both are satirical fantasies about the power of the governed.

There is a bleakness to this comedy, as there usually is in Capra's films, although we sometimes stigmatize Capra as a gung-ho, Pollyannaish American flag-waver. Kawin and Mast (1992) comment:

> But there is a dark side to the Capra films as well, despite their eventual affirmations. Mr. Deeds must endure the courtroom malice of his accusers for an agonizingly long time, until the judge finally pronounces him the sanest man who ever entered his courtroom. Mr. Smith suffers another ordeal, a Senate filibuster that pushes his physical and moral endurance to their limits, until his enemy finally capitulates to the strength of his will and courage. In *Meet John Doe* (1941), Capra demonstrates that the folksy slogans of an ordinary John Doe (Gary Cooper again) are uncomfortably close to the fascist slogans of an Adolf Hitler (personified by the American millionaire, D. B. Norton, and played by Edward Arnold, Capra's inevitable representation of plutocratic oppression). Like so many Capra heroes, John Doe is a Christ figure who must endure a painful Gethsemane, and it eventually takes a miracle to save him from crucifixion [p. 214].

Smith's father, an honest newspaper publisher, was murdered for telling the truth, shot in the back, while sitting at his editor's desk. Smith trusts his father's former colleague, Paine, but he has been corrupted by the forces who were behind his father's murder. (The free press seems to be a common theme among several of the films of 1939: Gringoire gets his pamphlet out because King Louis waffles on destroying the new printing presses and saves Esmeralda; Zee's Uncle is an editor who tries to save Jesse.) Paine is jolted to his senses and finally behaves in a moral manner — in fact Capra suggests that it was Paine's reconnection with his earlier ideals which is the central moral focus of the film which got him interested in the project; Jeff gains some insight into practical matters; and Saunders learns that compassion and idealism are not just masculine traits.

Conclusions

The year 1939 was good for men in the movies. (It was also a very good year for women in the movies.) In just the five films we have examined here we see a wide variety of characters: the heroic Rhett Butler whose domestication is thwarted by a selfish wife; the dreamy, noble, but fundamentally ineffectual Ashley Wilkes; the intelligent Scarecrow; the sentimental Tin Man; the fallible but resourceful Lion; the obsessive murderer Frollo; the idealistic poet Gringoire; the disfigured, emotional Quasimodo; simple, honest Jefferson Smith; cynical Senator Joseph Paine; stalwart, conflicted Will Wright; and heroic Jesse James spiraling toward catastrophe. We have outlaws (Rhett and Jesse), farmers (Ashley and Jesse), kings, judges, poets, senators, boy guide leaders, beggars, bell ringers, and scarecrows.

The allegory of *The Wizard of Oz* suggests that a whole man combines intelligence, compassion, and action. The other films confirm this 1939 psychology. Rhett Butler, Gringoire, and Jefferson Smith come closest to this medley of attributes.

The other men in these films are incomplete according to this equation: Ashley is smart and compassionate but also fundamentally miserable because, in the words of Rhett Butler, he "cannot make up his mind." Frollo is smart and active, but his lack of compassion makes him a monster. Quasimodo has compassion and can take action — as when he rescues Esmeralda — but his deafness and his isolation diminish his ability to understand.

There is a fundamental heterosexual message to the films of 1939: men are incomplete without a woman. We are still in a Tocquevillian vision of America where the integration of domestic (female) and public (male) spheres is possible only in a marriage of separate but equal spouses (although *Mr. Smith Goes to Washington* turns the sexual equation on its ear). Happily ever after is only possible when Prince and Princess resolve their conflicts and join together.

So there is both diversity and similarity in the portrayal of men in 1939. Some of these themes continue throughout the next six decades. Others are modified or abandoned. In the next section we will see how the necessity of war changed the cultural concept of masculinity. In the following chapters we will see how some of the components of that concept were changed quickly and permanently at the end of that conflict.

PART II

Heroes

Now, having a baseline against which to compare them, we will concentrate in the next three chapters on the movies made during a pivotal period in 20th century history, 1942 though 1945, when America was involved in World War II. These are an exceptional group of films. Using Sackett's (1990) box office figures, the 20 highest grossing films of the period were, in 1942, *Bambi, Mrs. Miniver, Yankee Doodle Dandy, Random Harvest,* and *Casablanca*; in 1943, *This Is the Army, For Whom the Bell Tolls, The Outlaw, The Song of Bernadette,* and *Stage Door Canteen*; in 1944, *Going My Way, Meet Me in St. Louis, Since You Went Away, 30 Seconds over Tokyo,* and *The White Cliffs of Dover*; and in 1945, *The Bells of St. Mary's, Leave Her to Heaven, Spellbound, Anchors Aweigh,* and *The Valley of Decision*.

We will concentrate first on two genres of films, musicals and the so-called "weepies," women's films which focused on the suffering of women separated from their sons and husbands because of war. By doing so, we will discuss 11 of these films. We will also devote our fifth chapter to the most enduring classic of their period, *Casablanca*. What remains are a diverse collection of films, from the Disney animated heartbreaker, *Bambi*, which we will discuss in a later chapter, to Howard Hughes's bra-Western, *The Outlaw*, and David O. Selznick's fine religious biopic of St. Bernadette, to Hitchcock's psychoanalytic thriller, *Spellbound*.

Many of these films have reputations as flag-wavers, but as in the case of *Mr. Smith Goes to Washington,* there is often much more there as well. A good deal of recent criticism about the films of World War II has concentrated on the propagandistic and alleged racist content of many of the films (e.g., Doherty, 1993). But the films which portrayed Germans only as Nazi thugs and the Japanese as google-eyed freaks failed to find a wide audience. We must make a distinction between Hollywood product and viewership. The fact that films were made which we now regard as racist is one thing. Had many Americans spent their dollars to see these films *may* indicate a racist culture. But when audiences seem to have *rejected* those films, this might better be construed as evidence of nonracist feelings in the general American culture. By looking at popular films, we feel we are at a better vantage to understand American popular values than analyses of films selected without attention to audience. The films that large numbers of people went to concentrated on the home front and on the character of the American fighting man. And that character is what we will be interested in.

What was genuinely startling to us as we viewed these films is the extent to which the popular films of World War II directly addressed the issue of war, and particularly the war in which Americans were involved. This is in distinct contrast to films made during later American wars. Kawin and Mast (1992) point out that only Samuel Fuller made films about the Korean conflict during the war years, and those films only made their money back because of their low production costs. During the Vietnam War, the war and its resistance were barely covered by Hollywood.

Three — Musicals of World War II

Griffith and Mayer (1957) estimate that 40 percent of the films Hollywood produced during the War were musicals. Seven musicals were box office successes, *Yankee Doodle Dandy, This Is the Army, Stage Door Canteen, Going My Way, Meet Me in St. Louis, Anchors Aweigh,* and *The Bells of St. Mary's.* The last film was not really a musical, but a sequel to one. Except for *Meet Me in St. Louis,* all of these films had a contemporary military theme.

In her analysis of American musical films, Jane Feuer (1993) suggests that if you "peel away the tinsel ... you find the real tinsel underneath" (p. ix). The musical films of the World War II years have a good deal of tinsel, but we contend that if you peel away the tinsel, you find some important societal concerns there as well. As mentioned in our discussion of the *Wizard of Oz,* characterization must be limited in musicals. Characterization is developed by splendid performances or by relying on common stereotypes. Four of the films, *Yankee Doodle Dandy, Going My Way, Meet Me in St. Louis,* and *The Bells of St. Mary's* are enlivened by rich performances by the central actors. The three others rely heavily on stereotypes and production numbers.[1]

Yankee Doodle Dandy

Yankee Doodle Dandy, Michael Curtiz's biopic of George M. Cohan, appears to be a film confirming straightforward American values. James Cagney's Academy Award winning impersonation of the highly successful vaudevillian was supervised by Cohan himself, and the musical performances are considered highly accurate, although the biographical details are sometimes changed to make a better story. The frame of the film is based on two

43

incidents late in the playwright's life. Cohan had come out of a lengthy retirement to portray a singing and tap dancing Franklin Roosevelt in Kaufman and Hart's *I'd Rather Be Right*, and Cohan was concerned that impersonating a current President would not be thought appropriate. Among the opening night telegrams is a summons to the White House. Cohan meets with Roosevelt and tells him his life story. Rather than being reprimanded, he receives the Congressional Medal of Honor at the end of the film.

Cohan begins his story by telling FDR that he was born in the "beginning of the Horatio Alger age," and the parallels to a typical Alger story are reinforced throughout the story, such as when a "classy" actress initially declines to appear in a play because his first play was a naive rags-to-riches story. Cohan's life story *was* a rags-to-riches story, but the screenplay is sensible enough to temper it, primarily by the constant comparisons between Cohan and his father (Walter Huston), a talented actor and decent man who lives on the edge of financial catastrophe until rescued late in life by his son.

Like the Horatio Alger hero, George M. Cohan is a family man, first as a vain and energetic juvenile in his family's act, then as an attentive husband. Yet the "family values" of this film are startling upon inspection. This is a family where everyone works, including father, mother, and children. George and his father spat about who is the better actor, and the father has to prompt George not to steal his mother's scenes. Later, George argues against his parent's retirement, because it will break up the act, and he tries to convince his sister to keep working after her marriage. When the Four Cohans are broken up, George sullenly retires and spends his time traveling with his wife, haunting European theaters. As portrayed in the film (although not biographically correct), Cohan's greatest successes are in the context of his family. In this picture there is no conflict between family and work: they are the same thing.

Also characteristic of the Alger hero, Cohan is ambitious. The classy actress' manager describes his main attributes as "ambition, pride, and patriotism." Cohan describes himself with uncharacteristic understatement as "persistent." Yet, as an adolescent and young man, his energy and ambition are coupled with a conceit which places those around him in jeopardy: his girlfriend is fired because of his meddling, and his family's act is blacklisted because of his brashness. An emblem of this conceit is in the scene where we see young George nailing a star onto his dressing room door *before* opening night. Later that evening George will be set upon by local toughs for his arrogance, but he does not learn from this experience — his conceit soon leads to the loss of a lucrative New York deal with a producer.

While Cohan is undeniably talented and ambitious, he is also something of a con man: he convinces his future wife that he is elderly on their first meeting; he gets his first Broadway production by a ruse. In other situations, he exhibits tremendous bravado—which works for him from time to time—but he cannot tap dance his way into the army around age restrictions.

Yankee Doodle Dandy is a far better film than it is often given credit. It is clearly inaccurate in some details, but the film creates an impressive document of vaudeville and the beginnings of the American musical comedy, and in the characterization of Cohan, it creates a rich portrait of a kind of American male that appealed to the viewing public at the beginning of the War. Ambition and energy, when tempered with concern for others and refined of self-promotion, are portrayed as American values. Fame, wealth, and patriotism are promoted, but so are honoring one's father, finding a life's companion, and working hard in one's area of talent.

This Is the Army and *Stage Door Canteen*

In *This Is the Army* and *Stage Door Canteen* we have plots of little substance or conflict. They have no love triangles. *This Is the Army* was the title of Irving Berlin's fund raising all-army show which had toured successfully throughout the United States and Europe. As the show was closing in 1943, Warner Brothers volunteered to film it and donate the profits from rentals in small cities and towns to Army Relief. *This Is the Army* had the largest box office of 1943, despite the fact that one had to buy war bonds as well as pay an admission to see it.

There are only about 20 minutes of plot in this film, with most of the two hours of running time devoted to the show itself. At the opening flashback, Jerry Jones (George Murphy) is the singing and dancing sensation of Broadway at the beginning of World War I. At intermission during a matinee, he receives his draft notice. His first duty is to produce Irving Berlin's morale building show, *Yip, Yip Yahank,* and then he is sent to the trenches of Europe where he is wounded in the leg. Several numbers from Berlin's World War I army show are included.

In the present, Jones has become a theatrical agent in New York after his dancing days were ended by his war wound, and his son Johnny (Ronald Reagan) is a recent draftee. At a reunion of the cast of *Yip, Yip Yahank,* conveniently held at the base where all the sons of the World War I cast are stationed, the old commanding officer suggests a new show.

The show itself is remarkable, containing half a dozen songs which have become standards. There are three entertaining drag numbers, and a nearly offenseless blackface routine. The acrobatic and magical numbers still are interesting to watch, but the references in the patter comedy acts are too obscure. Likewise, for old film buffs the impersonator is funny, but many will not understand the references to Ethel Barrymore, Lunt and Fontaine, and Herbert Marshall.

The men in the show are a long way from home, a rowdy lot who shape up into a precision military unit. Being a long way from home, they are lonely. Memories of the girls back home are prominent in several of the songs. Social rules which protect women from their pleasures and men from their passions are poked fun at, but are seen as necessary, particularly in an extended parody of the other vaudeville film, *Stage Door Canteen*. Like the characters in the film, the boys in the show are draftees chafing under the demands of military life, but anxious to see action.

Jerry Jones expresses his frustration at being assigned to a show rather than getting to the front, but the tour allows him time to straighten things out with his girl. On the eve of being inducted into the army, he visits the widow of one of the soldiers from his father's WWI show. Her son has just been killed in action, and the mother talks about the problems his wife and infant son are facing. Later that night when his girl proposes they get married immediately, Jerry asks her to wait until after the war. She sees no reason to wait and leaves him in a huff at the night club. She sees him at the Old Boy's Reunion and returns his engagement ring. Finally, she gives him an opportunity to explain himself on the night of a performance of the show in Washington for the President. After the performance — their last, it turns out, before returning to their combat units — she shows up with a chaplain, and they marry.

Stage Door Canteen has even less of a plot. Boys on leave go to the Canteen where they mingle with stars and ordinary hostesses. The rules say that the hostesses cannot be seen with servicemen outside of the canteen, but one couple meets and falls in love. Again, most of the running time is give over to musical numbers and cameos by movie stars. Film buffs will enjoy these cameos, and the professional musical numbers are often interesting. But our preference is for the amateurs in *This Is the Army*.

The male characters in both of these films are untried soldiers, and they are concerned about whether their mettle will be up to the testing. But in the simple formula of these films, because they have found their girls, they now have a reason to fight, in contrast to the formula from the *Four Horsemen of the Apocalypse,* where it is the man who is free from emotional entanglements who can risk his life. Both films also stress that falling in love is not merely a relationship between a woman and a man: there is the expectation that there will be children and that children are best reared by two parents. War interferes in love because of this additional commitment.

Going My Way and *The Bells of St. Mary's*

Going My Way was the most popular of the wartime musicals. James Agee's synopsis of it in *Time* suggests something of the way in which the film was received:

The story, without rich characterization, would be nothing much. A young priest (Bing Crosby) is sent by his bishop to help out an old one (Barry Fitzgerald) in Manhattan's mortgage-ridden St. Dominic's. For awhile they do not get along; but young Father O'Malley fixes up everything else almost too easily. He deals with a delinquent girl so silkily that before long she is married. He handles the jail-fodder kids of the street so astutely that before long they are singing Mozart's *Ave Verum* and liking it. He even teachers old Father Fitzgibbon how to play golf. He also writes songs which, with the help of an old friend who sings in opera (Metropolitan diva Rise Stevens), he sells so effectively that the parish, despite a disastrous fire, rises clear of all financial problems. And just before he leaves St. Dominic's to troubleshoot for another decrepit priest, he brings Father Fitzgibbon's mother across on a surprise trip from Ireland, for the picture's unusually valid and powerful tear-jerking climax [Agee, 1958, p. 347].

Father O'Malley, despite a bit of buffoonery at the beginning of the film, stands for competence and compassionate action. His list of abilities is almost as long as those of James Bond: he sings, plays the piano, conducts the choir, composes hit tunes, balances the books, and plays golf and baseball at the professional level. But he is competent in the human relations area as well. He deals in a low-key but effective way with police, the banker who holds the church's mortgage, the banker's amorous young son, a runaway girl, juvenile thieves, an unpleasant widow who cannot pay her rent, and music promoters. Perhaps his most difficult task is to convince Father Fitzgibbon that he still has worth upon stepping down from his pastorate, which his does with only a little more trouble than he accomplishes his other tasks. While he is also a priest, we are lead to suspect that there had been a successful courtship between him and the opera diva.

The sequel to *Going My Way* was *The Bells of St. Mary's* (1945). Here, Father O'Malley continues in his fixer role, this time called upon to determine the fate of a run-down parochial school. The musical numbers play a back seat to an essay on the socialization of children, and the difficulties of single parenthood. The topic of this essay is introduced when a woman delivers her daughter to the care of the school. The woman was abandoned by her musician husband (?) before the birth of her daughter. The daughter is now on the brink of adolescence, and she is beginning to wonder how her mother makes a living. Father O'Malley takes her under his wing. He soon discovers he needs the assistance of the mother superior (Ingrid Bergman). Mother Superior has her own test case, a boy who is being bullied. At first, she tries to teach him to turn the other cheek, but later instructs him in the manly art of self-defense from a boxing manual, before being almost KOed by her success. Yet, finally, she must turn to Father O'Malley for help with her charge. The message here is clear: it takes two parents to raise a child: particularly, it takes a man to raise a son and a woman to raise a daughter.

The solution to the school's problem is to dupe the miser next door out of his new office building. The nuns' tactic is to pray for a miracle, but Father

O'Malley, abetted by a physician who breaches professional ethics in several ways, convinces the geezer to donate the building. Again, Father O'Malley is resourceful and agentive.

In the conclusion of the film, Father O'Malley sends Mother Superior away to a new school in a climate more conducive to her recovery from tuberculosis. This time he follows the doctor's confidentiality and does not tell her why he has decided to move her, because the doctor has suggested that if Mother Superior knew about her condition, it would hinder her recovery. Mother Superior, of course, first assumes that she is being sent away because of their previous conflicts, but, at last, intuits the truth. O'Malley has kept faith ("loose lips sink ships"), but he is redeemed in her eyes when she understands his decision.

Both of these films present Father O'Malley as a model of male role behavior. He has skills; he take charge; he acts with compassion. He is the full realization of the Tin Man–Scarecrow–Cowardly Lion configuration. Contact with him allows other men in the film to become fully male. The thieves learn about their effects on others; the old priest learns that he can use his skills in other contexts; the miser learns that giving is better than receiving; boys become men. It seems unimportant that there is no romantic partner in this equation. But this is a time when romance was being put on hold by many; and so, a virtuous and active model was just what was needed.

Anchors Aweigh

Like *The Bells of Saint Mary's, Anchors Aweigh* (1945) deals with the theme of the socialization of children, and in a much more realistic way than in many other films of the early 1940s. Two sailors, played by Gene Kelly and Frank Sinatra, are on the town on a four day leave, looking for some female companionship. Both have just received the silver star. Kelly is sophisticated; he is trying at the beginning of the film to hook up with a fleet follower, Lola. Sinatra knows nothing about big city life or women. He has been an assistant choirmaster in Brooklyn, a fact he wants hidden. Early on, they encounter a young boy (Dean Stockwell) who wants to join the Navy to be like his father who has been killed in action. Reluctantly, the sailors take the boy to the home of his aunt Susie (Kathryn Grayson), an aspiring singer/actress who is working as an extra in a movie. She returns home late and dressed in her elegant movie costume. Kelly assumes she is the kind of woman he has been looking for — out for a good time — and angrily denounces her because of her responsibilities in raising a child. This misunderstanding, and several others, provide the plot for the film, but as in the other musicals, Kelly and Sinatra find girlfriends, push a little too hard, but then keep them. There are romantic misunderstandings but no conflict between the sailors, no competition among American men in arms. Because Kelly has Lola somewhere waiting for him, he fixes Sinatra up with Susie. Kelly and Susie eventually find they are attracted to each other, but Kelly refuses to break faith with his fellow sailor. Meanwhile, Sinatra has found his own girlfriend, but he feels an obligation to remain with Susie, because he had asked Kelly to fix him up. This kind of honor seems archaic, even incomprehensible, to us now in a time where following your heart wherever it may take you, regardless of the consequences, is the norm. One wonders whether this is an idealized cautionary tale or whether young fighting men of World War II actually realized that stealing the girlfriend of someone with whom you would be sharing a bunk for years might not be just too complicated.

There are two plot points which today seem misguided if the purpose of the film is to present Kelly and Sinatra's characters as admirable types. On the first day of their leave, in order to gain Susie's attention, the sailors pretend to know the classical pianist Jose Iturbi, who is the musical director of the studio where Susie works, and they promise to get her a private audition. Of course they don't know him, and while they try to arrange an audition, they are ineffective. Crowing to get the girl's attention has always been a ploy of men on the make. Here, everything works out, and perhaps we forgive them, because they try very hard to arrange the audition. The second scene is even more disingenuous. On the second day of their leave, the sailors are at Susie's house when her date arrives. He is the son of an important family who might help her out careerwise. While singing the song "If You Knew Susie," they imply that she is a promiscuous fleet follower, and the suitor leaves in a huff.

Anchors Aweigh is much a vaudeville show as *This Is the Army*. This movie attempts to have a serious plot, but it is continually derailed by musical numbers which have little to do with advancing the story — classical musical performances, lounge acts, and dream sequences. Most conspicuously is the film's most famous sequence, a dance between Gene Kelly and Jerry the mouse (a kind of stand in for the more famous Mickey whom Disney would not lend out).[2] At the end of the film, Kelly and Sinatra go off to war as part of a well-choreographed fighting unit, enlivened by having found the girl back home that will make the fighting worthwhile.

Meet Me in St. Louis

Meet Me in St. Louis is a dreamy recreation of the halcyon days of middle class turn-of-the-century America and the family values the country was fighting to maintain. The central characters are women, Mrs. Smith (Mary Astor), and her four daughters, Rose (Lucille Bremer), a high school senior who likes older men, Esther (Judy Garland), a high school junior who has

*The musicals of World War II often addressed the War itself, but in a fantasized way. Here Gene Kelly (*Anchors Aweigh*) in his sailor suit dances with a cartoon.*

set her cap for "The Boy Next Door," and two younger daughters, Agnes (Joan Carroll), and Tootie (Margaret O'Brien). There is also the wise-cracking maid, Katie (Marjorie Main). There are also men in the family, the father (Leon Ames), a lawyer, the oldest son (Henry H. Daniels, Jr.), who is on his way to Princeton, and an eccentric grandpa (Harry Davenport), who has a fetish for hats.

The film is justly famous for several production numbers, lovingly directed by Judy Garland's soon-to-be husband, Vincente Minnelli, including the upbeat "Trolley Song," and the moody "Have Yourself a Merry Little Christmas." It is 1903, and everyone has World's Fair fever. But Rose and Esther also have boys on the brain. Rose's boyfriend Warren is in New York, and the first scene of the film involves the women in the family trying to trick the father into an early dinner so that Rose can take her long distance call in private (the phone is in the dining room). Grandpa warns that they should let dad know what is going on. Sarcastically he says, "It's enough that we're letting him work hard to support the whole family." But his warning is unheeded. Dad is an autocrat and fails to make the necessary change, and so the telephone conversation goes nowhere, because Rose is being watched as she tries to wrangle a proposal out of Warren. When dad discovers the ruse, he is genuinely hurt, particularly when he realizes that everyone in the family is in on it. "When was I voted out of this family?" he fumes.

The next sequence is about Lon Jr.'s going away party for Princeton. Esther has arranged for John from next door to be invited. Prior to the party, she announced to Rose that she will maneuver John into kissing her. Rose tells her that she should not do this before becoming engaged. "Men don't want the bloom rubbed off," she warns. Esther counters, "Personally, I think I have too much bloom." But despite her best maneuvering, John only gives her a handshake.

Tootie, the five-year-old, is perhaps the most interesting character in the film. If this were a 1990 film, she would certainly be thought to be emotionally disturbed. She is obsessed with death. She buries her dolls in a backyard graveyard after lengthy illnesses. She comes to the forefront in the Halloween sequence, in which the main themes of the plot come together. While we are led to believe that things were simpler back in upper middle class St. Louis in 1903, Halloween was a great deal more sinister. The children are burning furniture in a bonfire, and trick-or-treating is nonexistent. Rather, the children "kill" people by throwing flour in their faces when they answer the door. One neighbor is particularly sinister because he boils cats, hits his wife with a red hot poker, has a dog who will bite you to pieces, and perhaps worst of all, has empty whiskey bottles in the basement. The older kids don't want Tootie around, so she goes to this neighbor's home alone. Of course the old man smiles after being "killed," and his bulldog is not vicious, but Tootie becomes "the most horrible" child of the evening.

Then suddenly, Tootie is brought into the house, nearly unconscious and badly scarred. John has attacked her. Esther goes next door and blackens his eye and rips his clothes. But this is a 1940s musical, so by the time Esther returns, the truth has been sorted out. Agnes and Tootie had made a dummy and placed it on the trolley tracks so that it looked like a dead woman's body. Tootie was injured while John tried to hide her from the police. Esther goes next door and apologizes. John asks her out for the following evening and then kisses her. She goes into a trance. The trance is broken only when her father returns home and announces that the family will be moving to New York.

The complications of the plot resolve themselves over the next months. John and Esther plan to marry, but when they think through the consequences, they realize that it is not really feasible. John needs to go to college, Esther needs her family. Rose and Warren connect, and after Tootie once again goes berserk, this time in the backyard hacking up a family of snowpeople, dad realizes that going to New York is a bad idea.

Three themes emerge from this film which are consistent with the war musicals: deception in romance, the rational side of love, and dislocation.

Just as in each film we have considered, romance here is construed as "tricking" the object of one's affection into falling in love (Cohan pretends to be old when he meets his wife; the sailors pretend to know Jose Iturbi). Rose needs to be alone on the phone to be able to lead the conversation where she wants it to go. With her family watching and listening in rapt attention, she cannot do this, and Warren merely inquires about the weather. Esther must first act cold and then ask John to help her put out the lights. She wants a kiss, but she needs to think when this might be appropriate in her scheme. In the other musicals, it is the men who are most likely to be the tricksters, but this film suggests that this is an equal opportunity activity. Apparently, tricking is also involved in late marriage, as well. Yet, while everyone in each of these films seems to operate under the assumption that such trickery is necessary, in every case, it is honest communication which wins out.

Male-female relations are not just about the spontaneous expression of emotions in this film. There are constraints that must be considered, social forms that must be observed. Were Esther and John to marry, it would solve the immediate problem — she would not have to leave St. Louis, but the long-range results would be disastrous. There is a nice balance here between head and heart, just as Ronald Reagan in *This Is the Army* wants to postpone his marriage until after he comes home.

Finally, the most memorable theme of this film — although not introduced until well over halfway through it — is the great sadness that the women in this film feel about the possibility of leaving their home. School, friends, the home, loves, even a graveyard of beloved dolls, hold them to place. As tens of millions of Americans were being displaced because of the War, these losses must have resonated deeply with the audiences of the times.

Conclusion

In some ways, the musicals of the war years present comfortable stereotypes of male behavior. Male sexual energy exists, but it can be harnessed by the right woman, or by a political or religious commitment (or by some natural combination of the above). Again and again, the story line is the domestication of the rogue male, or in the idiom of the time, the wolf. The plots are so devoid of romantic conflict that they seem simple and naive by today's standards.

Male heroes are skillful and energetic (similar to the dimensions of intelligence and activity developed in the previous chapter). Cohan can write a full-length play or a song, dance, sing, act, direct, and run a string of theaters. Father O'Malley can compose, coach both singers and ball players, solve economic and interpersonal problems, and hear confession. The sailors in *Anchors Aweigh* can deal with children, get friends career breaks (almost), and sing and dance. When they find their girl, they become emotionally anchored.

In one departure from the five films of 1939, in each of these films, men are also seen as devious. While pretending to be one thing while really being another is a staple of comedy from Aristophanes to Shakespeare, there is a particular American twist in all these films. The pretender appears to be what he knows his co-actor wants. These men are con men. Cohan pretends to have a play already written to conform to what the producer says he wants. Father O'Malley pretends to be only the assistant to Father Fitzgibbon, the adversary to mother superior, and a healer to the misanthropic millionaire. The sailors in *Anchors Aweigh* pretend to be professional entertainers. The servicemen in *Stagedoor Canteen* and *This Is the Army* pretend to be what the women want when they discover that they have aversions to what they really are. Men in these films are heroic liars in the tradition of Odysseus. Their ends are noble or at least innocent, but their means are devious.

Two more troubling themes emerge, the untried draftee concerned about his skill and bravery and the problem of children in war-torn families. But the audience never leaves the theater with any doubts that these men, fortified by finding the right woman, will prove themselves. Also, while both boys and girls are seen to need the nurturance of both male and female role models, we are left with the hope that priests and teachers, aunts and even sailors on shore leave, will pitch in and provide something approaching the family guidance available in St. Louis on the brink of the Centennial Exposition when things were more or less as they should be.

Four — Men as Objects: Men in the Weepies

In addition to the six musicals just discussed which had military themes, five of the top 20 films of 1942–1945 were concerned with themes of the War: *Mrs. Miniver* (1942), *Casablanca* (1942), *Since You Went Away* (1944), *Thirty Seconds Over Tokyo* (1944), and *The White Cliffs of Dover* (1944). Because of its importance, we will devote the next chapter to *Casablanca*. Three of the remaining films fit under the category of "weepies," and so that genre will be the focus of this chapter. *Thirty Seconds Over Tokyo* is a combat film sandwiched between two very effective episodes about the home front and returning home, so it would be fair to discuss this film here as well.

By and large, Hollywood produced action films about the naval war in the Pacific and social dramas set against the land war in the European theater. This distinction may reflect a number of realities about the times. West Coast Hollywood was certainly more concerned about the military threat from Japan and more aware of the actual warfare in the Pacific. It may also reflect the government's restriction on the film industry that each scene in a movie could only cost $5,000, and miniature naval battles and submarine interiors were less expensive to produce than land battles (although the army routinely lent its men to serve as extras in war films).

World War II produced an original form of film entertainment, disparagingly called "weepies," films that were women-focused and meant to show the strength (and the suffering) of the women back home. Male characters serve primarily as the focus of the women's affections and as cannon fodder, so in most of these films the male characters are simply and flatly drawn: their main roles are to be handsome and brave and dead. They are objects, objects of affection, for both the female actors and the audiences.

The White Cliffs of Dover and *Since You Went Away* have not aged particularly well, although both have recently been restored and released on video and sold well. Students of popular culture may find they are sources of information about the kinds of concerns expressed by people of that time. The third, *Mrs. Miniver,* is a classic which can still be watched with pleasure at many levels.

The White Cliffs of Dover

The White Cliffs of Dover surely has one of the most contrived plots in the history of cinema. The daughter of an American newspaper editor (Irene Dunne) — she says she's from Rhode Island, but she also says she misses her Green Mountains — goes to England on vacation in 1914 and falls in love with an English peer, Sir John Ashwood (Alan Marshal). Susan's stay in England is initially disappointing, because she spends most of the time taking care of her father (Frank Morgan), who has caught cold when an Englishwoman on a train insists on opening the window. Father Hiram is an Anglophobe. He dislikes the food, the weather, and the people. His daughter, however, feels a strong connection between English and American culture. It would probably be accurate to say that one of the primary reasons for this film is to convince the audience of the need to intervene in the European war, which seems redundant by the time of its release in 1944.

An eccentric elderly Englishman who lives at the boarding house where Hiram and Susan are staying decides to take her to a ball on the evening of their departure back to the States. There she meets Sir John through a case of mistaken identity, which has been arranged by her escort . Susan does not clarify the misunderstanding (romance requires trickery, as we saw in the previous chapter). Sir John is immediately smitten, and he almost forces Susan to stay on in England. He takes her to his ancestral home, where she discovers that it is not only her father who harbors xenophobic tendencies: Sir John's family (mother, nurse, sister-in-law) have negative attitudes about Americans. Susan finally has had enough and explodes, accusing them all of unintentional prejudice. Then everyone just adores Susan. There also is a bit of business about the Ashwood women hearing ghostly horse hoofs when Ashwood men are killed in battle as Sir John and Susan look at the gallery of family portraits.

As the first war with Germany arrives, Sir John takes his hereditary position as head of the local military unit. The women wait anxiously for any word. Susan hears horse hoofs, but it is Sir John's younger brother who has been killed.

Nanny (Dame Mae Whitty) is concerned that no heir has been produced, and so she is excited when a program is announced which allows wives to visit the troops. Susan and Sir John rendezvous in a hotel in Dieppe, France, overlooking a park with a bandstand. Like Ashley's visit to Atlanta, this one, too, produces an heir. Back home, Susan holds her son proudly at the window when the Americans arrive in London. This scene seems ludicrous today, not only because the American army is composed entirely of an enormous marching band, with several of those most American of musical instruments, the sousaphone, but because the panorama of London is distorted to include all the most well-known monuments — Westminster Cathedral, the Houses of Parliament, and St. Paul's Cathedral — in an impossible configuration.

Predictably, Sir John is killed on a battlefield in France. Afterwards, Lady Ashwood remains in England, mourning the loss of her great love and overseeing the rearing of her son, John Ashwood II (Roddy McDowall). There are some interesting scenes in which her bourgeois American values come into conflict with British aristocratic ones, and others in which her son flirts with a beautiful local commoner (Elizabeth Taylor, in an uncredited juvenile role). The fortunes of the Ashwoods decline, and Susan decides to take Sir John II home to America, but he understands his social responsibilities, and on the train to London, he convinces her that they should remain in England. He must take care of his tenants.

Prior to the train scene, Sir John II has been entertaining two classmates at tea, German lads, and when the conversation turns to politics, their Nazism surfaces. They are two "blondies" who are intent upon world domination and revenge for the humiliation of the Treaty of Versailles. But the real conflict comes when it is time for her son to follow father's footsteps in the second war against Germany. Mom believes she has given (and suffered) enough, but she is told that peerage demands sacrifice. This is all comfortably couched in conflicts between American ideas of self-interest and English ideas of duty.

When World War II arrives, Susan becomes a nurse in a London military hospital. Now grown, and having assumed his father's place in the military, John II (a young Peter Lawford) passes through town, with his old commoner girlfriend. She suggests that he might want to see his mother, but John thinks she'll understand if they don't stop. John follows his father's footsteps much too literally and is mortally wounded in the exact same spot where he was conceived, the little hotel in Dieppe. He dies in London, in his mother's hospital, while Susan looks out the window at a new American military band which has arrived to rescue England once again.

Since You Went Away

Since You Went Away is another film difficult to appreciate, although Leonard Maltin gives it 3½ stars. Maltin's summary is worth quoting:

Tear-jerker supreme with Colbert at her valiant best. Story of family suffering
through WWII with many tragedies and complications dates a bit, but still is very
smooth film.

The family is the Hiltons. The father Tim (seen only in a photograph)
has volunteered for the armed services and leaves behind his wife Anne
(Claudette Colbert), and his daughters Jane (Jennifer Jones) and Brig (Shirley
Temple). The story begins an hour after he leaves for training and it ends the
following Christmas Eve, when, after months of being missing in action, the
army calls to say that he is safe.

The complications the female Hiltons face are mostly financial. Immediately, Anne must discharge their maid, Fidelia (Hattie McDaniel), who later
returns as a nonpaying tenant. Shortly thereafter, they take in a paying
boarder, Colonel Smollett (Monty Woolley). After Jane graduates from high
school, she cannot afford to attend college. Food shortages and gas rationing
intrude on their domestic lives, and they plant a victory garden in the back
yard. Jane becomes a nurse's aide at the local veterans hospital—which is
located next to the country club's golf course, which serves both as a reminder
of how far the family has fallen and to create a sense of irritation with those
who still have leisure to play golf—and Brig becomes an avid collector of war
scrap and seller of war stamps.

The male themes in this film are simple, but they add to our picture of
what it meant to be male during this period. The most pressing male theme
is the financial implications of the absence of the Good Provider, but there
is also the issue of the missing husband/father as the Companion.

Smollett provides the necessary financial resources to the family for them
to be able to survive, but he is a bitter curmudgeon, a role Woolley had per-
fected in earlier films. He is career military, but he is too old to serve except
in some ill-defined advisory capacity. His bitterness is exacerbated by the
presence of his grandson Bill (Robert Walker), the son of his dead son. Bill
has failed to make it at West Point. Bill desperately wants the old man's attention and affection, but the Colonel seems incapable of giving it. The Colonel
is set up to be that typical incomplete male of the period: active—or at least
wanting to be—and smart, but uncompassionate.

But both men are transformed by their relationships with the Hilton
women to become compassionate, and to some degree to become companions to the Hilton women. The Colonel first tries to run the Hilton household like a military camp. He wants breakfast sharply at seven. He despises
their dog Soda who insists on sleeping in his room. But over time he becomes
a sensitive human being by his connection with the expressive emotional dis-
orderliness of the Hilton women. He even becomes willing to express his
fondness for Bill, but, in one of many moments of extreme bathos in the film,
he arrives at the train station too late to see Bill off to war: he has come

around, but three minutes too late. Late in the film he can be a surrogate father for the family, offering them restrained emotional support when they receive news that Bill has been killed in Italy.

Bill and Jane gradually fall in love, and Jane encourages him to be confident in himself. In a scene that tells us much has changed in society and in male-female relationships since 1944, Bill asks Jane if it is okay if he smokes while they are in a soda shop. Jane chastises him for asking her permission: as a man he should do as he wishes, and not ask for a woman's permission. When he leaves for battle, Bill has his confidence. He is a Smollett, after all, he says. Grandfather gets his heart as surely as the Tin Woodman did by knowing Dorothy Gale, while Bill gets his courage like the Cowardly Lion.

The other prominent male character in this film is Lt. Tony Willett (Joseph Cotten), Tim and Anne's best friend. Tony is a wolf. He is an artist, but his subjects are pin-up portraits of women. He comes on to Anne a half a dozen times in the film, but only to a point, flirtatious and only half serious. Anne is adept at deflecting his advances. During the beginning of the film, before she meets Bill, Jane has a serious crush on Tony. Although in the movie he encounters two very young women with whom he has clearly had a fling, he knows that involvement with Jane would not be proper. He is in many respects like Rhett Butler in the first half of *GWTW*, decidedly not a gentleman, but not completely a rogue, either. He tries to deflect Jane's attentions, but he has not had much practice at restraining himself around young women. He is saved by the appearance of Bill and Jane's case of mumps. Genuinely predatory males are not shown in this film, and we later find out that Tony is a hero, the recipient of the Navy Cross. But he is at least a partial wolf.

There is another small wolf role in this film. While Bill and Jane are bowling, they encounter Hal Smith (Guy Madison). Hal tries to pick up Jane by making fun of Bill, but when Hal finds out that there is a serious relationship between them, he stops his advances, and they become friends for the evening. When they see Hal off in his bus, Bill cautiously remarks to Jane that Hal is handsome. Jane, tactfully, says she hadn't noticed. (But the young women in the audience noticed, and Hollywood noticed that the young women in the audience noticed, and this ten minute role is often credited to leading to the casting of younger and sexier men in leading roles in later films. Guy Madison in this movie looks remarkably like Brad Pitt.)

Mrs. Miniver

As the title suggests, *Mrs. Miniver* is focused on a central female character, Kay Miniver (Greer Garson), whose family, according to the introduction, is representative of the British middle class. The stratum she represents is surely economically high within in the middle class. The nature of the household's financial status is shown in contrasting scenes at the opening of the film in which Kay buys an expensive hat and her architect husband Clem (Walter Pidgeon) buys an expensive sports car. Both are reluctant to share their extravagances with each other, but in the quiet of their bedroom, they conclude that the good thing about being middle class is having enough money to buy things you do not absolutely need. The Miniver household is rounded out by their university-student son Vin (Richard Ney), two younger children — a nearly silent girl who practices her piano and a precocious, mischievous, and talkative boy — a maid, a cook, and a cat named Napoleon.

The movie attempts a commentary on social class. On the way home from her hat-buying spree in London Kay shares the train compartment with Lady Beldon (Dame May Whitty) who complains bitterly about having to deal with crowds of middle class shoppers. She uses phrases like "their betters" without a blink of an eye. In contrast, the next day Vin comes home for holiday from Oxford, where he is currently a sociology student of Marxist persuasion. Sitting in their huge dining room in formal attire being served by a uniformed maid, he critiques the feudal nature of British rural society. During this comic (but actually sound Marxist) harangue, they are visited by Lady Beldon's granddaughter, Carol (Teresa Wright). The purpose of her visit is to ask Mrs. Miniver to speak to the station master, Mr. Ballard (Henry Travers), about withdrawing his entry in the flower show. Her grandmother has always won the rose contest, and Carol fears that Mr. Ballard's rose, which he has named for Mrs. Miniver, will win. Vin sees this as just another aspect of repressive feudalism. Kay and Clem try to shut him up, but Carol can take care of herself. She admits that she more or less agrees with him, and she asks him what he is doing about it. "Do?" he asks. She tells him about her philanthropy which he dismisses in favor of a thorough analysis. By the time Carol leaves, Vin is clearly in love.

Of course there will be difficulties in a love affair between a commoner and a member of the aristocracy. The memorable image of this social chasm is when Vin looks across the aisle in church and sees Lady Beldon and Carol. Behind them is the medieval tomb of their ancestors. There is a good deal of truth to Vin's sophomoric analysis of British society.

The central part of the film is driven by Kay. While Clem is ferrying the boys from Dunkirk, she encounters a downed German fighter pilot in her garden. The pilot is wounded and starving, but murderous. She subdues him. She also deals effectively with Lady Beldon's objections to the marriage between Carol and Vin, helping her recall her own early marriage, over her family's objections, to a young man killed in war.

While Clem and Vin take a backseat to Kay, they are far more interesting than most men in the weepies. Clem is industrious and brave: he is among those who cross the Channel to rescue the forces at Dunkirk. He is more or less an attentive and affectionate father, although he refuses to listen to his daughter's piano piece even when her teacher begs that it will bolster her self confidence. Enduring a direct assault with his family in a bomb shelter, he shows strength and keeps the children calm, even though he himself is clearly frightened. He accepts the indignities of war, including the destruction of their grand home which he had designed himself. He is at ease with both the aristocracy and his servants. He grieves, although quietly, when Carol is killed.

Vin is an Americanized version of the young British gentleman, a kind of Hugh Grant prototype. He is hilarious as the deadly earnest Marxist, spouting revolutionary slogans in a gentleman's accent, dressed in a tuxedo. The night after Carol has come to his house, he follows her to a dance and apologizes for the manner, but not the substance, of his outburst. Carol mentions dancing, and Vin admits enthusiastically that he is a good dancer, but he engages in righteous Marxist self-criticism and asks, "Is this the time for frivolity?" Carol replies, "Is it time to lose one's sense of humor?" After the honeymoon, however, he is impressed that Carol has heraldry emblazoned on her luggage.

Vin is young and enthusiastic. Love and military experience moderate his brashness, but he fails to see the danger in his rushed training. He is eager to see combat, but he is concerned about his family and arranges a signal to his mother when he flies overhead. Like his father, he restrains his obvious grief when Carol is killed. In the final scene in the sandbagged and bombed out church at the memorial service for Carol, the station master, and a choir-boy killed in the same raid, he is able to overcome his history with Lady Beldon, and he comforts her.

Vin is a character that deserves thought. He is in a long line of comic "English" stereotypes in American films. Yet his maturation in this film is far from stereotypical. He is incomplete in each of the three dimensions of masculinity that have been defined thus far. He is intelligent (although clearly misguided by his Marxist inclinations — book smart, but not really smart). He is active, wanting to get into "action" as soon as possible, but unable to see how his liberal feelings for the poor could lead to action in their behalf: he would rather analyze social class than help the poor. And he is compassionate at his core, but his English reserve interferes with his putting his compassion into action. Vin seems much like the Scarecrow: sentimental rather than caring, unaware of how to help, even though he is willing, and often unaware of what is going on around him, though fundamentally bright.

In the current climate, the weepies seem an overly sentimental form of entertainment. But more than their calculated bathos, the popularity of these films which mirrored the worst of the period's reality strikes us as strange: why would audiences pay money to watch their worst nightmares acted out in front of them?

Part of the reason is a changing social function of film over the past 50 years. Movies and radio were the great national media in the 1940s, just as television is today. An evening at the cinema not only entertained, it informed though newsreels and short documentaries. While television has its Thursday night sitcoms after the evening news, it also broadcasts Sunday night social-problem-of-the-week movies.

The weepies may also have served as a precursor of modern phenomena such as support groups which are not merely support, but ritualized times for expressing emotions. It seems not too much of a stretch to suggest that two hours grieving with Greer Garson or Irene Dunne facing troubles might be just what the doctor ordered, so that in the morning women could get up and get on with their interrupted lives. These films are little different than Oprah.

Thirty Seconds Over Tokyo

Thirty Seconds Over Tokyo was the highest grossing combat film of the war years. Based on a book and a widely read article in *Collier's,* the film follows the crew of the Ruptured Duck, a B-25 involved in the Doolittle raids on Japan early in 1942, from their training through their return to the United States.

The captain of the crew is Ted Lawson (Van Johnson) who joined the army in 1940 to study aeronautical engineering. Although he has been married for just six months, he has volunteered for a dangerous secret mission. His wife (Phyllis Thaxter) joins him in Florida for the training phase of the mission. Ted and Ellen have a close relationship, even though they have spent less than two weeks together as man and wife. Like the other men, Lawson speculates on the nature and location of the mission. No one suspects a direct attack on Japan.

The other fully realized character in the film is Thatcher (Robert Walker), the gunner who never gets over being airsick. He is from a small town in Montana and is a vocal proponent of his state and small town life. Regionalism is a conspicuous theme in this film, which emphasizes how it is important for people of different backgrounds — and military personnel from all branches of the service — to unite to get the job done.

The movie is divided into five sections: training, time aboard the carrier *Hornet*, the mission, hiding in China, and the return home. The training section shows the bonding of the men from different regions and backgrounds. The time on the *Hornet* emphasizes how the army and navy personnel come to respect each other, mostly through lightly comic touches as when they gamble together and when the army fliers explore the alien maze-like territory of a carrier. The mission segment is full of special effects of a low flight over Japan, which shows how the team works together and the bravery of the men who take off in a plane with a problematic left engine and a faulty communications system.

It is the segment in China which separates this film from other run-of-the-mill combat films. The carrier is spotted by the Japanese, and the mission must begin hours too early. There are two problems with this change in plans: the strike on Japan must take place in daylight, and the landing in China must take place at night. After scoring direct hits on its military targets, the plane runs out of fuel before it can reach the landing site in China and crashes along the Chinese coast. Except for Thatcher, all the crew are all seriously injured, but with the help of groups of Chinese and two British missionaries, they are finally lead to safety. But if the audiences at home wanted to be assured that everything would be all right, this episode of the film does not confirm it. Lawson's injuries are serious, and he must be moved several times to avoid capture. He receives no medical attention for several days, and his injuries worsen to the point that when a doctor arrives, he must have his leg amputated above the knee. Lawson is not an ideal patient: without medical treatment or medication for the pain, he comes close to despair as he drifts in and out of consciousness. But during some of his dreamlike hallucinations, he recalls Ellen, and he reconnects with why he is fighting. This section of the film assures the audience that the world appreciates what America is doing: the Chinese risk massacre (the first town that shelters them is burnt to the ground) to assist the Americans.

Throughout the film Doolittle (Spencer Tracy) is a cool, dispassionate leader. He does not join in on the camaraderie of his crews. But during the final section of the film, it is he who informs Ellen of Ted's return and his injury, and he brings her to Washington, against Ted's wishes. He understands that Ted's healing is not just learning to use an artificial leg, but he must reconnect with his wife to become whole again. The reunion scene is unforgettable, perhaps a little maudlin for current tastes. Ellen is pregnant and concerned that Ted will not find her attractive. Ted wants to postpone the reunion until he can use his new leg well enough to take her dancing. Though they have each talked about how deep their love is, each worries that the other's affections are skin-deep. When Doolittle leaves Ted's hospital room, having assured him that there is still a place for him in the war, Ellen enters. Ted rises from his wheelchair and collapses on the floor. Ellen rushes to him, and after their exchanges, we are left certain that this is one returning serviceman who will have the emotional base from which to recover from his harrowing service experience.

Perhaps too much has been made of a gentle scene in Dalton Trumbo's script on board the *Hornet* where Lawson and his friend Bob Gray (Robert Mitchum) discuss their motivations for fighting. Lawson says that he doesn't hate the Japanese. "I don't like them," he concedes, "...but it's a case of drop a bomb on them, or pretty soon they'll drop one on Ellen." There is nothing in the film to suggest a pacifist undertone. Doolittle does register the hope that this will actually be the war to end all wars, but that sentiment was alive in *Going My Way, This Is the Army,* and *Since You Went Away,* as well.

Conclusions

In the four films we have considered in this chapter, we have moved from the periphery of the war directly into it. In the musicals, no one we know dies, although in *This Is the Army,* we encounter a grieving mother and Jerry Jones' dancing career was ended by a injury in World War I. Those were musicals. These films are dramas (or melodramas). Death, which does not come at convenient points in the plot, is omnipresent in these films.

Those who die must have some substance for their deaths to mean much in these films. But as we mentioned earlier, the male characters are typically flatly drawn in these films. In *Since You Went Away,* we have gotten to know Bill rather well, and our sorrow for his death is because he was still in the process of realizing his potential. While he had gotten his confidence, he had just gotten it, and he had not reconciled with his grandfather. We wish that he had a month or two before going away so that he could have grown more. Likewise, we regret that Sir John, Sr., had not gotten to see his son, and that Sir John II, who seemed so responsible with regard to his tenants had been more caring toward his mother as he passed through London before shipping out. *Mrs. Miniver* strikes us today as the best of the three weepies discussed. Carol and Mr. Ballard are skillfully drawn characters, and non-combatants, and it outrages us that the Hun in the garden will have a chance to grow old, while Carol will not. That the gentle station master was killed is pathos in a fine tragic sense.

Today we may demand more well-developed victims for films of these kinds to work. But during the period of 1942 through 1945 it probably required very little for the audience to identify with the situations of Kay Miniver, Ellen Lawson, or Susan Ashwood. Everyone knew or was related to or loved someone in combat, and it took little more than an appealing actor who shared the common characteristics of the American soldier or sailor (youth, unrealized potential, flaws) for the audience to sympathize with the situations on the screen. Even someone as eccentric as the tuxedoed, middle class Marxist, Vin Miniver, probably reminded many audience members of someone they knew.

Five — Casablanca

Casablanca is a movie which has been held in remarkable esteem. It was the fifth most popular film at the box office in 1942. It was reviewed enthusiastically by most major newspapers. It won the Academy Award for best picture in 1943, as well as for best director (Michael Curtiz) and best screenplay.[1] It is the most often shown movie on television, and the 50th anniversary reissue on video has been a consistent high seller and rental. It is the only serious contender with *Citizen Kane* among English-speaking critics for the best picture ever made.

When one of us developed a summer program a few years ago to help foreign students adapt to American college life, it seemed that there were four films which could be considered primary cultural texts. *Casablanca* was one of those four films, along with *Gone with the Wind*, *The Wizard of Oz*, and *Star Wars*. Lines from *Casablanca* are repeated every day: "Here's looking at you, kid," "I stick my neck out for no one," and "This is the beginning of a beautiful relationship" are said with the expectation that the hearer will understand their film context. The song, "As Time Goes By" (originally written for a 1931 musical *Everybody's Welcome* by Herman Hupfeld and included in the play on which *Casablanca* was based), is as culturally meaningful as any American song. On one hand it conveys deep romantic involvement and on the other the profound loss of that involvement. There have been many positive references to the film in other films (*Last Tango in Paris* [1972]) and extended satiric references (*Play It Again, Sam* [1972], *Top Secret* [1984], and *Barb Wire* [1996]).

There was no obvious reason for this extraordinary reputation. The film did not represent a vision of a gifted *auteur*. Michael Curtiz was a utility director of comedies, musicals, and action pictures. It was based on an unproduced play by Murray Burnett and Joan Alison, and was one of many studio films in the year in which it was made. Many of those who worked on it were reluctant to do so (Harmetz, 1992, chapter 4). George Raft and Ronald Reagan were early choices for the character of Rick. Its immediate reception may have been enhanced by the Casablanca Conference between Churchill and Roosevelt coincidentally held at the same time as its release, but that certainly cannot account for its sustained popularity. The tension and ambiguity brought about by the fact that the final resolution of the plot was not determined until a day before the final scene was shot led to an honesty of emotion among the principal characters which is rare in Hollywood cinema.

The Political Context

It is tempting and perhaps useful to view *Casablanca* as a political allegory. Bernard F. Dick (1996) has sorted out much of the movie's political iconography for the reader whose grasp of the political situation in 1941 is limited:

> Even if Burnett and Alison had not made Laszlo a Czech, the screenwriters might have, since they were at pains to make each character's background plausible. Czechoslovakia was a logical homeland for Laszlo since it had two resistance movements — one for officers, another for activists and intellectuals, to which a political writer like Laszlo would belong....
>
> ...To achieve the right geographical and political mix, the writers could not leave the national origins of the characters to chance.... Like her husband, Ilsa should be from an occupied country. Although Ingrid Bergman was Swedish ... she could not appear as one of her countrywomen in *Casablanca*. Sweden was neutral, and the wife of an underground leader should not be from a neutral nation. On the other hand, if Ilsa were Norwegian, she should share in the growing sympathy for occupied Norway....
>
> The care taken in establishing the national backgrounds of the characters was not limited to the leads; it also extended to the supporting cast. The screenwriters rounded out the cast with some additions of their own: the "good Germans" are represented by a couple en route to the United States; the Soviet Union by Sascha, the anti-Nazi bartender; Free France by Berger the Norwegian, who has responded to de Gaulle's call and proves it by a ring that opens to reveal the Cross of Lorraine. Annina appears in the play, but the film makes much of her desire to immigrate to America with her husband since their homeland, Bulgaria, had joined the Axis in March 1941. [p. 169].

But despite this kind of helpful insight, what we are interested in here is the portrayal of male identity and masculinity in this film, not its political significance. There is a strong message in this film, however, that part of being masculine is to be political. As we suggested in the Introduction, the definition of masculinity to include political involvement represents a major step in the transformation of the American male.

The film begins with the image of a swirling globe with a voice-over narrative identifying Casablanca as the next-to-the-last stopover for refugees trying to get from Nazi-occupied Europe to America. We are told that most of the refugees will have to wait and wait and wait. A montage of scenes (directed by Don Siegel) then follows which blend the corruption of Casablanca with the danger of waiting: people stroll through exotic markets in white suits while their pockets are picked and police shoot those with expired credentials. In this montage, we also learn that two Nazi officers have been killed on a train to Casablanca and letters of transit, allowing anyone who has them to leave for Lisbon without question, have been stolen from them. The montage ends with the plane to Lisbon flying just over the sign to Rick's bar.

We then go to Rick's Café Americain. In the deep Moorish interiors we see all the diverse people who are in conflict outside during the day tolerating each other at night. Particularly, we notice the several different uniforms interspersed among the evening clothes.

The real action of the story begins when Ugarte (Peter Lorre) confesses to Rick (Humphrey Bogart) that it was he who killed the couriers and is now in possession of the letters of transit. He is going to make a deal that evening for them which will leave him rich enough to leave Casablanca. While he reveals his dirty dealing to impress Rick, he knows that Rick despises him, and because of that disdain, Rick is the only person he trusts to hold the letters. Before the deal can be made, however, Ugarte is arrested by the French police as a sign of their willingness to cooperate with the recently arrived agent of the Third Reich, Major Strasser (Conrad Veidt). Ugarte appeals to Rick for help as he is being led away, but Rick can offer none and appears unlikely to have done so had he an option.

The intended customer for the letters is Victor Laszlo (Paul Henreid), a leader of the Eastern European Resistance who soon enters the bar dressed to the teeth (in a yellow suit in the colorized version!) and moving elegantly through the crowd. He is accompanied by Ilsa Lund (Ingrid Bergman). Ilsa is surprised to see the pianist Sam, and while Laszlo goes to have a drink with a fellow member of the underground, Berger, she chats with Sam and asks him to play her favorite song "As Time Goes By." At first Sam claims to have forgotten it, but he caves in when she keeps on asking him. Within a few minutes Rick reappears, and when he notices what Sam is playing he storms angrily over to him. Sam gestures in Ilsa's direction with his eyes, and the romantic plot of the film is underway.

Until this point in the film, there is so much music it could be mistaken for a musical. Music will later precipitate the political crisis in the movie when some German soldiers take over Sam's piano and begin singing nationalistic songs. Laszlo rushes to the bandstand and calls for "La Marseillaise."

Rick signals the band to follow Laszlo's lead, and eventually the French national anthem drowns out the Hun's music. Strasser is indignant and demands that Renault close the bar. Tolerance is clearly a threat to the Third Reich.

The Main Men

There are three important male characters in this film: Rick, a self-described saloon keeper, Victor Laszlo, a Czech journalist and leader of the anti-Fascist resistance, and Captain Renault (Claude Rains), a corrupt policeman. Each of these men undergoes a series of transformations by the events of three days in Casablanca early in the war.

There are other interesting male performances by Conrad Veidt (who had played Cesare the somnambulist in *The Cabinet of Dr. Caligari* [1919]) as a representative of the Third Reich sent to "Free France" to keep an eye on Laszlo; Peter Lorre, as the blackmarketeer Ugarte who has murdered two couriers with "letters of transit," the magical device which sets the plot in motion; Sydney Greenstreet as Ferrari, the unctuous head of the black market; and Dooley Wilson as Rick's friend and pianist Sam, who has a distinctly personal view of the action of the film. But these are fundamentally stock, flat characters: Strasser remains unredeemedly evil; Ugarte is murdered early in the film; Ferrari stays self-interested and slippery, and Sam seems motivated entirely by keeping Rick emotionally in line.

And there are important and interesting women, too, in this film, because this is as much a movie about love and its aftermath as it is about war and politics. Two minor women characters are important in advancing the plot. Yvonne (Madeleine LeBeau) has recently been involved with Rick, but he is tired of her, and she shows her distress at being ignored, first by drinking too much at the bar and then by going over to the Germans. Rick's cavalier treatment of her occurs before Ilsa returns to his life. The fact that he can be so heartless toward her tells us that he is wounded. More poignant is Annina Brandel (Joy Page), the teenaged Bulgarian newlywed who considers sleeping with Captain Renault so that she and her husband can get the necessary papers in order to get to America. It is Rick's rescue of her from the sexual predation of his friend Renault that signals the effect that Ilsa (or perhaps to some extent, Victor Laszlo) has had on his conscience. He allows her husband to win at roulette so that the necessary pass can be purchased semi-legitimately.

And of course there is Ingrid Bergman (Ilsa Lund). Even with a focus on men in this book, it is impossible not to comment on what Bergman brings to the screen. The transformations that Rick undergoes in Paris, after Paris, and in Casablanca seem altogether reasonable when it is Bergman who is the cause of his joy, despair, and redemption. Whether she was intended to be read as a symbol of "Europe" or not, she is a nexus of beauty, feeling, and intelligence for which a warm-blooded man can give all. Bergman's onscreen presence makes both the political and romantic meaning of this movie palpable.

Victor Laszlo

Victor Laszlo is not the most stereotypic of underground leaders. He is well dressed, urbane, and emotionally constrained. Two adjectives come to mind when trying to describe him: elegant and relentless. He has a calmness about him that is difficult to understand, given the intense personal threats on his life. He is always polite, even to Major Strasser. And yet, despite this low-keyed manner, he will insist on going to the underground meeting and pursuing the letters of transit. In the police office, he will demand his rights. He is a man with a mission, but a dignified man. He will not stoop to the barbarianism of his enemies. (We should remember Dick's [1993] comments about an intellectual resistance in Czechoslovakia.) One does wonder where he gets his money and clothes after his escape from a Nazi concentration camp, though, and he certainly does not conform to the American stereotype of the hard-drinking journalist in well-worn clothes.

Although Laszlo is entirely dedicated to the overthrow of Fascism, we only gradually discover his intense love for Ilsa. No one — until Ilsa admits it to Rick — knows that they are husband and wife. When Ilsa makes this revelation, we wonder whether the marriage has much fire, because there has been some reserve between them. But Laszlo must protect Ilsa by pretending that they are merely traveling companions (who nevertheless share a hotel room). Ilsa will be in jeopardy if their marriage is known to the Gestapo because she is intimately connected with his work.

Laszlo's reserve sometimes makes it difficult for the audience to believe the intensity of his devotion to Ilsa, but actions and words must tell us more here than flamboyant display, which is not Laszlo's style. Even when he overheats and leads the house band in the playing of the French national anthem to drown out the Nazis' singing of "Watch on the Rhine," he displays little emotion. Rather, he sees the necessary occasion and he takes it, come hell or high water. Yet he has lingered in his flight from the Nazis because of Ilsa's health, and everything he says to Rick underscores his love for Ilsa. His hatred of the Nazis is not merely a political abstraction, it is reified in the persona of his wife.

Captain Renault

Renault is a comic character. He is in some ways a child (he always refers to Rick as "Ricky") who chases skirts and money like a Gallic 15 year old. He is proud of his amorality: He tells Major Strasser that he bends with the prevailing winds and those winds are currently from Vichy. He bets that Laszlo will not leave Casablanca, when the decision for him to do so is entirely in his own hands. When Strasser demands that Rick's be shut down after the French anthem incident, he does so on the basis that gambling takes place on the premises, and then collects his evening's winnings.

Renault has no background, which serves his amorality well. Somehow he has come to Casablanca and become its police chief. He views Rick's decision to let the young Bulgarian couple win at roulette as "sentiment." He advises Rick not to throw Yvonne away, because women may become scarce. Yet amorality is not that far away from morality — certainly not as far away as immorality. At the airport, he can recognize that Rick's shooting of Strasser is for a higher good, and he can tell his lackeys to "Round up the usual suspects," allowing him and Rick to flee to a free French garrison across the desert. He cannot bring himself to drink Vichy water at the climax of the film, because Vichy is the emblem of collaboration with the Nazis.

Rick

Rick (or Richard — his name in Paris) is, except for his African-American pianist friend Sam, the only American in the film. His moral, political, and romantic transformations are the center of the film. His character defines masculinity in this film. For those who notice the calendar in the police station, the film takes place on the three days preceding the bombing of Pearl Harbor, and Rick's decision to get back into the fight is just a heartbeat ahead of his compatriots in recognizing the world threat of Fascism. Like the country itself, Rick is still attempting to be neutral — everyone is welcome at Rick's; and isolationist — he drinks with no one. Twice, early in the film, he states, "I stick my neck out for no one." This kind of political and emotional isolationism is viewed negatively. It is typical of male behavior, but it is not admirable masculinity.

Rick has three pasts. In the remote past, he has left America under some sort of duress, and he cannot return. Renault tries to get him to explain in a comic scene. Renault imagines that he stole from the church fund or seduced a senator's wife or killed a man. Rick says that it was a little of all of that, but Rick is always evasive about his American past. He tells Major Strasser that his nationality is "drunkard."

In exile, Rick became an anti-Fascist freedom fighter, first against the Italians in Ethiopia and then against the Spanish Fascists. He seems to have been conspicuous in these activities, as Renault, Strasser, and even Laszlo know about them. He dismisses them as paid mercenary activities, but Renault reminds him that the Fascists would have paid him more. In this regard, as in several other scenes, there seem to be direct parallels drawn between Rick and Rhett Butler: Rhett was a paid blockade runner. Like Rhett, he admits to being "a sucker for the underdog."

His most recent past is his life in Paris immediately prior to the invasion of the Germans. It is never clear what Rick is doing in Paris, other than romancing Ilsa, but as the Germans are about to enter the city, Rick shows a knowledge of German artillery, and Ilsa is concerned that if he stays he will be a target of the Gestapo. In the Paris flashback, Rick seems younger and more handsome. He dances in nightclubs and drinks champagne in trendy bars. Sam is with him, but in what capacity we are left out. He has cars to drive through the city and into the countryside. He is a freedom fighter in the same decidedly upper class way that Laszlo is. That he and Laszlo are attracted to the same woman, and she to them, is not all that outrageous.

This most recent past in Paris has left Rick cynical. As the Nazis invaded Paris, he and Ilsa planned to escape together. But she left him standing on the train platform, in the rain, with a note about her absence which tells nothing. Of course, they had agreed to tell each other nothing about their pasts, but this abandonment leaves Rick morose and cynical. What is left for the morose and cynical American is to become a successful entrepreneur. Rick's American bar is a big hit in Casablanca. Everyone comes to Rick's.

But Rick may be less of a cynic than he wants people to believe. He excludes some Nazis from the premise — not the military who have clout, but the civilians. He abets Ugarte. He rescues the young Bulgarian wife. When his bar is closed, he promises to pay his staff (all conspicuous anti-Fascists) for as long as he can. And at the end of the film he arranges for his employees to retain their positions and for Sam to receive a share of the profits — interestingly a bigger share of the profits than he is paying himself.

Rick is a richly drawn character: we see him as a businessman, as a friend, as a patriot, and as a lover. In none of these roles is he completely admirable. He pays bribes to keep his casino open, and the tables in the back room are rigged. He deceives his friend Renault and later is clearly willing to shoot him. He describes his previous heroics as self-interested acts. His actions toward Ilsa and particularly Yvonne are sometimes offensive.

In one of the most famous scenes in all American movies, Rick is drinking alone in his closed bar. He drunkenly and angrily commands Sam to play "As Time Goes By," which occasions the flashback of their days in Paris. When we return to the present, Ilsa silently enters the bar to a twisted minor key version of "As Time Goes By." She wants to explain, but Rick is drunk and abusive. When she sees the hatred in his eyes, she leaves. Rick, unaware at the time of the true relationship between Ilsa and Laszlo, maliciously predicts that she will be back.

We have seen the man as the spurned and hurt lover in popular films before this time. There is something almost as pathetic as Quasimodo, hanging on the gargoyle, in the understated acting of Humphrey Bogart or as dismayed as Jesse James when he returns to find his wife and new-born child have gone back to civilization. But in this scene the hurt is less mythic, more personal, and more complete. Compared to the smiling and youthful Rick of the flashback, Rick in Casablanca is old, morose, and wasted. He is seriously damaged goods. There is nothing hopeful about him as there is about Rhett Butler when he walks out on Scarlett in Atlanta.

The following day, Laszlo learns from Ferrari that Rick probably has the letters of transit and he begins to piece together the fact that his wife has had a relationship of some sort with Rick. Rick meets Ilsa in the bazaar and tries to apologize for his conduct of the night before, but Ilsa is not that easily won over.

One of the mysteries of *Casablanca,* and one of the reasons that we can return again and again to the film, is discovering what triggers Rick's reconnecting with his masculinity and what Ilsa's motivations are when she returns to the bar for the second time, after the police have shut it down. Ilsa first appeals to his better nature to give Laszlo the letters. When that doesn't work, she pulls a gun on him. But Rick dares her to shoot him, and she cannot, and the love that has been put away in both of them resurfaces. An ambiguous cutaway suggests more may happen between them than a passionate kiss. Now each understands the whole story, but Rick comments, "It's still a story without an ending. What about now?"

> ILSA: Now? I don't know. I know that I'll never have the strength to leave you again.
> RICK: And Laszlo?
> ILSA: You'll help him. You'll see to that, and then he'll have his work, all that he's been living for.
> RICK: All except one: He won't have you.

Ilsa's descriptions of her love for Laszlo until this time have been tentative. She says she was young, and he was her teacher. He is a great man. She admires him. Rick by this time recognizes that Laszlo's love for Ilsa is more passionate, the thing that keeps him going. It has not only moral resonance, but personal fire. Ilsa's response to his challenge reflects genuine ambivalence and confusion: "I can't fight it any more. I ran away once. I can't do it again. I don't know what's right any longer. You'll have to think for both of us ... for all of us."

Because they have both put Laszlo back into his proper place in the equation, and since marriage had more permanence then than now, Rick pauses for a few moments, and then he says emphatically, "All right. I will." From this point on Rick manipulates the situation. He misdirects Laszlo, Ilsa, and Renault, leading to the final confrontation at the airport when he puts Ilsa and Laszlo on the plane and goes off to rejoin the resistance, killing (or merely

Richard and Ilsa in better days, if that can be said of the time of the Nazis in Paris.

wounding?) Strasser along the way. His final "hill of beans" speech to Ilsa echoes, we think intentionally, Rhett's speech to Scarlett on the bridge to Tara — we are living in crazy times and no one will be happy until we individually act to make things better. But Scarlett was "free" to marry Rhett, and Ilsa is not. Rick sees a barrier he cannot cross, or at least in the moral context of war, should not.

Other Readings of the Film

Casablanca is a postmodernist's dream. Almost any approach to it seems to produce insights. As we suggested, the film can be read as political allegory about a cynical isolationist America (Rick) which has lost its European roots (Ilsa), only to find strength of will by reconnecting with them/her. At the beginning of the film Rick is both politically and emotionally isolated from the events in Europe. But as the events of the film run their course, he becomes more concerned with the moral implications of the situation in Casablanca.

First he uses his rigged casino to save the Bulgarian girl. Then he arranges for the escape of underground leader Victor Laszlo. Then he shoots Major Strasser, and finally sets off to join the fight. The audience in 1943 could identify with Rick's stages of involvement.

Certainly having the hero of the film an American capitalist will not warm the hearts of serious Marxist critics, but at the end of the film Rick sells his business and joins the anti-Fascist revolution. The singing of the "La Marseillaise" is modestly revolutionary, and the way that scene is edited is an extended homage to Eisenstein.

The film may not reward feminists as generously. If one is looking for a strong "role model," Ilsa is not that. She is said to be involved intimately in her husband's work but in most scenes, she is tentative. Yet within the political and psychological context of the film, Ilsa is a believable character who makes realistic decisions. She is overwhelmed by the conflicts in her personal and political life. She relinquishes control because of that confusion. Certainly Rick's behavior toward her has not given her much guidance about whether she should abandon a world-famous freedom fighter husband. She is, after all, up against the Third Reich, not a glass ceiling.

Nor is Rick a masculinist hegemonic villain. He's a man, comfortably licking his wounds, when both romance and politics some crashing down on him all of a sudden. Carole Gilligan (1988) has posited sex differences in moral reasoning. Women, she maintains, make moral decisions out of the relational issues of a situation, while men make moral decision more from absolute principles. In this film, however, Ilsa's decision in Paris to return to Laszlo seems to be a conventional, absolutist one. It is, interestingly, one she made entirely on her own. Those critics who balk at Rick's statement in the hill-of-beans speech that he has been doing the thinking for both of them need to recall that Rick is only doing as she asked him to three scenes earlier. And that Rick's decisions involve Laszlo, as well. It is Rick who places personal relations into the equation to come out with a solution.

The often insightful and highly influential critic Umberto Eco (1986) has written provocatively about *Casablanca*, which he denigrates as a "cult movie." (Perhaps we should not react so negatively to this description, as, for example of other cult works, Eco give the examples of *The Divine Comedy* and Gaudí's Sagrada Familia church.) He describes it, though, as: "...a very modest aesthetic achievement. It is a hodgepodge of sensational scenes strung together implausibly, its characters are psychologically incredible, its actors act in a mannered way" (p. 197). Among other charges against the film, he suggests that the various rooms in Rick's bar segregate various nationalities and treats them in a stereotypical way.[2]

We would like to address Eco's specific charge that "its characters are psychological incredible." (Clearly we do not agree with *any* of Eco's evaluations of this film.) Eco is correct in asserting that Laszlo is not a typical underground leader. He is certainly not like those in films of Rossellini (although he is similar to the anti-Fascist intellectuals in Bertolucci's *Il Conformista* [1970]). Eco asserts that one nonrealistic element is that Laszlo drinks four different beverages — but most of them are bought for him or ordered at different times of the day. This is a minor point. Any bartender will tell you that there are some customers who have a regular drink, while there are others who change drinks on every order.

Eco's (1990) description of Rick, however, is more important to address:

> Rick slowly shows up, first by ... his hand, then by ... the check. The various aspects of the contradictory (plurifilmic) personality of Rick are introduced: The Fatal Adventurer, the Self-Made Businessman (money is money), the Tough Guy from a gangster movie, Our Man in Casablanca (international intrigue), the Cynic. Only later he will be characterized also as the Hemingwayan Hero (he helped the Ethiopians and the Spaniards against fascism). He does not drink. This undoubtedly represents a nice problem, for later Rick must play the role of the Redeemed Drunkard and he has to be made a drunkard (as Disillusioned Lover) so that he can be redeemed. But Bogey's face sustains this unbearable number of contradictory psychological features [pp. 204–205].

Indeed, any movie plays with stereotypes/archetypes. To the audience of 1943, Bogart was primarily known as a minor player in gangster movies. But in 1941, he had broken out of this mold as detective Phillip Marlowe in John Huston's *The Maltese Falcon.* Marlowe is many of the same things that Rick represents: tough, cynical, self-made, adventuristic, and heroic. He is even an incipient disillusioned lover. If one is going to view these qualities as a hodgepodge of "contradictory psychological features," what is problematic about Rick is his most distant past. If Rick's enforced leaving of America is due to criminal activity, then his taking on the role as the anti-Fascist champion of the underdog *is* unbelievable. One can imagine a more likely scenario, and if one does, there seems to be nothing contradictory in Rick's character. Leaving the U.S. in the height of the Depression, Rick's reason for leaving may have been political. Politics rule him, until he falls in love. When love fails him, he becomes apolitical and cynical.

One thing that Eco asserts here is inaccurate: that Rick does not drink; he is drinking when we first see him. He merely drinks alone. Drinking alone has an American cultural meaning of "trouble."

Viewed decades later or through odd captioning or subtitles, the dialogue may seem unnatural, but this film still strikes younger American audiences as psychologically meaningful.[3]

Casablanca is a film to which we will want to return. The centrality of Rick's character in our culture and the sustained popularity of the film suggest that there are qualities in Rick that have remained common to what it means to be a man throughout the period described in this book.

PART III

Antiheroes

While we have had several reasons to refer to the work of the Plecks in their social history of masculinity in America, we take an exception to their chronology of the 20th century. They view the period from 1920 until 1965 as being the period of the Companionate Provider. We believe that the films of the late 1940s, 1950s, and 1960s, however, disclose a new period.

In the films we have describe thus far, men were more than companions and providers, they also acted in the world beyond the family. Julio in *The Four Horsemen*, the Sheiks, Rhett, Ashley, Gringoire, Jeff Smith, the soldiers and sailors of the World War II musicals and weepies, and Rick Blaine were all men who risked their lives in one way or another for a cause. And they were all successful. They were heroes. But until Rick Blaine, these men became "political" out of domestic concern. Julio joins the army because everyone else is doing so. The sheiks act to protect their women. Rhett and Ashley act despite their larger perceptions of the Civil War, and most of the men in the movies of World War II are acting to protect their "American way of life," which means their families, to a large extent. Rick transcends this domestic form of politics in the "hill of beans" speech: he is acting not as Rhett does in his own similar speech on the bridge to Tara to "save face," but to fight Fascism.

Now something else enters the picture. We may want to call it the sensibility of the antihero. Success will elude most of the principal male characters put on screen from 1945 until 1970—in the home as a companion and as a provider, and outside the home, too. In the next chapter, we will have a less heroic version of the World War II fighting man. We will see returning servicemen struggling with alcohol and suicide. We will see cowardice and prejudice in those same fighting men we have just examined and a military wracked with social inequality and petty bureaucracy. In chapter seven, we will see that heroism can still be portrayed on screen, but not by contemporary men—heroism must be in the distant past and acted out by men with divine callings. In chapter eight we will examine the most positive popular film of the period about family values, *Shane*. But the homesteading Starrett family in *Shane* is up against relentless nature, ruthless ranchers, and a villain for all times, and can only be rescued by a gunslinger of epic proportions. In chapter nine, we will look at what has happened to the vision of the family, once thought of as the refuge for men, women, and children, but now portrayed as a cauldron of both lust and repression, greed, violence, and perhaps worst of all, indifference.

In chapter ten we will see one way out: a fantasy hero, James Bond, who has expensive cars, beautiful women, money, power, and prestige. But James Bond is a hero for an antiheroic age. He has no family of origin and establishes no family. He defends a dead ideal: British colonialism. And when night falls, on most days, he has nothing but his job in which to establish his masculinity. He provides for no one but himself; he is only fleetingly a companion; and because there must be sequels, his triumphs are inevitably momentary and incomplete.

Six — Revisioning the War

The remarkable focus on the war in popular films produced during the war changed suddenly. The studio bosses assumed that the public wanted to get the war behind them. In 1946 the most popular film was Disney's now politically incorrect *Song of the South,* a retelling of Joel Chandler Harris's Uncle Remus tales. The third most popular film was the psychoanalytic western, *Duel in the Sun.* Fourth and fifth were musicals, *The Jolson Story* and *Blue Skies.* The second most popular film of the year was, however, one of the most challenging films about the role of the military in democratic society ever made, *The Best Years of Our Lives.* The next two years produced a variety of popular films, all of which ignored the war experience. The final year of the decade revived interest in the war.

Freed from military production codes and censorship, the military and the country itself were viewed with a critical eye, although not an acerbic one. That kind of criticism would take longer. The role of the soldier also changed. In the films we have discussed thus far, there is less emphasis on individual heroics than on accomplishing group goals, less emphasis on fear and frustration with military regulations than on an eagerness to "make the home folks proud."

The Best Years of Our Lives

The Best Years of Our Lives is one of the great American movies. Visually stunning and impeccably acted, it traces the return of three combat veterans immediately after World War II. The first is Al Stephenson (Fredric March) who was a mature, successful family man and banker when called up for service as a sergeant in the Pacific. The second is Fred Derry (Dana Andrews), a young Air Force flyer forced to return to his job as soda jerk after being a hero and an officer. Most memorable is Homer Parrish (Harold Russell), a sailor whose hands were burnt off when his ship was sunk. Never being merely sociological, each of the primary characters becomes a vivid individual.

The film opens with Fred Derry trying to get a flight home to Boone City. The airline openings for returning servicemen are filled for several days. He is bumped by a fat businessman with golf clubs (golf seems to be the ultimate antithesis of the soldier, as in *Since You Went Away*), and he is referred to military transport. There he meets Al and Homer, and they share a B-25 home, sitting in the glassed-in nose of the plane, reacquainting themselves with America. These flying scenes are astonishing even 50 years later, photographed in both sharp foreground and background focus by Gregg Toland. The men are mesmerized by the beauty of the flight, particularly Homer whose service had kept him deep in the bowels of a ship. He has never flown before, nor has he understood the magnitude of his country before.

Once in Boone City, the men are reluctant to face their families. Homer is the first to be let out of the taxi. They drive by his uncle's (Hogey Carmichael) bar, and Homer suggests that they meet there sometime. Al and Fred watch his reunion with his family. His family is delighted to see him, but his mother collapses when she sees his hooks. Next, Al is dropped off at his posh apartment building. He is almost detained by the lobby attendant who doesn't like the looks of his sergeant's uniform, but he gets to the apartment and first sees his son and daughter Peggy (Teresa Wright) and then reunites with his wife (Myrna Loy) in a particularly moving scene. Finally, Fred is let out in a derelict part of town where he meets his father and his father's wife and learns that his own wife has moved out some time ago and is working in a nightclub. Later, Al takes his wife and daughter out on a toot, ending up at Homer's uncle's bar. Homer has escaped there from his family and his girlfriend. Fred, who has been unable to locate his wife and is on alcoholic automatic pilot, is also there and comes on to Peggy.

Although yet unidentified, Post Traumatic Stress Syndrome is clearly portrayed in this film: Al develops a serious alcohol problem, which remains unresolved at the end of the film; Homer has difficulty in reestablishing a relation with his girlfriend, explodes with anger, and nearly commits suicide; and Fred experiences night terrors, divorce, violence, and unemployment. But in 1946, people were hopeful that these symptoms were just a phase, and that back in warmth of home, healing would just take a little time.

Homer is reluctant to impose his handicap on his girlfriend. Like Lawson in *Thirty Seconds Over Tokyo*, he cannot imagine that she can love him because he is not physically "whole." In a heart-wrenching scene, he takes her up to his room and shows what his nightly ritual is like. While he can remove his artificial arms, he, of course, cannot put them on again, and during that time he is completely vulnerable: he cannot even open the door in case of fire. When she has viewed the worst and still indicates her desire to marry him, the morose cloud he has been walking around in lifts, and he decides to marry her.

Fred is the most complexly drawn of the men. After high school he took a position as soda jerk and worked until he was drafted. As a bombardier, he became an officer, and his wife (Virginia Mayo) fell in love with the officer's uniform and the officer's paycheck. She wants to go out to restaurants and nightclubs every night. After his money runs out, she become restless. He takes an assistant job under his former assistant, after a humiliating interview with the new boss of the drug store who carefully points out his complete lack of qualifications. Later when a customer suggests to Homer that he lost his hands for nothing, Fred decks him and loses his job. Shortly thereafter his wife, who was apparently doing more than working at the nightclub while he was away, leaves him.

Abandoned by his wife and jobless, stripped of the two masculine roles of the time, companion and provider, Fred takes a walk out to the graveyard of hundreds of aircraft which we first saw in the early aerial scenes. These useless giants now have a different meaning than when we first saw them from far away from the airplane. Like Fred, these have become relics of a war that the country would like to put behind. Once the hope of democracy, they and Fred have become junk. Fred climbs up into the nose of one of the planes. However he might intend to do it, it is apparent that he is contemplating suicide. Suddenly the austere silence is shattered by the sound of machinery. A man steps forward and angrily tells him to get lost, but within a few moments Fred has a new job — recycling junked aircraft — and with a job he can take the first step in rebuilding his masculinity.

Throughout the film the attraction between Fred and Al's daughter Peggy grows. Al steps in when Peggy admits her resolve to become a homewrecker and demands that Fred bring a halt to the relationship. By the end of the film, at Homer's wedding, Fred is now free from his wife and beginning a new career, and so he can develop a relationship with Peggy. This is one of the first casual — perhaps even positive — treatments of divorce in American film. We are not scandalized at the end of the film when Fred and Peggy are together. Whatever the audiences of 1946 made of these events, today we are happy he is rid of a selfish and unfaithful wife and about to make a life with the generous and understanding Peggy. He can now be a provider and a companion and he now has his masculine identity back.

This film also introduces another new theme into American film: ordinary work. We see Fred making sandwiches and selling cosmetics in the drug store. We see Al making loans and meeting with his boss. Work rather than home will increasingly become the major theme in the portrayal of men in films.

1949

The year 1949 saw the return of movies about World War II itself. Studio executives from Louis B. Mayer to Howard Hughes had resisted war films for several years, but independently, MGM, Republic, and Fox produced films about the war which became three of the top five box office hits that year. Two were serious combat films, *Battleground* and *The Sands of Iwo Jima,* about pivotal and costly battles in the European and Pacific theaters, respectively. Also that year the first successful romantic comedy about the war and its aftermath was produced, *I Was a Male War Bride.*

The two combat films are easily distinguished from the films produced during the war in showing outright fear among soldiers, mistakes made which produce loss of life, conflict between professional military and draftees, and the staggering human cost of combat. Death in the films made during the war happen relatively rarely. Death in these two combat films arrives often and capriciously and unexpectedly. Both *Battleground* and *The Sands of Iwo Jima* show stark contrasts between what is necessary for an effective military and living in a free society. The draftees constantly chafe under the demands of military life, but the fundamental message of both films is that such demands are necessary in the reality of combat against enemies as lethal as Nazi Germany and Imperial Japan.

Battleground follows one platoon through the grueling days of the Battle of the Bulge. The narrative is episodic and in some respects almost chaotic: there is no sense of purpose to the film which is normally given to combat films by the strategy of the battle it is following, fundamentally because there was no strategy during the Battle of the Bulge. As the days pass in a blizzard, under thick fog, the men react to whatever happens to wander into their small field of action. The soldiers do not even know what country they are in.

Battleground won the Oscar for best black and white cinematography in 1949, and the scenes in the snow and fog which comprise the bulk of the film are mesmerizing. Although most of the scenes are clearly shot on the limited confines of a sound stage, this small, claustrophobic space is important to the mood of the film. Because of the fog and blizzard, the men are only aware of what is going on a few yards around them. All action is in the foreground. At any moment rescue or death can intrude. The climax of the film is less an heroic act or other specific behavioral event than when the fog lifts and there is finally a background to the action of the film. Depth of focus is the hero of this film.

No less impressive is the soundtrack of the film composed of deadened ambient sounds of war — airplanes flying overhead, gunshots, bombs falling and exploding, German propaganda radio, tanks plowing through the snow. There is no orchestral score to supply the emotional context as in *Casablanca,* until the last 30 seconds of the film, when the survivors march back to Paris. One imagines that this is what it must have sounded like in the field. The soldiers are always ready to interpret sounds, and the audience becomes edgy doing the same.

The film would now be described as having an ensemble cast which we meet as they are preparing for a three day leave to Paris. No single character becomes the focus of the film. As they plan what they will do in Paris, some of the men want to drink, one wants to take a bath and check into a hotel room to be alone, most want to meet women at Place Pigalle, certainly a contrast to the war period films when the boys are faithful to their girls back home. Each character has a hook to establish his identity: one man clicks his government issue false teeth (perhaps about 40 times too often), one man, wearing shoulder pads, wants to stay behind to play football, one wants to go to the art museums. A new recruit, Jim Layton (Marshall Thompson), cannot find a cot to sleep in. Pop Stazak (George Murphy) has just gotten permission to return home, not because of his arthritis, but because his wife is too sick to care for their children. The next morning, leave is canceled for everyone, and they are sent off into battle. Like the groups in the combat films produced during the war, this is a conspicuously multiethnic group (a Jew, a Latino, several soldiers with Polish names, as well as many WASPs — late in the film there will even be black soldiers).

Holley (Van Johnson) is perhaps the central character of the film. He complains less than most of the others. He meets a French woman before the battle, whom he does not hit on, after some consideration. He does a very extended bit of screen business with eggs he steals. Of course his selfish act never leads to his actually eating the eggs. When the sergeant is wounded, he receives a field promotion. With this promotion, he becomes more military, but his one substantial act is ambiguous: he may be running away when he dispatches a nest of Germans.

A more complicated character is Jarvess (John Hodiak) who at first is standoffish from the bumpkins in the platoon. He is the one who wants to be alone in a hotel in Paris. He is a journalist whose wife has assumed his duties at his hometown paper. He is constantly irked by the fact that he knows nothing of what is going on around him, although he is sure his wife is being well informed by the wire services. He has been teamed up with the most bumptious of the soldiers, L'il Abner, who is shot in the most pathetic moment in the film, crying out for his mother. Abner has left his boots outside of the foxhole to dry because he was unable to find galoshes big enough, despite the fact that he has been warned not to do this. Jarvess has been critical of Abner's hick diction, but he adopts it late in the film.

Jim Layton is also a strongly etched character. We first see him encountering a friend from home. Later, on the battlefield he goes to find this friend but discovers he has been killed. The friend had been with his unit so short a time that the sergeant doesn't know his name: Layton resolves not to be an anonymous kill.

The Sands of Iwo Jima is better known than *Battleground,* justly famous for its skillful integration of footage from the actual battles it portrays into the narrative of the film. As a gimmick, the three surviving marines who raised the flag on Mount Suribachi have bit parts in the film, which are easy to note because they are conspicuously bad actors.

The film follows the training-to-battlefield formula, and focuses on three characters. The central character of the film is PFC Pete Conway (John Agar), the son of a general killed at Guadalcanal. Conway has eschewed the family tradition of a military career, like Bill Smollett in *Since You Went Away.* But he has joined the marines out of a sense of family duty. He is uncomfortable with military life, particularly with his sergeant, Stryker (John Wayne), who had served under his father's command and who greatly admired the old man. During the course of the film Conway comes to appreciate the necessary hardness of professional military men and through his begrudging acceptance of Stryker, reaches a posthumous rapprochement with his father.

Conway's understanding of his father also comes from his meeting a woman during his leave in New Zealand, marrying her, and finding out shortly before battle that he has a son from whom he will be removed for some time, and whom he may never see. Conway's absent fatherhood connects him with Stryker and his own father. Although he and Stryker nearly came to blows on the night before combat, he accepts his duty to follow Stryker's command.

Forrest Tucker plays a coward. He has done something prior to the action of the film which has lead to his demotion. During the first battle in the film, he pauses to drink a cup of coffee rather than returning to the foxhole with new ammunition, and one of his buddies is killed because of his tardiness. But after Stryker whips some sense into him, Tucker's character becomes a brave man.

Stryker is a complex character for Wayne. He received an Academy Award nomination for this performance. Stryker is estranged from his wife and child. Writing to his son or waiting for letters from his son which never come throws him into alcoholic despair. When he's drunk, he's mean, and even when he is sober, he's mean. But after he is killed on the summit of Mount Suribachi, a partially complete letter to his son in which he anticipates his own death finally humanizes him to Conway.

I Was a Male War Bride begins a process in which the war can be mined for comedy, particularly comedy about the stupidity of military life. Like *Mr. Smith Goes to Washington,* it derives its humor by turning traditional sex roles upside down. Directed by Howard Hawks who had invented the "screwball comedy" in films such as *Bringing Up Baby* (1938), the movie divides neatly into two distinct parts. The first half is a tepid screwball comedy about the relationship between a French officer, Henri Rochard (Cary Grant), and his WAC driver/interpreter, Lt. Catherine Gates (Ann Sheridan). Hawks' earlier comedies derived their energy from a rich cast of eccentrics and fast pacing. The pacing here is relatively slow and the cast during the first half of the film is largely Rochard and Gates. The energy is further deadened by many scenes being filmed in bombed out locations in Germany.

Rochard and Gates have worked together successfully before, but with a great deal of conflict. Gates early admits that she likes fighting with Rochard, but she states she has had it with his octopus hands. She ascribes his behavior to his being French; he ascribes her reluctance to typical American female coldness.

Rochard's mission — his last before being separated from the French army — is to find a German lens maker and convince him to move to Paris. On this mission, Gates gradually assumes the more masculine role in their relationship, first by becoming the driver of their motorcycle and sidecar, because Rochard has not been checked out for such a vehicle. She disappears and returns wearing trousers. Later, she solves problems in getting them beyond roadblocks and will save them from going over a waterfall. Unlike Jefferson Smith who has no difficulty in surrendering to Saunder's expert hands, Rochard cannot accept her as a full partner in the mission, but at the end, it is she who finds the lens maker and convinces him to move to Paris. Along the way Rochard's high-handedness leads to his being caught on a train gate, falling out of a window, being arrested, and plowing into a haystack. But inside the haystack, he finally reasserts his masculinity and teaches Gates how to kiss.

The second half of the film is more high-spirited. By the time they return to post from their encounter in the haystack, they have decided to marry, and the comedy from that point on derives from Rochard's Gallic inability to deal with American red tape, somehow ignoring the fact that *bureaucracy* is a French word and a French invention: they must fill out reams of forms in quadruplicate; they must wait as the forms circulate from office to office; and they must be married three times. The final insult is that Rochard can only get to America as a "war bride." The legislation which authorizes his emigration allows for "spouses," but the procedures seem only to accommodate women. Just as he must gradually accept Gates' "masculine" roles in the first part of the film, he must accept his own feminization in the second. He must complete a gynecological questionnaire, and he can finally get to America only by entering the ship in drag, wearing a wig made of a horse's tail. His feminization is only partial: several soldiers and sailors comment on his bad face, although they also think he has "good gams." As they are left alone in their room on the ship, finally on their way to America after half a dozen bureaucratic interruptions of their wedding night, the audience remembers that he is wearing a skirt.

Changes in Masculine Images During the 1940s

World War II is often credited with making America an international rather than parochial culture and a nation rather than a confederation of regions. The War involved everyone in some way. People who had never ventured outside their county of their birth were scattered across the country and the globe and forced to share bunks and foxholes with other Americans from different regions and social and ethnic backgrounds.

There is a tendency among social critics to describe the war films made during the war as naive or sentimental. We sometimes say that these were simpler times. We berate ourselves because of words or actions in works of fiction which we now call sexist or racist or homophobic or culturally insensitive. That these dramas, comedies, and musicals dealt with death and maiming, reflected the day-to-day reality of the times. One of every three men in the country between the ages of 18 and 30 was in service. Receiving good or bad news was part of life, not maudlin plot building.

Entering the world of the 1940s through these films should tell us these were not simple times. If anything, we live in simpler times. Life changed dramatically day-to-day, in unpredictable ways. Families were decimated, and others were changed beyond recognition. Three of the films we have considered (*Mrs. Miniver, Since You Went Away, The Best Years of Our Lives*) chronicled middle class adjustment to loss of domestic help, which seems to us a small and good change. But there were equally inconvenient and disrupting effects on those thrown out of domestic service into factory work or other less honorable ways of life. Women assumed roles they had never considered, and men returned with disabilities they had never imagined. Those of us who did not experience the horrors of the Nazi and Japanese ethnic purges during the 1930s and 1940s might need to be cautious before labeling the term "Jap" as racist or a wolf-whistle as sexist. Our dominant philosophy of multiculturalism should not ignore the reality that at times many cultures have been committed to the annihilation of other cultures — including our own relatively tolerant one.

There are differences in representation of male behavior the films made during the war with those made about the war after 1945. During the war, men are faithful to the women back home. After 1945, men are faithful in their minds to the women back home, although their bodies may check out Place Pigalle when they are on leave in Paris. Likewise, by the time of *Best*

Years of Our Lives, men may have to consider that the women waiting back home did not actually wait.

Men in both groups of films are committed to the military and political objectives of the war. Because of their commitment to these objectives, they do the unnatural thing of bonding together as a unit. (Male bonding as an important social role was not "discovered" until the 1960s; the primary social role for men from 1920 through the 1950s was within the family; what is going on in these films is temporary and against nature; these men really belong *home*.) But the men in the later films are more constrained by military life. They complain. They try to get out of combat. There is recognition by the filmmakers, if not the characters, that the "arbitrary rules" of the military are not at all arbitrary — Abner loses his life because he leaves his boots outside the foxhole, against orders.

Between the representations of male behavior in 1939 and the films made during the war, there are few differences, however. The factors which will change our conceptions of masculine role behavior are just being put in place: a national if not global orientation, women in higher echelons in the work place (Anne likes her factory job in *Since You Went Away*, as does Gates in *I Was Male War Bride*), a new view of child rearing (no maids for the working mothers), a replacement of Mom and Pop businesses with corporations (Fred Derry's drug store has been bought by a "chain").

We called an earlier version of this chapter "Wolves, Lone Wolves, and Team Players." In that title we wanted to convey the idea that during the 1940s we saw a male role which was male- and team-oriented. Teddy Roosevelt's notion of America as a nation of rugged individualists was suspended. The fighting unit (or even in the musicals, the chorus) was what was important. The war imposed this cultural change. Wolves (which preyed on women) or Lone Wolves (individuals interested in personal glory) were pariahs, at least in the most popular films of the decade.

We also used the image of the wolf as a reference to Joan Mellen's (1977) book *Big Bad Wolves: Masculinity in the American Film*. In that work, Mellen announces:

> This book is about the fabrication in American film of a male superior to women, defiant, assertive, and utterly fearless.... Hollywood has demanded that we admire and imitate males who dominate others, leaders whom the weak are expected to follow. The ideal man of our films is a violent one. To be sexual, he has had to be not only tall and strong but frequently brutal, promising to overwhelm a woman by physical force that was at once firm and tender. Male stars are people manufactured from the raw material of humanity to appear as supermen overcoming women and lesser men by sheer determination and will, involving, in varying permutations, competence, experience, rationality — and charm [p. 3].

Mellen acknowledges that there are other images of men in films, particularly the comedians like Chaplin, and musical comedy stars whom she says "fall outside the stereotype of the self-controlled, invulnerable, stoical hero who justifies the image of unfeeling masculinity as a means of winning in a world that pounces on any sign of weakness" (p. 5). But the "big bad wolf," Mellen contends is the dominant film image of men in American films. Mellen's book has been widely popular and consists of a great deal of intelligent writing about films.

But there is a stark contrast to what she finds in films and what we have described so far in this book. The most obvious reason for this difference is the contrast between our methods of selecting films. Mellen selects films which exemplify her thesis, while we have looked for commonalities within a group of rationally selected films — the most popular films of 1939 and the most popular musicals and social dramas of the 1940s, and the most popular films about the war from 1945 to 1949. In her discussion of the films of the 1940s, she mentioned only one film which we have discussed, *Casablanca*. In addition, she concentrates on *The Maltese Falcon* (1941), *Blood and Sand* (1941), *Gentleman Jim* (1942), *Across the Pacific* (1943), *To Have and to Have Not* (1944), *Back to Bataan* (1945), *Body and Soul* (1947), *Red River* (1948), and *The Set-Up* (1949).One thing which strikes us about these films is their high rate of violent acts perpetrated by the characters, compared to those which we selected based on popularity, in which the characters are more likely to be the recipients of violence. Moreover, the men in her films are far more individualistic/isolated than those in the films we have discussed. The men in Mellen's films are not only sexually predatory "Wolves," they are also "Lone Wolves."

Mellen is interested in Hollywood "product." We are not only interested in the product but what of that product the public bought. If one looks across the whole range of films produced each year, one would be able to find men and women fitting every possible image. Popularity allows us to focus on the prevailing images of the times — not just what producers and directors wanted to make and distribute but which people embedded in the values and attitudes of their times wanted to see. And what audiences paid to see — for nearly the last time in popular cinema — were men who were family-oriented. Beyond the 1940s, male behavior is not moored in family, but, increasingly, in self and work, where the wolf and the lone wolf are valued and the team player and homebody receive little recognition.

War Films of the 1950s

During the 1950s, Hollywood returned to World War II for a number of popular films, including *From Here to Eternity* (1953), *The Caine Mutiny* (1954), *Mister Roberts* (1955), *Battle Cry* (1955), *The Bridge on the River Kwai* (1957), *South Pacific* (1958), and *Operation Petticoat* (1959). All turned a much more jaundiced eye toward the military, and a much less sympathetic eye on the behavior of soldiers, sailors, and marines. With the exception of the last, all were based on literary sources, and these were mostly observations of the military from the perspective of civilian draftees. With the immediate threat of the Japanese and the Germans over, each ask, in one way or another, *is the military somehow incompatible with the democratic way of life it is designed to defend?* More to our purposes, each of these films eschews the portrayal of soldiers as heroes, and even questions the nature of heroism. In the next chapter, we will see how the idea of heroism was kept alive in historical dramas, but in these films the contemporary fighting man seems to have shrunk in stature.

The war films of the 1950s reflect other contemporary views of the times. Sex was much more commonly depicted in cinema, although in ways that today seem rather indirect and almost "in code." Extramarital affairs were a wellspring of plots, but compared to today's unambiguous portrayal of sex and sexuality, they seem quite tame. If extramarital affairs exist, then there is the possibility of bad marriages, something barely considered in the popular films of the 1930s and 1940s. The fighting man was not only a sexual being, he was capable of cowardice, desertion, and even violence toward fellow soldiers. Part of what was to blame for all of this sex and bad behavior was the flawed nature of the military. How much of this critique of military life was due to the personal experience of soldiers who wrote novels which got turned into films reflecting on their war experience, or how much the military was a convenient metaphor for the outmoded class structure of society or whether people were just shell-shocked by the prospects of another nuclear war, the revelations of the Holocaust, or the fears generated by the Cold War, is difficult to determine. What results are very popular films in which there are no heroes, but antiheroes, and in which the real enemy may not be the Japanese or the Germans, but ourselves.

We will examine three movies, *From Here to Eternity, Battle Cry,* and *The Bridge on the River Kwai,* because these are the three we feel speak most directly about the nature of the military "hero." *The Caine Mutiny,* for example, is more about the nature of mental illness than about the nature of heroism or masculinity. *Mister Roberts* is primarily a comedy of manners set on an insignificant navy ship, and although it makes keen observations about the nature of leadership in the contrasts between the bullying Captain (James Cagney) and intelligent and compassionate Lieutenant Roberts (Henry Fonda), the film suffers from being almost an exactly filmed version of Thomas Heggen and Joshua Logan's stage hit. *South Pacific,* a musical, deals with the issue of interracial love more centrally than the issue of heroism or even military life.

From Here to Eternity is just barely about World War II, and the conflicts that exist here are not between professional army and the civilian recruits, but between officers and enlisted men and between men from different regional and ethnic backgrounds. It shows the military as a society that would fall apart if it were not for a strong disciplinary code and a few honorable men.

From Here to Eternity is full of compelling performances, the casting of which is part of the legend of Hollywood. Originally, burly Aldo Ray was to play Robert E. Lee Prewitt, the company bugler, but slender, nervous Montgomery Clift was eventually cast. Clift is mesmerizing as the former middleweight boxer who blinded a sparring partner and refuses to box for the company, despite the sadistic pressure of fellow enlisted men, encouraged by his commanding officer. Burt Lancaster portrays Milton Warden, the sergeant who holds everything together in the company, but cannot hold together his own personal life by avoiding an affair with his commanding officer's wife (Deborah Kerr). Originally Robert Mitchum was cast in this part. Eli Wallach was first cast as Angelo Maggio, a New York wise guy who irritates many around him and whose inability to back down from a fight leads to his death, but Frank Sinatra eventually got the part and an Oscar for best supporting actor. He claimed that it did not involve the decapitation of a studio producer's horse, as portrayed in *The Godfather* (1972). Deborah Kerr got her chance to portray Karen Holmes when Joan Crawford had a fit about her wardrobe.

The story of *From Here to Eternity,* set during the weeks before the bombing of Pearl Harbor in Hawaii, revolves around a minor character, the commanding officer of Company G at Schofield Barracks, Captain Holmes (Philip Ober). Holmes is obsessed with his own career, to the point that everything else, military order, individual rights, and even the very lives of his men are compromised. He and his wife are irresolvably estranged, because he was with another woman on the night she miscarried. She begins an affair with Sgt. Warden, when he comes to her house to cover up one of Holmes' meetings with another woman. She clearly knows about her husband's infidelities but no longer cares. Her affair with Warden culminates in one of the most seen film scenes in American movie history. Although Holmes carries on with other women with little care about being observed, it is his wife that has "the reputation." Although warned of this reputation by a fellow noncom who had slept with her, Warden and Karen meet in a park near the beach. They both have bathing suits under their clothes. They take off their outer clothes and plunge into the surf. In the next cut, the camera follows a gentle wave sweeping across the sands until it splashes over the couple as they lie in each other's embrace on the shore.

But the film is depicting a time when marital infidelity, regardless of the provocations, would be regarded as unambiguously wrong, and so the affair will come to nothing, and this scene comes to an abrupt end. The only solution Karen can see for them is for him to become an officer, and then for her to divorce her husband. Warden loves the military and certainly has the ability to become an officer, but he hates officers, and when he refuses to take the Officer's Candidate School exam, their passionate affair comes to a depressing halt.

Prewitt, too, loves the military, but he is in no way a military man. At one point he says, "I love the army. When a man loves a thing, that doesn't mean that it has to love him back. I left home at 17; I didn't belong no place until I joined the army." He is far too independent, even though his self-image is bound up in being part of the military. Holmes believes that a good showing at the intercompany boxing competitions will give him the edge on a promotion, and he suggests that his men "encourage" Prewitt to box by giving him demeaning details and by picking fights with him. "Prew" gets "the treatment," which includes digging holes, only to fill them up again, being tripped in bayonet drill, and marching for miles. Prewitt would rather endure a beating than use his fists against a fellow soldier. Eventually, it is this sanctioned abuse of Prewitt that leads to Holmes' downfall, when a hazing of Prewitt at which he is present is observed by a senior officer.

Prewitt and Maggio are buddies, and Maggio takes Prew to a thinly disguised house of prostitution, the New Congress Club, where he meets a hostess, Alma (Donna Reed). This affair is as doomed as Warden's, and as his own relationship with the army, because Alma wants a proper life, including membership in a country club and a big home in the best section of her hometown. Her ambitions are a kind of social class revenge. She wants to return home successful to show the man who took her virginity but would not marry her because she was not from the right family that she could have lived in his world. But Prewitt loves the military life, and has no intention of a civilian life in the Pacific Northwest. One doubts that he could make it there, either. It is interesting that both Prew's and Warden's relationships are doomed not only because of the unsanctioned sexual nature of them, but because the women both have higher social ambitions than the men.

Like Prewitt, Maggio is a "hardhead." He and the stockade sergeant (Ernest Borgnine) come in conflict several times early in the film, but when he is sentenced to the stockade, the conflict, which seems to be ethnic in nature, comes to a lethal head, and Maggio is killed. Prew seeks out the sergeant and kills him, and then goes AWOL at Alma's. While there, the Japanese bomb the harbor. The scenes of the bombing of Pearl Harbor are spectacular, and while we may be shaking our heads about military life up until this point in the film, we are reassured that the threat of a real enemy will bring the fighting community together. The bombing also serves very conveniently to wrap up all the loose ends of this episodic story. In a tragic ending, Prewitt, who does not quite grasp the fact that now that it is wartime, the rules have changed, tries to sneak back onto the base, and is shot. Prew never quite grasps the reality of the demands of the military life he so much loves in the abstract.

Of the seven films based on the experience of World War II which achieved blockbuster status during the 1950s, Raoul Walsh's *Battle Cry,* based on Leon Uris's bestseller, is the most positive in its depiction of military life. *Battle Cry* is framed as a story about how a group of very different young men come together to become a fighting unit and how they mature as men. But the movie has a nontraditional structure which makes it as dark as *Thirty Seconds Over Tokyo.* The story of the group is told in three sections (boot camp, assignment in New Zealand, and battle), where the stories of individual soldiers come to the forefront for a period of time, and then recede. Sometimes the stories end abruptly because the particular episode comes to an end or because the character dies. For example, during boot camp, the middle class kid from Baltimore (Tab Hunter) becomes involved with an older, married woman to the point that he stops communicating with his family and girlfriend back home and becomes derelict in his duties. When the family contacts the commander of the unit, Major Huxley (Van Heflin), he arranges a leave back home. There Hunter's character patches things up with his girl and they elope. Now that this issue has been resolved, he almost disappears from the film, except for a brief moment in combat and in the film's final scene.

One of the most compelling stories is the romance between Andy (Aldo Ray) and Pat (Nancy Olson). Andy is a Swedish lumberjack. For the first half of the film he ridicules the others who abstain from female companionship because they have girlfriends back home or who become involved seriously with women. He sees all women as available and can hit on more than one woman at a time (he can be arranging a date with one woman while striking a match on the backside of another). In New Zealand he meets Pat, whom he believes is the wife of a soldier, but, in fact, her husband has been killed in action, as well as her brother. When he understands her true position, he apologizes for his forward behavior — he says this is the first time in his life he has apologized for anything, and they begin a very tentative romantic relationship. Pat is afraid to commit to a relationship — she does not want to be hurt again, and Andy, too, has some misgivings. After his first taste of battle, Pat nurses him back to health after he comes down with malaria and refuses to go to a hospital. Eventually he decides that their best solution is for him to defect, and he leaves the ship the night before it is due to move out. But eventually he faces the reality of life as a defector, particularly when it comes to facing a wife whose first husband was a war hero and when he thinks about the prospect of having a son.

The Bridge on the River Kwai does nothing more or less than question the basic legitimacy of war. The film follows the fate of a regiment of British soldiers, forced to surrender to the Japanese in southeast Asia, who are enlisted in the building of a bridge. The film consists of two basic conflicts: the first between Colonel Nicholson (Alec Guinness), the leader of the British, and Colonel Saito (Sessue Hayakawa), the commandant of the camp, for control of the souls of the British soldiers. Saito attempts to break the morale of the men by taking away the structure of the fighting unit and by making the British dependent on him for food and rest. Nicholson refuses to allow the officers to work beside the men, insisting to his fellow officers that if the structure and discipline of army life breaks down, the men will go from being soldiers to being animals, and insisting to Saito that the rules of the Geneva Convention do not permit officers from working in such a capacity. Today, such an insistence seems elitist and self-serving, but we learn from Saito that this is exactly his plan. Perhaps the most memorable scenes in this movie are those of the torture that Nicholson endures before Saito caves in — standing at attention in the sweltering Burmese sun covered with flies and then contained in a torture cage for days with little food or water. His absence bonds his men together.

But Nicholson begins to veer off from a rational path once Saito relents. Not only does he nix the development of an escape plan (indeed an escape into the jungle would be foolish) but he decides to actually help the Japanese build their bridge. On the one hand, his decision is commendable. He envisions a time in the future in which a well constructed bridge will serve as a reminder of British will and skill, but on the other he seems to have lost sense of himself as a soldier in his efforts to keep that identity for his men: the bridge has a military mission. He is aiding the enemy.

Like most things military in this film, the Japanese plans are flawed. They have picked a location to build the bridge where the ground will not support it. Nicholson uses the engineers in his unit to reconceptualize the bridge and build an even finer one than had been planned. He outlaws attempts to sabotage its construction, and as he becomes successful in building the bridge he gets more and more accommodations for his officers and men: they eat well, have days off, and even throw an occasional party. He turns the tables on Saito, who is not a mindless stereotype, but a man of culture, and strips him of his identity as a military man.

The second conflict is an internal one, within the American Shears (William Holden). Shears reminds us of Rick in *Casablanca*, particularly in his initial state when the British arrive at the camp. He is a cynical outsider whose primary motive is self-preservation. He is particularly scornful to Nicholson whose actions he comments on: "That's the kind of courage that will get us killed."

Colonel Nicholson is dragged from his torture chamber. Before 1945, no popular film portrayed the horror of war quite as graphically; no hero looked so unheroic.

Shears escapes and makes his way back to a British outpost, aided by natives. While recovering from his ordeal, he swims in the ocean, dates a beautiful woman, and enjoys his freedom. But since he knows the way from the bridge to the outpost, he is drafted into going with a party to blow up the bridge. He tries every way out of going on the mission. He discloses that he is not Shears at all: he adopted Shears' identity because Shears was an officer who was killed and he expected better treatment as an officer in the camp. His transformation into a "hero" is never quite complete, and so he is a perfect 1950s character.

But he reluctantly goes back. After a harrowing journey, they must fight nature (the river dries up disclosing their explosive wires), the Japanese, and even Nicholson, who is so invested in the bridge that he almost succeeds in defusing the explosives. Only at the last moment does Nicholson realize how misguided he has become, and when he is shot from behind, he falls on the detonator. In the final frame of the movie the British medical officer says again and again, "Madness. Madness." They are *all* quite mad: war is the madness in this film.

Either driven mad by the cruelty of war or sidetracked by his pride in a job well done, Colonel Nicholson tries to stop the demolition of the bridge, despite its strategic use to the enemy.

Conclusions

There are two main themes that run through the movies we have examined in this chapter: the first has to do with a redefinition of heroism and the second has to do with the emergence of social class as a pivotal lens through which to view society.

As for heroism, we may note a change between thinking of heroism as a deliberate choice that many men made to a perspective that heroism is a decision a few are forced into. During the war, we have depictions of everyday men rising to the challenge of the situation — domestic or military. Mr. Miniver ferries soldiers from Dunkirk; the soldiers in *Thirty Seconds Over Tokyo* help each other survive; even the soldiers and sailors in the musicals grind their teeth together and volunteer for combat. Most often this decision is motivated internally and domestically: the man looks inside himself, largely because of an investment he has with a woman or his family. This devotion to a wife or girlfriend, father or mother, becomes transformed into a low-key patriotism. This patriotism further leads to overcoming personal and regional and ethnic prejudices.

In the films of the later 1940s, heroism becomes something more supplied from the outside: most often by the military itself. None of the men in *Battleground* want to fight, but the enemy provides the necessity for being brave and violent: Van Johnson may be running away, but when he sees the enemy, he knows what to do. In *The Sands of Iwo Jima,* Stryker's men may dislike him, but they know they can count on him, and they come to realize that they must rely on each other, despite their natural prejudices.

By the films of the 1950s, we come to realize that it was almost a miracle that the conflicts among the various enlisted men and between officers and enlisted men allowed the military to function at all. We have moved from men and their officers who are capable of both heroism and cowardice, to sheer scoundrels. Families and women cannot be counted on for much other than as additional conflicts in one's life, and officers are almost universally flawed. That miracle is most vividly symbolized by Nicholson's almost chance fall on the detonator.

Many of the films we looked at in earlier chapters dealt with the upper echelons of American society. The O'Haras, Wilkes, and Butlers were among the social elite. The Minivers are very upper in the upper middle class, and Vin marries into the aristocracy, like the American in *The White Cliffs of Dover.* The most successful series of films of the 1930s, the *Thin Man* films, is based on the preposterous marriage between a wealthy socialite and a policeman. All of these films convey the idea that while social classes of dizzying differences existed in American and British society, the barriers between social classes were relatively easy to surmount. Nick and Nora Charles can come together because of mutual attraction and a mutual love of alcohol and adventure. Ignoramus Jeff Smith can make it in the Senate.

The division between officers and enlisted men is a much less permeable boundary, and so this boundary may be seen as a metaphor for the realization among certain elements in society by the 1950s, that some boundaries, particularly those based on race and ethnicity, are in actuality extremely difficult to broach. Nicholson's *leitmotif* is that officers cannot work with the enlisted men, or both the officers and the men will become brutes: social class structure has real meaning than cannot be haphazardly done away with.

The officer/enlisted man conflicts also reflect real differences in society in the war films of the 1950s. In *The Best Years of Our Lives,* middle class Al Stephenson can take his wife out boozing in a working class bar and champion loans for working class vets, but when his daughter wants to marry a soda jerk, it takes him some time to come around. But he does come around. Only a few years later, such class tolerance is missing. Alma and Karen in *From Here to Eternity* need middle class husbands, Alma because she needs to overcome barriers in her hometown that cannot be overcome otherwise, and Karen, because she is decidedly middle class. The working class men find working class women and the middle class men find middle class women in *Battle Cry.*

And then, of course, there are the sexual politics. If we look over the dozen and a half films we have discussed that deal with the representation of men in World War II, we note that over time it becomes increasingly difficult for men and women to come together to form a lasting bond. Happily ever after is becoming the stuff of fairy tales. Even when we have romantic couples (Fred Derry and Peggy Stephenson; Pat and Andy; Tab Hunter and his Baltimore girlfriend), we doubt that they will be happy forever.

In the three following chapters, we will look at how these three themes, heroism, class conflict, and love, are portrayed in other films of the 1950s. In the next chapter we will look at the biblical epics, where men are strong and love must be compromised between an earthly woman and a jealous God. In the following chapter, we will look at what we feel is the most representative film about masculinity of the 1950s, *Shane* (1953). Joe Starrett in *Shane* would like to be a hero, but he cannot overcome his higher class enemies without the gunfighter Shane, and Shane disrupts his secure family configuration. And finally, we will look at the deteriorating picture of the family during the 1950s and 1960s, beginning with the tempestuous lives of Texas ranchers in *Giant* (1956) and Southern planters in *Cat on a Hot Tin Roof* (1958), ending with the fractioned version of family life in the 1960s films *Psycho* (1960), *Who's Afraid of Virginia Woolf?* (1966), and *Love Story* (1970).

Seven — Saints and Sinners: Masculinity in the Biblical Epics of the 1950s and 1960s

Beginning with *Samson and Delilah* (1949) and ending 17 years later with John Huston's *The Bible ... In the Beginning* (1966), Hollywood produced a string of blockbuster biblical epics, the most popular of which were *Quo Vadis?* (1951), *David and Bathsheba* (1951), *The Robe* (1953), *The Ten Commandments* (1956), and *Ben-Hur* (1959).

"Fifties epics" has become a cliché among film buffs, but there had been a long tradition of spectacle in the cinema set in biblical times, going back at least as far as Pathé's *Samson and Delilah* (1903). What is of interest in this book is to examine why they became so immensely popular at this particularly time and to discover what they tell us about the changing image of masculinity in popular American movies.

The most common explanation for the popularity of the genre is that it competed with television. Producers believed that in order to lure customers away from the small glowing boxes to be found in ever increasing numbers of American homes, color, stereophonic sound, big, wide screens filled with costumed extras, long films full of special effects and action were necessary. This was also the period of the great blockbuster musicals, like *Annie Get Your Gun* (1950), *Showboat* (1951), *Oklahoma!* (1955), *South Pacific* (1958), *The Music Man* (1962), *Mary Poppins* (1964), *My Fair Lady* (1964), and *The Sound of Music* (1965), another effort in the "bigger is better" phenomenon.

But "bigger is better" is only part of the story. There were many other biblical epics made during this period, including *The Queen of Sheba* (1953), *Slaves of Babylon* (1953), *Salome* (1953), *Demetrius and the Gladiators* (1954), *Noah's Ark* (1959), *Solomon and Sheba* (1959), *Joseph and His Brethren* (1962), *Sodom and Gomorrah* (1963), *Saul and David* (1965), and the hilariously miscast *The Greatest Story Ever Told* (1965), none of which attained blockbuster status. There were also dozens of other films set in the ancient world, of which only two, *Spartacus* (1960) and *Cleopatra* (1963), became hits, although Steve Reeves's first Greco-Roman muscle film, *Hercules* (1959), came close. What was it about some of these movies which resonated with movie goers of the period and made them hits and which did not make others that popular?

One obvious possibility for the popularity of religious epics was their religious themes. Most critics have dismissed these films as seriously religious films. Unlike the hit film *The Song of Bernadette* (1943), which tackled the doctrine of the Immaculate Conception and asked the question of whether revelation is possible in the modern age, or Fellini's *La Dolce Vita* (1963), the only hit foreign language film of the period, which questioned the legitimacy of received religious institutions, the fifties epics dished out healthy servings of lighter fare: angelic choirs singing in the background as the heroes engaged in otherworldly gazes, miracles/special effects, familiar tales rendered in highly touted authentic detail.[1] There is most often little religious substance to them. Perhaps these movies served the same religious function that coffee table books about angels and CDs of chanting monks do today: they evoke individual religious sentiment without engaging us in divisive sectarian thinking. To be less sanguine about them, they are like the great billowy interiors of Baroque churches, designed to create a general sense of awe, and less like the cerebral frescoes of the Renaissance, with their more specific doctrinal references.

But we think that there is more to these films than an ecumenical religiosity. Each of these films is about a moral decision made by the central male character, a decision to give up being a sinner and to become a saint. In this sense, these films are not a contradiction of the films discussed in previous chapters, but another aspect of a time which viewed masculine action against a moral background: Moses, becoming aware of his Jewish background, revisions his understanding of the treatment of Hebrews in Egypt in much the same way that Bic Benedict comes to understand the plight of Mexicans in Texas once he is connected to them by marriage. Ben-Hur chooses not to go along with the corrupt power structure he finds himself in and must suffer the consequences, just as Milton Warden does when he chooses not to go to Officer's Candidate School in *From Here to Eternity*.

But in one way they were quite different from the social dramas: they were about larger-than-life heroes. The main male characters of the social dramas would better be described as "antiheroes." The heroes of the biblical epics are the precursors of what Susan Jeffords describes in her analysis of films in the 1980s as "hard bodies," representations of the traditional — perhaps even reactionary — masculine values of action, bravery, and moral certainty. And the display of muscular, male skin by these actors (Steve Reeves, Victor Mature, Stephen Boyd, and most importantly, Charlton Heston) changed the way in which American heroes should look. They had to be big enough to compete with spectacular special effects. So it is probable that these films give rise to two genres of films which will become prominent in the 1970s and 1980s — the muscle-bound patriotic films of which the *Rambo* films are the most prominent examples, and the superhero films, such as the *Terminator, Star Wars, Superman,* and *Batman* series.

In a later chapter, in discussing the social dramas of the 1950s, we will note that while these films did not address the major social issues of the time head on, particularly the issues of race and poverty, many of these films did tangentially touch on these issues in subplots. Here, too, we have indirect references to these contemporary issues by focusing on a controversy from ancient times, slavery.

Samson and Delilah

While Cecil B. DeMille had built his career on historical movies, *Samson and Delilah* began the craze for biblical epics that would become prominent for the next decade and a half. There was nothing particularly unusual in the making of *Samson and Delilah*— DeMille films always did well — but this one turned out to be the highest box office non-animated film of the decade, even though it had less spectacle than other DeMille films. Immediately after its reception, all the major studios all put a biblical epic into their production calendar.

As we described in the last chapter, 1949 was the year in which three of the most popular films revisited World War II, this time with an eye toward the terror and tragedy of war and the flawed soldier in *Battleground* and *The Sands of Iwo Jima.* Samson (Victor Mature) is a flawed hero, and his flaws, too, lead to terror and tragedy.

The biblical story is followed rather rigorously. Samson, a Jew, falls for the sexual wiles of a Philistine, Delilah (Hedy Lamarr). He betrays his race and his religion and after becoming her lover, he becomes a slave of the Philistine. Shorn of his long locks (psychoanalysts can make of that what they will) and blinded, he becomes weak. But significantly, unlike actual rather than symbolic testicles, hair grows back, and with his power and religious faith restored, he is able to seek revenge.

This is one of the first films to be fundamentally about the male physique. Mature's nearly naked body is prominent in most of the scenes in the film.

(He later complained that he was tired of being a male striptease). Publicity on this film invited women to come to the film to gaze at Mature, and the *New York Times* review used, for the first time, the descriptor "hunk" to refer to an actor in a major film.[2]

DeMille films often lavished much more attention on the pagan orgies than on the moments of individual Judeo-Christian faith, and *Samson and Delilah* is no exception. Yet there comes across a set of conservative values from this film which are not incompatible with Judeo-Christian tradition: be strong, live simply, and keep the zipper up, particularly when faced with foreign women.

Quo Vadis?

Quo Vadis? is a film about the complications in the love between Marcus Vinicius, a brash young Roman soldier (Robert Taylor), and Lygia (Deborah Kerr), a Lygian hostage and a Christian. Their marriage is mixed in many ways: different ethnicity, different religion, different social class (in Rome, he is a well-connected officer and she little better than a foreign slave; outside of Rome, she is royalty and he is middle class). Religion is conspicuously highlighted by the filmmakers, but this is a 1950s film, and so social class and sex also emerge as the central themes.

The film begins as Marcus is met at the gates of the city of Rome with an imperial order to wait. He is a hero and has been away from home for three years, so he impatiently crosses into the city and demands an audience with the emperor Nero (Peter Ustinov, in his best/worst over-the-top acting). The Emperor informs Marcus that the reason for the delay is so that he can be joined by other returning heroes for a big production number in the forum. Marcus' temper is controlled by his cynical uncle Petronius (Leo Genn), the Emperor's chief flatterer. Petronius has his nephew quartered with old friends, a retired general and his wife, who have adopted Lygia. Marcus seems not to notice anything unusual when a vagabond named Paul of Tarsus drops in for the afternoon or when he finds Lygia sketching fish in the dirt. He's been out of town forcing the Britons and the Gauls to be loyal Roman subjects and seems not to have heard of this new Christian menace. But once he lays eyes on Lygia, he has only one idea in his head: getting her, however he can.

Rome in the first century was a genuinely patriarchal society. When Lygia rebuffs Marcus for being too confident, too violent, and too condescending toward her (he tells her she is too beautiful to think), he quickly decides that because of her status as hostage and, therefore, ward of the Emperor, that she is his for the asking. He asks and receives, but not before we discover that there is some attraction for him on her part. She dismisses attending his triumph and the banquet afterwards when they first meet, on pacifist ground, but there she is in the crowd, admiring him, the next afternoon.

And what a crowd it is! Trailers for this film proudly proclaimed that there were 30,000 extras in this film and 32,000 costumes. The entire resources of Rome's *Cinecittà* were used for six months. And here are most of the extras, seething around a huge reconstruction of the forum. Of course there is an irony here — audiences of the 1950s being lured to the theater to watch the debauched citizens of first century A.D. Rome lured to the Colosseum and Forum to watch a spectacle. Clearly no connection between the audience and what the audience was watching was intended to be made — we would need to wait for Fellini's *Satyricon* (1968) for that.

When Lygia returns home there are Praetorian guards to take her away, first to the banquet at Nero's Golden House and then to become a permanent member of Marcus' household. At the banquet, she is "romanced" by Marcus. She informs him that the way to a woman's heart is not through abduction.[3] He tries to interest her in gladitorial combat, but she is repulsed by the violence. After the banquet, abetted by her bodyguard Ursus (Buddy Baer), Lygia escapes into the community of Christians, hiding in the catacombs. Marcus follows her with a gladiator for bodyguard but they are overcome by the gentle giant Ursus, who tosses the gladiator into the Tiber, and then, remembering the Christian virtue of forgiving one's enemies, nurses Marcus back to health.

Marcus' conversion takes place late in the film, so through most of the two hour and 50 minute running time, Marcus is a negative example of masculinity. While there is something which attracts Lygia to him immediately, we are unsure what is good about him. Certainly one of the bases for Lygia's attraction is his physical good looks. But she is also simultaneously drawn and repelled by his assertive confidence. She seems to admire his Roman confidence in Roman law, even though she is a victim of that law. She wants him to turn the other cheek. She wants him to be less ethnocentric, to understand that those coerced to live under Roman law are not necessarily happy with that honor. She wants him to get beyond the naive assumption that everyone benefits from order, an assumption being made almost daily in the papers of the 1950s by proponents of segregation and Jim Crow laws.

There are three points in the film where Lygia's and Marcus' perspectives clash significantly, and it is perhaps at these points that we can find the most direct commentary on masculinity in the film. The first, already mentioned, is when Lygia will not look at the gladiators at Nero's banquet. The second is after recovering from his wounds, Lygia and Marcus exchange statements of love. He condescends to her (again) by saying that he will allow her to put up a Christian shrine in his Sicilian home, but when she says that part of her heart will always be reserved for Jesus, he storms out, saying he must be loved completely or not at all. Yet, he has taken the first step in his "Christianizing": he has agreed not to pursue her return to his household. In the third scene he is told that to be a Christian, he would need to free his many slaves. He says that if you want to be rich and powerful, you need slaves. That's the point, she tells him, you have to give up your desires to be rich and powerful, but he is a man/pagan and doesn't get it — at least not yet.

In the films which we are discussing there seems to be a solid association among four traits: Judeo-Christianity; bravery; heterosexual fidelity; and anti-slavery sentiment *versus* paganism, cowardice, promiscuity/effeminacy, and slave ownership and abuse. Forgetting his religion, Samson becomes promiscuous, becomes a slave himself, and is weakened and displayed as a coward. Marcus gradually loses his pagan traits — while he is brave in a military sense, he does not stand up to the excesses of Nero until late in the film, after he renounces his affair with Poppaea and joins the Christians. His renunciation of slave ownership comes last. If slavery and segregation can be equated, it is no wonder that this renunciation is the last and most painful.

When they are married in the holding tank at the Colosseum by Peter, Marcus admits to Lygia an admiration of Christian bravery, facing death by lion. The audience is by now aware of the differences in Roman and Christian views of courage: the Romans are active and savage, while the Christians have a passive courage, they smile and sing as they are lunched upon by big cats.

A secondary plot derives from Nero's wife's attraction to Marcus. Poppaea is one of the great villainesses in history, a former prostitute whom Nero installed as Empress, after dispatching his mother and wife (neither of whom were particularly nice ladies themselves). Poppaea's hold over Nero, according to Suetonious, was both in arranging orgiastic evenings for her husband and ignoring his penchant for boys. She is known to have taken many lovers, whom she disposed of if they grew tired of her before she grew tired of them.

After Lygia disappears into the Christian underground, Marcus becomes Poppaea's lover, but when Nero sets fire to Rome, Marcus dashes off to rescue Lygia and her friends. Although he is not a Christian, he has thrown his lot with them. Poppaea arranges for a contest between Ursus and a bull in a reenactment of Theseus and the Minotaur (apparently she didn't know the plot of the myth), with Lygia as the sacrificial damsel tied to the stake. Ursus handily dispatches the bull, and Marcus pulls free of his fetters and helps the crowd demand their release, setting off the riots which bring about Nero's downfall.

History is manipulated, particularly at the end of the film when the time between the burning of Rome and Nero's suicide is presented as four days rather than four years. Poppaea outlives Nero in the film, rather than being kicked to death by him. There are also deliberate attempts to make parallels between Nero's Rome and Fascism (Marcus had returned from getting the recalcitrant British and French in line; he is joined by those working in the areas of Poland and the Czech Republic). Of course it is easy to make these connections, as Hitler and Mussolini both borrowed imagery heavily from imperial Rome. The portrait of the self-indulgent tyrant who was a failed artist would have been particularly chilling in 1951.

Quo Vadis? has a happy ending of sorts. Of course, most of the Christians have been eaten by lions or used as torches to light Nero's after-the-fire party, and Peter has been crucified upside down after having the *Quo Vadis?* vision on the Appian Way. Likewise Petronious has committed suicide after finally declaring his love for a slave girl, who shows her love for him by slashing her own wrist, in a kind of double love suicide which was considered romantic at the time. But Nero is dead before he or his wife can think of another way of offing the lovers, and at the end of the film Marcus and Lygia are moving to Sicily.

David and Bathsheba

David and Bathsheba is darker and smaller than many of the other films we are discussing here. The biblical story, found in chapters 11 and 12 of second Samuel, is a straightforward episode of sexual infidelity in the life of Israel's most famous and most flawed king during another period of privileged patriarchy:

> And it came to pass in an eveningtide, that David arose off his bed, and walked upon the roof of the king's house: and from the roof he saw a woman washing herself; and the woman was very beautiful to look upon. And David sent and inquired after the woman. And one said, Is not this Bathsheba, the daughter of Eliam, the wife of Uriah the Hittite? And David sent messengers, and took her; and she came in unto him, and he lay with her; for she was purified from her uncleanness: and she returned unto her house. And the woman conceived, and sent and told David, and said, I am with child.

While the story is basically intact in the movie, there are many additions which speak about the attitudes that the audience of the time could accept about the relationships between men and women. David invites Bathsheba to dinner, allegedly to give her a reward for her husband's service in the army. Gradually, he tells her of his desire for her, after first ascertaining that she is caught in a loveless, arranged marriage (she has spent only six nights with her husband in seven months of marriage: Uriah seems to be avoiding her, preferring martial male companionship to her). David says that he does not have sexual privilege "like the pharaoh." Israel is a civilized nation where such things are no longer possible. Moreover, it turns out, as they each reveal their mutual attraction, step by step, that Bathsheba's bath was a deliberate attempt to gain David's attention. After admitting that they will be breaking Moses' law, they finally kiss. There follows a number of pastoral scenes of a developing relationship before the awful news of her pregnancy is revealed.

David, too, is caught in a loveless marriage (actually many marriages), most prominently to Michal. One of the dividends of this film is Jayne Meadows' cranky portrayal of David's spurned first wife. She is an aristocrat, and even as she tries to rekindle some interest in her husband, she seems incapable of not throwing their differences in social class (he is a shepherd/usurper) up in his face.

As mentioned previously, while these biblical epics do not seem to be deeply religious, they do involve moral dilemmas: it would not be unfair to suggest that the moral quandary of *David and Bathsheba* is what to do about loveless marriages when an opportunity for true love arises. This is a continuation of the Fred Derry story from *The Best Years of Our Lives,* but this time both parties are encumbered by bad marriages. Bathsheba is ignored by her company man husband — even when in town for the night, he chooses to spend it with the guys, next door in the palace. David's first wife is an upper-class shrew who has cut him off sexually. What are a guy and gal to do? Recognizing that an extramarital relationship is morally wrong, they still find romantic love to be a transcendent good. The second half of the film, involving flashbacks which flesh out the story of David from shepherd boy to reluctant military hero and ruler, is basically a trial in which romantic love is the defendant. Yes, extramarital love is wrong, so their love child dies in infancy, but after David arranges for Uriah to have the hero's death he dreams about, he and Bathsheba can marry and have Solomon.

We have previously had many reasons to refer to Pleck and Pleck's (1980) analysis of changing social roles of American men. During the period from 1920 until 1965, they describe an era which they call the Companionate/Provider Period. This period is characterized by: 1) the primacy of the heterosexual romantic bond, brought about by love matches and marriages involving husbands and wives of more nearly equal ages; 2) an emphasis on the husband as the provider, with only modest involvement as a father — within the family, he is primarily the companion of his wife; she raises the children while he is at work; 3) a de-emphasis on friendships with other men, partially due to the competitiveness of men in the workplace; and 4) an emphasis on the joys of sex, both inside of marriage and outside of it, particularly prior to marriage.

While *David and Bathsheba* attends to many authentic details about life in the court of ancient Israel, there is little authenticity concerning male-female relationships. David's domestic situation is virtually a case study of the problems of the Pleck's Companionate/Provider family: 1) he risks everything for the relationship with Bathsheba, because he is a "man" who needs someone to look him directly in the face and hold his hand, rather than a king who sees only the tops of subjects head's bowing, and sees only hands turned up for handouts; 2) his relationships with his sons are distant — he *provides* them with land and money, but he really does not understand what is going on in their lives; 3) he seems incapable of understanding Uriah's decision to stay with his men, when he has an opportunity to be with his wife; and 4) he seems more governed by his penis than by his head or the Law.

But the requirements of the biblical text insert some other issues into this film which are worth considering. David is tormented by his relationship with Jonathan, Saul's son and Michal's brother. The relationship between David and Jonathan borders (at least) on the homoerotic, and there is something deeply disturbing to David in his betrayal of Jonathan in the scene when he has an aural flashback about the death of Jonathan. This is certainly a negative commentary on the problem of male friendship and competition for those familiar with the whole biblical story. Those fully aware of what awaits David at the hands of his two competing older sons, also know that just providing is certainly insufficient — in this respect, David is a kind of ancient Jewish Big Daddy (in *Cat on a Hot Tin Roof*: see chapter nine) who will find these two fighting over his legacy. And recreational sex certainly has its complications. Unwanted pregnancies are a constant theme in the movies of the 1950s, whether set in the present or in the distant past.

The Robe

The Robe is more horror movie than biblical epic, and this horror-religious film, like so many hyphenated movies, verges toward the ridiculous at times. Richard Burton plays — need we say it — the brash young pagan Roman soldier, Marcellus Gallio, who is sent off to the garrison in Jerusalem. One of his first duties is to supervise the crucifixion of Jesus, and it is he who wins Jesus' robe in the craps game. On the way home from the crucifixion, he wraps himself in the robe and suffers a dreadful reaction to it, which causes nightmares, delirium, as well as a severe case of overacting.

Tribune Gallio had been sent to godforsaken Palestine after a public disagreement with the emperor Caligula (Jay Robinson) over the slave Demetrius (Victor Mature). Marcellus recognized him as an educated Greek who would make a good companion, while Caligula saw him as meat for gladitorial combat. Even worse, Caligula wants to marry Lady Diana (Jean Simmons), but she loves Marcellus.

When Marcellus goes robe-nuts, Demetrius takes the robe and abandons him, having become a convert to Christianity after a single glimpse of Jesus. When Marcellus returns to Rome, Diana sticks by him, and they decide he must go back to Palestine to find the robe to remove the curse, in a kind of classical version of psychoanalysis. In Palestine, Marcellus comes to know Peter (Michael Rennie), becomes a Christian, frees Demetrius, and returns to Rome with the robe and an evangelical spirit. The latter brings him in conflict with the Emperor again — Marcellus will not deny Christ's kingdom, and he walks off to execution, joined at the last minute by Diana, accompanied by those ever-ready cherubic choirs.

Although reviewed poorly at the time, *The Robe* was a major box office success, riding, perhaps, on the coattails of the best seller it was based on. It had spectacle, and it clung to the religion-bravery-sexuality-slavery formula. There was a sequel made, *Demetrius and the Gladiators*, but it failed to do well in the box office, not only because it was a fairly quickly put together production, but it also received a "Condemned" rating by the Catholic Legion of Decency for doctrinal errors and a little too much skin.

The Big Ones: *The Ten Commandments* and *Ben-Hur*

The Ten Commandments and *Ben-Hur* were the blockbusters of this period, earning more than $43,000,000, and $37,000,000, respectively. Only the Disney films *101 Dalmatians* ($69,000,000), *Mary Poppins* ($45,000,000), *Cinderella* ($41,000,000), *Lady and the Tramp* ($40,000,000), and *Peter Pan* ($38,000,000), the musical *The Sound of Music* ($80,000,000), and the Cold War epic *Doctor Zhivago* ($61,000,000) earned more through the 1960s.

On the surface, what these two films have in common are Charlton Heston hurtling through the spectrum of social class, going from royal pagan to slave to middle class saint. One is, however, a reasonably faithful recreation of a biblical episode, while the other is a work of fiction about a contemporary of Jesus whose life intersects with Him on two important occasions. Both films show a lot of skin, particularly muscled male skin, and both are serious anti-slavery (pro–civil rights?) tracts.

The second half of *The Ten Commandments* is a faithful retelling of the story of the life of Moses (Charlton Heston).The repeated showing of this film may actually cloud our recollection of the biblical story of Moses. While rescued from the bulrushes by the sister of Pharaoh, there is no biblical suggestion that Moses was afforded the position of prince of Egypt, a potential heir to the throne. There is no love triangle involving Moses, Rameses (Yul Brynner), and Nefretiri (Anne Baxter). But half of the film is taken up with invented material. Almost everyone loves Moses — his adopted mother, her brother, the sitting pharaoh Sethi (Sir Cedric Hardwicke), and Nefretiri. The people love Moses. Even the Hebrew slaves whom he oversees love him because he gives them food to eat and Saturdays off. But two people do not. The first is Rameses who sees him as a potential threat to obtaining his future wife (whom he seems not to love but sees as a necessary acquisition in his bid for power and to the throne). The second person who doesn't like Moses is the anti–Semitic slave Memnet (Judith Anderson). She believes in hereditary patriarchy, and a Jewish slave just should not become pharaoh.

When the possibility of such a thing happening becomes real, Memnet precipitates a crisis by revealing Moses' racial/social class background to Nefretiri, who reacts to the news by throwing Memnet over the balcony to shut her up. Nefretiri then tells Moses that she doesn't care who he really is, she loves him. Moses, in a much more late–20th century reaction than ancient one, sets off to find his roots. He finds his "real" mother and enthusiastically becomes a slave.

Throughout the first part of the film, there has been much concern at court about a Messiah, and Rameses finally identifies him in court, in rags and chains and considerably buffed up by his work in the brick pits: Moses. Sethi has him banished, and Nefretiri enters into a hate-based marriage with Rameses, after calling Moses "First friend of Pharaoh, keeper of the Royal Seal, Prince of Ammon, Prince of Memphis, Prince of Thebes, Beloved of the Nile God, Conqueror of Ethiopia, General of Generals, Commander of the Eastern Host, a man of mud." All of this is extra-biblical.

Of course the idea is for Moses to die in the desert, but he survives, ingratiates himself into the home of Jethro by saving his daughters against the onslaught of thieves, marries himself a good Semitic woman, and is called by God to go and rescue the Hebrew slaves. Like Elsa Lanchester beholding the visage of the Monster in *Bride of Frankenstein*, Moses' hair becomes streaked with gray after being in the presence of God. Then commences the contest between Moses and Rameses and the special effects. Solomon (1978) comments:

> A man of subtleties as well as hokey showmanship, DeMille creates a powerful change in mood by filming Egypt's plagues in even less colorful atmospheres (than the Hebrews in bondage, compared to the brilliance of the Egyptian court scenes). The darkened sky from which the ominously silent hail begins to fall, the deep red blood that swims out from Aaron's staff into the now contaminated sacred waters of the Nile, and the sickly, pervasive green smoke of the Angel of Death persuasively and impressively change a wealthy kingdom into a dying land [p. 91].

Of course, Rameses does decide to let Moses' people go, but then changes his mind, setting up the most famous special effect in cinematic history before George Lucas: the parting of the Red Sea and the drowning of pharaoh's army. Once in safety in the Sinai, the Children of God begin kvetching. While Moses returns to the mountain to get the Law from God (in the film, God does not burden Moses with the entirety of Levitical Law, but only the Ten Commandments), they make the golden calf and worship it, in one last display of pagan sensuality for DeMille to film.

Charlton Heston's portrayal of Moses was one of the icons of masculinity of the 1950s. He was handsome and muscular. He was brave and sure of himself. He showed a rational compassion: it seemed reasonable to treat slaves better if they produced more, as in the famous scene in which Rameses is recounting Moses' crimes by adding a weight to scales hanging in the tent for each crime: Moses raided the temple granaries; he gave the grain to the Hebrew slaves; and he gave them a day off. Moses places a brick in the scales and the balance changes. Now the slaves are content and produce bricks, he says. Then pulling back the curtain, he discloses the grand spectacle of the monumental city, showing that his methods have been able to complete Sethi's ceremonial city while Rameses' cruel ways had failed. This may not be egalitarianism in either a Marxist or Christian sense, but this is only a step along the way of Moses' redemption: he is still a pagan prince at this point—but he has a propensity for change.

What Moses seems to be, like George M. Cohan before him, and the Terminator after, is persistent. Once he understands what is right, he pursues it with a vengeance, whether it is building the old pharaoh's city, getting the new pharaoh to let his people go, or putting up with whining in the desert. Moses has a will that is unequaled. That was probably a good message for the 1950s. We seem to find America coming to awareness about the problems it was facing. World War II had brought Americans together in a way they had never been, and the growing diversity of its population might be held together by an outside adversary like the Nazis or the Japanese, but as social change took place after WWII—particularly the expansion of the middle class through educational and home ownership opportunities—race, ethnicity, regionalism, and social class were dawning on the American populace as issues it must address. But, it was just reaching consciousness: Americans could sit comfortably in the interiors of their larger movie houses in the fall of 1956 without necessarily connecting the story of the great Jewish liberator to their own times—like millions of slave-owning Miss Watson's reading the story of "Moses and the Bullrushers" to a naive Huckleberry Finn—unaware of how the events that had begun at the beginning of that school year in Little Rock and Selma and elsewhere would utterly change their lives over the next four decades.

Ben-Hur is less about the act of liberation than it is about the debasement of human life with enslavement. The novel on which the film is based has a credible pedigree as a parable about race in the United States. Its author was abolitionist General Lew Wallace, who freed the slaves of Maryland in 1863, after discovering that Lincoln's Emancipation Proclamation only freed slaves in the Confederacy. Bosley Crowther (1959) comments:

> This (the fact that the picture is the most stirring and respectable Bible-fiction picture ever made) is not too surprising when one considers that the drama in "Ben-Hur" has a peculiar relationship and relevance to political and social trends of the

modern day. Its story of a prince of Judea who sets himself and the interests of his people against the subjugation and tyranny of the Roman master race, with all sorts of terrible consequences to himself and his family, is a story that has been repeated in grim and shameful contexts in our age. And where the parallels might be vague in the novel, which was published, after all, away back in 1880, they could not be made clearer in the film.

(They could be clearer in the review — one wonders whether Mr. Crowther is talking about Nazism with its reference to "master race," or American race relations which would make more sense if one was expecting both the 1880 book and the 1959 film to be commenting on the same situation.)

Judah Ben-Hur (Charlton Heston) is a Jewish prince whose best childhood friend is the brash young pagan Roman soldier, Messala (Stephen Boyd). Tribune Messala has recently returned to Jerusalem and at first his reunion with his old friend is happy. But, like Sethi before him, he has heard of Messianic rumblings among the Jews, and since he sees these as threats to Roman hegemony, he would simply like his friend to provide him with the names of his friends and neighbors who are engaged in such treasonous talk. Judah says no, and their friendship is over (Messala is just following orders). Before their next meeting there is a parade, and a tile slips off the roof of the Hur mansion and is interpreted as being hurled with intention to do harm at the new tribune. Judah is sent to the galleys as a slave and his mother and sister are exiled.

Judah takes advantage of a number of opportunities to improve his condition (after bulking up on the rowing benches), finally becoming the adopted son of the Roman admiral Arrius (Jack Hawkins), whose life he saved, and for whom there seems to be some sort of oblique sexual attraction to Judah.[4] Eventually, a chariot competition in the Circus Maximus takes place which boils down to Judah and Messala. Although Messala cheats, Judah wins, but as Messala dies, he feels triumphant when he tells Judah his mother and sister have become lepers. Judah returns to Jerusalem and finds them living in a cave, being taken care of by a former slave of the family, Esther. After some coaxing, Judah gets them out of the cave in order that they may be healed by Jesus, but this is the day of the crucifixion. His family, however, is healed in the storm which follows Jesus' death.

Crowther wrote that Judah's essential qualities are that he is "strong, aggressive, proud and warm." Interestingly he says that Messala has "those same qualities, inverted ideologically." Indeed, of the films we have looked at here, this is the one which is most thoroughly "masculine" — by which we mean that the villains are not portrayed as sexually perverse or effeminate. In fact, for a three and a half hour long film, there is very little sex or romance. Judah simply uses those masculine traits described by Crowther for the right cause, while Messala is just plain wrong — a plot design we might expect from a general.

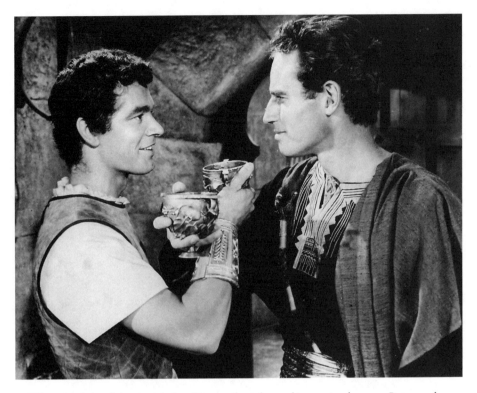

Whatever their adolescent relationship may have been, this reunion between Roman soldier and Jewish prince will not be a happy one for long. We are not yet at a time when male bonding can sustain a movie.

On the surface, what these two films have in common is a simple equation that (Judeo-)Christian belief coupled with middle class respectability and initiative and heterosexual fidelity leads to redemption, happiness, and prosperity. If this were all these films had to tell us, they would simply reinforce our stereotype of 1950s values. But these films also warn that if middle class prosperity relies on the suppression of a large segment of the population (here, slaves, in the society of the times, persons of color), then that prosperity can be toppled at any time. Like the social dramas of the 1950s, these are bleaker films than even the films made during the crisis of World War II. Moses is left wandering in the desert toward a land he would never be allowed to set foot in; Judah and his family are reunited, but they are poor outcasts.

Epilogue: And Then the 1960s

Not one blockbuster film of the 1950s is set in the future: we would have to wait a decade and a half before *most* of the blockbusters would be set in

*Male skin is a prominent feature of biblical epics, and no skin is more important than Charlton Heston's (*Ben-Hur*).*

the future. The human action blockbuster films of the 1950s are all set in the present, the near American past, particularly the 1940s, or the ancient past. In the present, men are dwarfed by social reality. Work, family, and society itself seem to overwhelm the man of the 1950s. Only in the distant past could men be heroes. While men could be heroes in the films of the 1940s, even in recreating those times in the films of the 1950s, the film directors filled the landscape with moody actors like James Dean, Montgomery Clift, Paul Newman, and Marlon Brando, actors whose "method" acting style was designed to register internal conflict, actors who were trained to feel.[5] Brando and Newman might sometimes fit Jeffords' classifications of physical hard bodies, but Clift and Dean certainly would not — these were antiheroes, liberals, life-sized (or smaller) men.

But men could be genuine heroes in the ancient past, a past where — so the reasoning went — there weren't as many ambiguities. The heroes of the biblical epics (and the classical and mythological films) were an antidote to the antihero mentality of the times. The strong, courageous, somewhat larger than life heroes, lead us to James Bond in a few years, and eventually to Indiana Jones and John Rambo, on the one hand — resourceful, courageous, talented, but fundamentally human heroes — and on the other hand, Luke Skywalker, with his magic sword, not unlike Moses' rod, and the superheroes of the next generation of films — Superman, Batman, the Terminator, among others.

The 1960s were a time which, like the 1950s, we may have mis-stereotyped. We think of the 1960s — or at least the late 1960s — as a time of rebellion, a throwing off of traditions with resulting culture clashes — particularly the generation gap, the youthening of American culture, the demise of high culture in favor of pop culture, a period of self-indulgence and self-expression. What we have found is that most of those changes had already been registered in the films of the 1950s (rebellion in Prew in *From Here to Eternity*; Nero in *Quo Vadis?* is a parody of self-expression, based in part on Beat improvisational poetry readings; generational conflict is at the core of *The Ten Commandments*), and sometimes as early as the 1940s (the youthening of actors in *Since You Went Away*). What we will find in subsequent chapters is that those changes also met with a backlash, so that the most popular films of the late sixties are often unexpected. For example, the two most popular "war films" of the period are the anti-war comedy *M*A*S*H* and the gung-ho John Wayne vehicle, *The Green Berets*. In the middle of the sexual revolution, the highest grossing romantic film, *Love Story,* was not only about heterosexual fidelity but about baby boom young adults trying to restore their relations with their parents, although the portrayal of the family was very dark.

So, the last of the big biblical epics was a mammoth hit in 1966. Surprisingly — because of the way we tend to recall the late 1960s — it is perhaps the most religious of the films we have discussed, with very little added to "modernize" the material. John Huston's *The Bible ... In the Beginning* is a curious film. Being faithful to its source materials, the first 22 books of Genesis, the film is episodic and characterization is thin. The episodes are The Creation, Adam and Eve, Cain and Abel, Noah and The Flood, The Tower of Babel, Lot, Abraham, and Isaac. With the exception of the Noah story — which is reinvented as a comic folk tale, with the first episode about Noah's lazy sons and the second about problems of zoo administration — the stories are told straightforwardly and without embellishment. The creation is a series of spectacular shots over an impressive musical score and John Huston's beautiful reading of the first chapter of Genesis. It is not unlike the first four frescoes in Michelangelo's Sistine ceiling. Michael Parks plays a muscularly lean Adam who lets a blonde Eve trick him out of Eden, a lush environment whose branches and fronds serve the same purpose as fans in a fan dance. Huston himself plays the silly old Noah. After the Tower of Babel sequence in which Stephen Boyd portrays a corrupt Nimrod in enough make-up to make

M. Beaucaire blush, the film stalls, partially because there is more dialogue and the characters throughout speak in King James and partially because there is a lot of plot to get through. There are few lessons about masculinity in this film.

Eight — The Good '50s Family: Shane

We often view the 1950s as simpler times. For evidence we turn to television sitcoms. The recent film *Pleasantville* (1998) uses the convention of television black and white in contrast to "real life" color to indicate the blandness of those sitcoms, in comparison to the vital sexual and creative life that time travelers from the present bring with them. While we may view the 1950s as the time of the middle class husband returning home from some undefined office to his well-groomed and fastidious housewife spouse, we also know the 1950s as the time of the beat generation, abstract impressionism, and the civil rights movement. One contemporary name for their own times was the "Age of Anxiety." These are conflicting images that at some point we will need to resolve.

Of the 50 most popular films of the 1950s, 17 are primarily concerned in family issues. Six of these films portray the family positively: *Cheaper by the Dozen* (1950), *Father of the Bride* (1950), *Shane* (1953), *Oklahoma!* (1955), *Old Yeller* (1957), and *Auntie Mame* (1958). Yet even in these films, the family is under stress. *Cheaper by the Dozen* is based on the life of efficiency experts Frank and Lillian Gilbreth. Dad marshals his troops in a highly regimented (although loving and comic) very efficient way, but at the end, Dad dies and mother must struggle on by taking her husband's position. *Father of the Bride* describes the emotional and financial tolls of the wedding of a doted-on daughter to pleasant effect. *Oklahoma!* has a very dark side about a psychotic barn-burner, and *Old Yeller* not only has as its climactic scene a boy having to kill his beloved dog, but the whole film is effused with the problems of a temporarily father-absent frontier family. *Auntie Mame* is a giddy romp about alcoholism, orphans, anti-Semitism, and unwed mothers.

Even darker are *Cinderella* (1950) which is primarily a story about child abuse; *Showboat* (1951), a musical about love interrupted by addictive gambling and race; *David and Bathsheba* (1951), previously discussed, in which the great hero of Israel become a modern cheating husband; *The Snows of Kilimanjaro* (1952), another story about a marriage on the rocks, despite an idiotically happy ending; *Peter Pan* (1953), the fantasy lives of neglected children; *Giant* (1956), an epic tale of how mistreatment of Mexicans, stifling of women, and class-prejudice can rot a decent family; *Peyton Place* (1957), based on the runaway best-seller about incest, class-prejudice, and illegitimacy; *Sayonara* (1957) which explains why interracial love might be a legitimate reason for suicide; *Raintree County* (1957), a gloomy story about gloomy Civil War families; *Cat on a Hot Tin Roof* (1958), which considers whether football, alcohol, denied latent homosexuality, and lying are equally bad and equally part of the American family; and *Gigi* (1958), a musical about preparing a young girl for life as a courtesan. Just where are June and Ward?

The western is a genre which we will not discuss much in this book, although it is the "male" genre most often written about. Most westerns were B pictures and not expected to reach into the realm of blockbusters. So between 1938 and 1999, only 11 westerns became big hits, with decreasing frequency: *Jesse James* (1939), *Boom Town* (1940), *The Outlaw* (1943), *Duel in the Sun* (1946), *Red River* (1948), *Shane* (1953), *Old Yeller* (1957), *How the West Was Won* (1962), *Butch Cassidy and the Sundance Kid* (1969), *Jeremiah Johnson* (1972), and *Dances with Wolves* (1990). We might include three "western-musicals" of the early 1950s, *Annie Get Your Gun* (1950), *Showboat* (1951), and *Oklahoma!* (1955), and Mel Brooks' "western-comedy" about race, *Blazing Saddles* (1974), but these hyphenated genres are more about the second term in their hyphenated term.

We will look at George Stevens's 1953 film *Shane* not just as a western but as the most complete representation of 1950s "family values" of any of the popular films of the time. These are not, however, the same family values of the Cleavers or the Nelsons. Like most popular period films, there is a blending in the values between those of the period depicted and those of the period for which it was made. To use the terminology of the Plecks (1980), *Shane* is set during the period of "strenuous living," while the movie appealed to an audience in the period of the "companionate provider," or as we contend in a period where this image of masculinity had come to be questioned. There are elements from both periods in the depiction of the families in *Shane*. Certainly, life in the valley is strenuous, but the home is the center of the primary family we observe, the Starretts. There is clearly a strong emotional bond between Joe Starrett (Van Heflin) and his wife Marian (Jean Arthur) that would be more typical of a 1950s family than among families on the range. Recreational sex is taboo. Although the "town" only consists of five buildings set on one side of a rutted, muddy street, the Starretts are suburbanites. In the town, there is a great deal of male bonding and violent male behavior, characteristic of the period of strenuous living. But in *Shane* we have a depiction of the situation of many 1950s families, set in the costumes and dilemmas of a previous period: there is a full-time homemaker wife, and work-involved father, and an only child. In their suburban farm, they are cut off from their extended family. The Starretts associated socially with other couples.

Shane looks like few other westerns. Even John Ford's best films shot in Monument Valley do not convey the scope of the landscape in *Shane*. Of course he didn't have the budget of *Shane*. The vastness of the land is made evident from the first shot of the valley under the opening credits into which Shane (Alan Ladd), the weary gunfighter, rides. Even Shane is dwarfed by the landscape. *Shane* was not intended to be a B picture. It was an expensive feature from a major studio, shot in CinemaScope, with major actors.

The gun, as tool or weapon, is the central image in Shane. In the middle of the film, preparing for Fourth of July festivities, Shane shows Little Joey (Brandon De Wilde) his expertise with a pistol. Joey's mother Marian objects. Shane says that a gun is a tool like any other. It is the person using it who defines whether it is a good tool or a bad one. One could be talking about any technology: telephone, Dictaphone, and even later, the computer. The gun become the iconography for the man using it in this film. We also may note that "the gun" is the basic metaphor, but there are two types of guns in *Shane,* the rifle, the legitimate working tool of a frontier farmer, and the sidearm, the symbol of the outlaw and the cattle rancher. Here the gun is not a phallic symbol: it is a gun, a technology. If it were a phallic symbol, the longer rifle would presumably be more potent and more primal.

At the beginning of the movie, we see young Joey stalking a deer with an unloaded rifle. Joey's education in what it mean to be masculine is the fundamental story of the film, and the way the film chooses to frame this education is in how Joey is instructed to use a gun. Joey will never use a loaded gun himself, although at the climactic moment of the film, Joey will cue Shane in using his. As Joey pursues the buck, Shane comes into the frame. The buck is the first to register the presence of the stranger by warily flicking his tail and then bolting (throughout the film, animals will express the emotional content of scenes). Dad is chopping wood. Marian peeks through the window at the approaching stranger. Joey greets the stranger, and admits that he has been watching his approach. Shane responds that he likes a man who watches things going on. "He can make his mark someday," he says.

As Shane pauses for water and makes very tentative contact with the Starrett family — he says he is surprised to see a Jersey (milk) cow — Joey gets his rifle to show Shane. He cocks his rifle, and Shane reflexively goes for his sidearm. Everyone is startled, and everyone knows (Joe, Marian, and the audience — but not Joey) what Shane is — a gunfighter. Like the buck, he is more primal and more disruptive. He is the thing that they are building fences to keep out.

Very soon the cattleman Ryker and his men arrive, trampling through the recently planted garden (the next morning, it will be the buck who is making havoc of the garden when Joey awakens; the parallel scenes equate Ryker, too, with the destructive, primal side of nature). On seeing Ryker approach, Joe assumes that Shane is a new member of Ryker's gang and tells Shane to leave. Joe is holding Joey's rifle, and Shane asks him to lower it so that his exit is voluntary. But he does not leave, and when the heat turns up between Ryker and the Starretts, Shane steps out from behind the cabin and changes the balance of power.

As soon as Ryker and his men leave, Joe is immediately apologetic and Marian gets Joe to invite Shane to dinner. There is a very understated attraction between Shane and Marian, which Joe at first seems completely unaware of: he seems puzzled that Marian has set the table with their better china. Throughout dinner he rambles about changing times; Joey admires Shane's guns; Marian admires Shane. She asks Shane where he is going. He responds "Some place I've never been." The Starrett's home place is clearly a place Shane has never been. Joe tentatively indicates that he needs a man around the farm.

After dinner, Shane goes outside and begins chopping a large stump, as an exchange for his bed and board. Joe is at first surprised and then goes out and joins in. He tells Shane he's been fighting the stump for two years. Joe and Shane attack the stump, and this collaboration brings the two men together. Shane sheds his shirt. His skin shines with sweat. Joe keeps on his tattered and soiled farmer's clothes. The two men might come together for a common goal, but they are distinctly different. Together, however, they can overcome this intrusive piece of nature in the middle of the yard, as eventually they will overcome Ryker together. They must do it together, by sheer muscle — they ignore Marian's suggestion that they get the team of horses together to finish the job. (It is of some interest that having drawn the huge stump out of the ground, they leave it sitting in the yard — it will become the place where the fight between Joe and Shane will end late in the film.) Marian and Joey observe the two men working together, and they notice the same contrasts as the audience. Both in their way are completely infatuated by the intruder. The nuclear family is threatened.

Joe makes it explicit that he wants Shane to work for him, not fight his fight. Shane retires to the barn. The next morning Joey rises when he sees the shadow of the buck in the garden. He finds Shane in the barn and asks him to teach him to shoot the gun. Later Joey will try to gauge his father against

Shane is about the education of Joey, and what he must learn about primarily is the use of the gun. While his father has too much work to do to show him, the intruder Shane demonstrates his skill. Joey seems not ready for the lesson.

Shane. He asks his father about teaching him to shoot a gun. Like a typical 1950s father, Joe will do it, when he has time. We wonder whether that time will ever come. He wants to know then whether his father can shoot as well as Shane and whether he could "whip" Shane in a fight. There are no answers, but we will find out the relative mettle of these two men later in the movie.

Clothes Make the Man

It is hard not to notice that Joe's clothes are tattered in the stump scene and to make a comparison to the elegance of Shane's costume. Shane arrives wearing buckskins (not, interestingly, the citified outfit in Jack Schaefer's novel on which the film is based), but over the first half hour of the film Shane is transformed in terms of clothing, much in the same way that clothing is used to register relative social status in Valentino's Sheik films. First he removes his sidearms, and then as he wrestles with the stump, he removes his shirt. (This is only four years after male skin had box office draw in *Samson and Delilah*.) The next day his transformation is complete when he buys a set of farmer's clothes in town. Not only will his physical appearance be transformed from the golden gunfighter to a pig farmer, he will be humiliated by the process. He is startled at the cost of his new outfit ($2.25) and admits that he has not bought clothes in a long time. He is being tamed, suburbanized.

Shane has gone into town to get fencing for Joe, but he has a subsidiary mission, to buy Joey a soda pop. Both missions turn out to be humiliating, at least on the surface. After getting the fencing (which must be read as an act of defiance toward Ryker and the fundamental purpose of his trip to town), Shane asks about getting a soda pop. The soda pop must be bought in the saloon adjacent to the general store. In moving from the mercantile establishment, which is the safe haven of both the male and female sodbusters, into the saloon, the realm of the untamed men, Shane crosses over the most important cultural boundary of the film. One of Ryker's men, Chris Calloway (Ben Johnson), begins harassing him by announcing "I thought I smelled pig." Shane is calm and deliberate, but he backs down from a fight. Chris throws a shot of whiskey on his new farmer duds, and so he is humiliated to those who observe him, but Shane leaves with the soda pop and the fence wire. This is not the time to defend his honor, but to do his job. Like most 1950s male employees, his primary allegiance is to his employer, not to his own honor.

The Progressive Western

Richard Slotkin (1992) in his analysis of Western literature, cinema, and television describes one form of western as "progressive." In this form of western, the various waves of Europeans represent a progress from the savagery of the Indians, to the unbridled masculinity of the cattle rancher, to the real civilizing of towns with schools, churches, and railroad stations. Almost every western, from *Stagecoach* (1939) to *Giant*, deals in some way with these waves of "civilization." Most westerns are progressive, seeing the next generation as an improvement. Occasionally, though, there are westerns, such as *Jesse James* or *Dances with Wolves*, which view the previous generation as better. Slotkin describes these as "Romantic" westerns. *Shane* appears on the surface to be a progressive western, but it is more ambiguous on this point than most. *Shane* is a film about shades of gray, not black and white, which is perhaps one reason that French critics — insistent that American films are simplistic — disliked *Shane*. Slotkin indicates that an important part of the progressive western formula requires that the forces of progress overcome the more primitive forces by violent action.

Just as the farmers in *Jesse James* meet for some collective action, the sodbusters assemble that night at the Starrett's home to decide what they will do about Ryker's threats. This is a claustrophobic scene, in contrast to the exterior shots, with the men huddled together in Starrett's front room, and driving rain keeping everyone inside, an annoying harmonica providing a commentary on the action. The collective action they decide upon is for everyone to go to town on Saturday. There will be a show of solidarity: they'll go shopping.

But the "progressiveness" of *Shane* is ambiguous. The sodbusters are weasels. They are portrayed by character actors (Edgar Buchanan, Elisha Cook, Jr., Ellen Corby, and Nancy Culp, among others) who can most generously be described as "plain," in contrast to Shane's masculine beauty. They are constantly throwing in the towel, piling their possessions on wagons and getting ready to scurry out of the valley at each of Ryker's actions. Several are alcohol dependent. They will criticize Shane at the meeting at Starrett's for not fighting Calloway, and Shane will leave the meeting to stand in the pouring rain, humiliated in front of Joey (who cannot believe his hero has backed down, acted like a typical 1950s antihero) and Marian, who completely understands. When on their collective outing to town, Shane goes back into the bar and takes on Ryker's men, they are equally condemning of this action. He is now a trouble maker.

Only Joe Starrett is an honorable man among the sodbusters. The others look to him for leadership, all the while criticizing him. Even Ryker recognizes that Starrett is a head above the others.

The Education of Joey

Joe Starrett is a typical 1950s father. He recognizes his duty to raise his son, but his work gets in the way: he will get around to teaching Joey to use a gun, but when he has time. Marian recognizes that Shane is a more available masculine model for her son, but she cautions Joey not to come to like Shane too much. For many reasons, she realizes that one day Shane will have to move on.

When the sodbusters go into town together, Joey returns his empty soda pop bottle for a peppermint stick. After everything else has been taken care of, Shane goes into the saloon. Now he has a different mission: Joey has overheard the sodbusters' criticism of him, and Shane now deliberately decides to show Joey what it means to be a man — he has other audiences, too — most notably Marian. He is also fighting to establish his masculinity in the sodbuster community as well. He must stand up to not only his personal humiliation, but vicariously he must show the sodbusters what it will take for them to be able to go into the saloon. Shane orders two drinks; Chris begins his intimidations again. Joey sneaks into the saloon and watches, while everyone else prepares to return home.

Many of the important scenes of the movie are shot from very low angles. Here and in the two other major fight sequences (between Shane and Joe and in the showdown with Ryker and his hired gun Wilson [Jack Palance]), these low angles are used to give us Joey's perspective as he watches them. In each of these fights, establishing shots of Joey show him to be mesmerized by the action, and passive. Here he sucks on his peppermint stick as if he were a 1950s child watching professional wrestling on TV.

All of the fight scenes in *Shane* are brutal and realistic. Fighting is hard and wearing and ungraceful. This is no martial arts fantasy. At first Ryker restrains his men so that the fight is only between Chris and Shane. When Shane appears to get the upper hand, Ryker offers Shane a job. But when he refuses, Ryker steps aside and lets his men fight as a group. Eventually, Joey understands that Shane is in trouble. Shane seems to be allowing his body to be brutalized to teach Joey a lesson. Before, Joey could not understand why Shane backed down, but now he realizes that there are just too many of them. Joey urges Shane to retreat, but when he doesn't, he runs to tell his father that Ryker's men are going to kill Shane. Only Joe responds to the call. Just as they were able to overcome the stump, together they appear to be holding their own against the combined forces of Ryker's men. But eventually the numbers catch up with them, and it is only when Grafton, the owner of the saloon and general store, intervenes that they escape with their honor. Back home, Marian is reluctantly proud of her two men as she patches them up, although she sees the danger in what they have done: "It was ugly, and you were wonderful." Soon Joey tells his mother a secret, which the whole household hears: "I just love Shane ... almost as much as I love Pa." When Marian has dispatched Shane and Joey to bed, Joe joins her in the main room. She tells him to say nothing, and just hold her. While Joe seems not to understand this action, if the audience has missed the subtle signs of Marian's attraction to Shane before, they now understand that she is infatuated, and that she is troubled by her feelings.

Evil

Ryker believes he has thus far been playing fair. He has merely tried to "buffalo" the sodbusters out of the valley by trampling gardens and cutting fences and generally creating mayhem. This is a kind of *mano a mano* confrontation which might be considered fair in the land of the cattle rancher. But he has not resorted to lethal force; that is, he has not used guns. But now there is a fat government contract for beef, and the sodbusters must go. So a gunfighter, Jack Wilson, is brought in. This was one of Jack Palance's first credited film appearances, and there is no other screen presence like him. His lean, slow moving, sinister presence is the Serpent in the Garden. He is, in this context, pure evil.

Of course, for their to be a Serpent, there must be a Garden, and this is represented by the Fourth of July party held by the sodbusters. "Stonewall" Torrey (Elisha Cook, Jr.) goes into town before the party, and with him we see the wild, male revelry going on. Ryker's men are having horse races and shooting guns. Torrey is a defiant little man, an unreformed Confederate, and prone to the sauce. He goes into the saloon to buy whiskey and drinks a toast to his native state of Alabama, and defies Ryker. Ryker seems to be extraordinarily tolerant of his rudeness. But it is a holiday.

Not only is it the Fourth of July, it is Joe and Marian's tenth wedding anniversary. Marian puts on her wedding dress and off the nuclear family (and their hired man) go to the festivities. Joe publicly professes his love for Marian, but it is Shane who ends up dancing with her. Torrey tells the sodbusters about Wilson. Shane seems to know who he is, and the weasels are now concerned that Shane knows about gunslingers.

When the Starretts arrive back home, Ryker and his men, including Wilson, are waiting, not to intimidate Joe, but to make him an offer. Ryker says that he will allow Joe to run his cattle with his and to give him a high wage. Shane already has his offer, he reminds them. Ryker states his case. He has spent his life and risked his life to tame the land, but the sodbusters have come in and fenced off the water and taken over his prime grazing land. For a while it is difficult not to be sympathetic with his position. He has a point. But Joe punches holes in his arguments: the cattle ranchers were not the people who "tamed" the West. Even though he is not ready to acknowledge the role of the Indians, he points out that the trappers and explorers also did their share, and the ranchers took advantage of what the earlier generation had done. And what about the other sodbusters? No, Ryker has no plans for them. They must leave.

While this exchange of versions of history is being made, Shane and Wilson circle each other in a silent, sinister dance in which they take each other's measure. There is something almost erotic in the way they check each other out.

At the Fourth of July festivities, Torrey and the Swede had decided to go into town together. Their trip days later is intercut with scenes of Ryker and his men talking about their plan to lure Joe into town to kill him. But they must make the killing seem right for Grafton. When Torrey and Swede arrive in town, Swede goes to the blacksmith's, and Torrey goes to the saloon. ("Nobody's going to buffalo me," Torrey says when Swede cautions him about the recklessness of this act.) A thunderstorm is brewing on the horizon. Wilson challenges Torrey by vilifying his Confederate heroes. They face each other for a shootout, and draw. Wilson has his guns pointed at little Torrey, whose gun is still in his holster. He has outdrawn him. Seconds pass, and then Wilson fires, and Torrey's small body is blown back into the black mud of the street. An anonymous laugh is heard on the soundtrack.

The Swede drags Torrey's body humiliatingly through the mud and puts him on his horse and leads him back through the community of the sodbusters. As he goes through each farm, the families react to the killing of Torrey. Some immediately begin to pack, but Joe convinces them they must stay at least for the funeral. The funeral is on a promontory above the town. After a forlorn service, highlighted by Torrey's whining dog, most of the sodbusters decide they have had enough. It turns out to be Shane who makes the most impassioned speech for them to remain: they must do it, not for themselves but for their children. For their families. Then Ryker goes one step too far, setting one of the houses on fire. They pull together to put out the fire, and to rebuild the farmhouse.

The Fifties Family

In the final episode of the film, completely frustrated in his efforts to get the sodbusters to leave, Ryker and his brother attempt to lure Joe into town to kill him. Ryker's brother goes to the farm and tells Joe that Ryker has given up and wants to come to an accommodation. Joe decides to go into town. Marian is frantic, but Shane will not intervene, not until Chris Calloway arrives and tells him about the plan to kill Joe. Chris has decided that the hiring of the gunslinger was beyond the pale.

We think that one of the central scenes of this film, in terms of its message about the family and 1950s masculinity is the scene in which Joe says good-bye to Marian. Joe, the Provider, sees his role as making sure that his family and the family's stuff is protected. He can risk his life to do this. He feels particularly able to do this, now that he has come to the realization that

At Stonewall's funeral, Joe says the eulogy, but it is Shane, dressed in his sodbuster attire, who must tell the sodbuster families why they are there: the man without a family can see in high relief the importance of family.

Shane and Marian love each other and that Joey loves Shane almost as much as him. This is complete selflessness, even though a completely tragic act: Joe must imagine his own death and his wife and son becoming Shane's family. But as his role of provider is the most important one, it makes sense.

Marian, in her role as keeper of the family, sees losing Joe as too much to ask. She suddenly exhibits almost venomous contempt for the farm. It is nothing but backbreaking work, and the house is a "shack." Joe is appalled at her language. He sees their crude little farm as "home," something he is willing to risk his life for.

Meanwhile, Shane returns to his buckskins and his side arm and determines to prevent Joe from going into town. He takes the role of society, wanting the nuclear family to survive, even thought he personally would like for Marian to become available. His fight with Joe to prevent him from going into town disturbs the harmonious universe of the farm: the cattle and the

Returning to his gunfighter clothes, Shane prevents Joe from walking into a trap in town. But to do so, he must violate the convention of the gun: he beats Joe over the head with it.

horses go crazy. We see much of the fight from between the legs of the livestock, stamping and flailing. The fight is pretty even, and Joe seems to get an upper hand, as he beats Shane into the stump they had pulled out of the ground. But then Shane brings out his trump card: the gun, the sidearm; he hits Joe unconscious with it. Joey is immediately outraged: this use of a gun is unfair; he rails against Shane, but Shane gets on his horse and goes into town, after making sure that all Joe's horses have been scared away. Marian is taking care of Joe, and tells Joey to be sure Shane knows that his rejection is not true, and so Joey runs the whole way from the farm to town after Shane, calling his name, again and again.

There are three people waiting at Grafton's for Joe: Ryker and Wilson on the first floor, and Ryker's brother upstairs. Again the outlaw, Shane enters the saloon. He confronts Ryker. He tells him his time has passed. Ryker responds by telling him his time has passed, too. Shane responds by saying that the difference between them is that he knows that he is out of date. And then there is the shootout. Shane gets those on the first floor, but he is slow against the brother upstairs: Joey, accompanied by Torrey's dog, looking in through the front door, warns him.

Joey has saved Shane's life, and Joey expects things to get back to normal. They will, but his view of what is normal and what must be are quite different. Shane has redonned his buckskins and taken up his old ways, and therefore must move out of the valley. The valley is safe for the sodbusters, but it is not safe for him: he has killed. The suburban family must return to its nuclear configuration, and the outlaw must move on. Shane is wounded, but he says he's okay. He rides away. Naive Joey yells after him: his father needs Shane. His mother wants him.

One wonders whether little Joey Starrett calling for Shane to come back is not the first peep of a call for more active and more masculine fathering that will eventually become the men's movements of the 1990s: Come back, Iron John!

Nine — Love Is Having to Say You're Sorry: Dysfunctional Families of the 1950s, 1960s and 1970s

Movies were driven by their female stars in the early years, but by the 1950s and 1960s, male stars drove box office, so much so that by the 1970s, we began to hear complaints by feminist critics and women actors that there were few interesting roles for women. Why did such a topsy-turvy situation develop?

It well may be that this situation came about because of some of the same social forces which gave rise to feminism: a decrease of interest in the home in favor of the workplace and a cynical attitude towards romance. We believe that this situation arose because of a view of the home as, at best, a prison, and often a torture chamber, good for neither men nor women. Romance became difficult to represent with any interesting conflict: it is simply dull to watch two people of equal status falling mutually in love. The tropes which drove romantic movies began to take on negative or even sinister properties beginning in the 1950s. For example, the persistence with which Katharine Hepburn pursues Cary Grant in *Bringing Up Baby* becomes potentially *stalking* to today's viewer. With romance and home minimized, other areas began to be the focus of film. And when the home was examined, it was examined critically.

This transformation came gradually. During the 1950s in films such as *Giant* (1956), *Peyton Place* (1957) and *Cat on a Hot Tin Roof* (1958), families were seen as conflicted places, but, in general, fixable. By 1960's *Psycho* and

126

1966's *Who's Afraid of Virginia Woolf?*, the families that we enjoyed watching were absolutely pathological. By the early 1970s in films such as *Love Story* (1970) and *The Godfather* (1972), the family could be represented as something worth getting completely rid of, even without psychotic relationships. We will look at these seven films as representative of this change in how families were depicted, particularly how the role of father was presented.

We should recall, however, that in the films we have discussed so far, good fathers have been few and far between. Certainly, the older Sheik in *Son of the Sheik,* is not a positive role model. Scarlett's father was too fond of horses and whiskey, and Rhett left much to be desired in terms of fatherhood. Many of the films about World War II focused on the father, but he was absent. The biblical epics were far more focused on God the Father than on earthly ones, and even the most positive father we have encountered thus far, Joe Starrett in *Shane,* was overinvolved in his work (providing), leaving too little time for his growing son and lonely wife (companioning).

We might want to remember that feature films are essentially about dramatic situations, and dramatic films imply conflict. When various groups bemoan the fact that there are few female (or male), African-American, Asian, gay, Latino, or older role models in films, we believe we should react by thinking that feature films are not really in the business of providing role models. To some extent, the war-focused films of the period 1942–45 consciously tried to provide role models — soldiers were never cowardly, never cheated on their girlfriends back home, and never fell in love with their buddy's girlfriends — but these films became stale and lifeless because of the lack of conflict. Propagandistic films of other periods likewise seem lifeless and contrived. So we should approach these films with a bit of caution. While the family was portrayed as increasingly miserable, this misery only works if we imagine a family as a potentially good, safe place. In most of the films we will describe, we want the husbands and wives, fathers and sons, to reconcile. We have not yet gotten to the romanceless superhero films of the 1980s and 1990s. Although, as we will see in the next chapter, we have created a wildly popular hero, James Bond, who is almost completely without family ties.

Giant

If we compare George Stevens's *Giant* to his earlier *Shane*, we can see how the view of the family, and particularly the role of father, changed quickly in the 1950s. We described the family in *Shane* as another example of individuals attempting to deal with quickly changing times. The Starretts were decent, hardworking farmers trying to reform and civilize the western range. They asked to be left alone to work their small patch of domestic soil. It is the sodbuster families who are the forces of progress. Joe Starrett could be a compassionate, loving father and husband, if roving deer, weather, and the Rykers would just cut him some slack. Some popular films immediately before *Giant* had reasonably good fathers and essentially happy families, *Cheaper by the Dozen* (1950) and *Father of the Bride* (1950) among them, although the fathers were portrayed as out of touch with their children and a bit dim. But at the same time, the biggest box office draw of the early 1950s was Disney's *Cinderella*, with its happily-ever-after theme of love. But Cinderella's family of origin is a bleak, abusive situation, although devoid of men. Even the merry *Hans Christian Andersen* has a dark minor plot about Andersen's (Danny Kaye) fascination for a woman trapped, he mistakenly believes, in an unhappy and abusive marriage.

The Benedict family in *Giant* is a relic of an earlier time, not a force for progress. They are the colonialists, wasters of the range, and users of the poor and those of color (a statement that might have seemed harsh, if not bizarre at the time). The central male character in the family, Bick (Rock Hudson), attempts to rule his ranch and his family in a way which no longer works in the twentieth century. He expects to say the word, and everyone will *obey* without question.

This epic about Texas begins in Maryland in order to give us some moorings against which to see the life in Texas. Bick Benedict has come there to buy horseflesh for his ranch. He gets more than he bargained for, not only in the horse, which is a thoroughbred with a mind of its own, but in a wife, Leslie (Elizabeth Taylor), also a thoroughbred with a mind of her own. Quickly, after returning to the flat, barren, vast landscape of Texas, Bick begins to understand that he has brought powerful elements of change into the well oiled machine that was his dominion. Leslie does not retire when the men talk politics. She believes Mexicans have a right to health care. Even Leslie's horse does not behave like an obedient cowboy's horse: he's a competitor.

The new generation of Benedicts do not want to follow either their father's orders or in his footsteps, either. His son Jordan (Dennis Hopper) wants nothing to do with ranching, but goes "back east" to become a physician. His older daughter does want to ranch, but on a more modest scale. Worst of all, his younger daughter Luz (Carroll Baker) decides to throw herself at upstart Jett Rink (James Dean). In fact, the second half of the film moves the focus away from the Benedicts and follows the sudden rise and very sudden fall of Jett Rink.

Of course one reason for watching this film is to look at James Dean in his final screen performance. (He was killed two weeks after the final shooting of the film in a freak car accident in the desert.) Dean's Jett Rink, a poor orphan boy who has been taken under the wing of Bick's sister Luz (Mercedes McCambridge), is either considered one of the best examples of method acting or the primary reason that method acting was a bad idea. Whether one buys into Jett's moody moods and slurred speech and jittery play with physical objects, it is difficult to take your eyes away from Dean when he is on screen. When Bick's sister Luz is killed by Leslie's horse, she leaves Jett a small piece of land. Like Ryker in *Shane*, Bick wants to keep his dominion together, so he offers to pay Jett an honest sum for the land, but Jett defers to "Madama's" wishes and decides to look for oil. Looking for oil is the functional equivalent to sodbusting in this film, and Jett's presence in the middle of his spread greatly annoys Bick.

Jett's decision to remain in the middle of Bick's domain has another purpose: Jett is not-so-secretly in love with Leslie. This becomes clear in a scene in which she stops by Jett's shack, and he serves her, of all things, tea. He is as completely out of place making this patrician beverage, as he is in engaging her in small talk. He takes a hit from a bottle to give himself courage. He has collected mementos of Leslie, and her presence turns him into a gangly boy.

If we were to regard *Giant* as an essay on masculinity, it might be seen in the contrast between sympathetic, naive Jett and overconfident, out-of-touch Bick. But the final resolution of the argument is not a standard liberal one. Jett is thoroughly corrupted by money, power, and his lack of understanding of how to use either. His gusher comes in, and he joins the Progressive forces. He builds the first major airport in the state (but incorrectly names it after himself). And he decides that if he cannot have mother, he will settle for daughter Luz. Jett has unfortunately become too reliant on the booze for courage, and in what should be his moment of triumph, he is incoherently drunk as he attempts to inaugurate the airport. At the same time, Bick moderates his authority-wielding and comes to accept a human scale role in his community and family.

In addition to the family context, this film deals seriously with an issue not much taken up directly in the films of the 1950s, race. The theme is introduced early in the film, when Leslie stumbles upon a Mexican community during one of her early rides. There she encounters a woman with a sick baby. On returning home, she asks the family physician to stop by the Mexican village and look after the child. Bick regards this request as several breaches of the social order. Leslie should not have been riding alone, let alone been in the Mexican village, and the white doctor should not treat Mexicans. Leslie seems not to notice the severity of her transgressions, and continues to insist that the doctor look in on the sick child. Of course, the doctor *does* see the Mexican child, as Leslie's quiet insistence on the rightness of all of her positions always wins over Bick's grumpy posturing.

Jordan not only gets a Harvard education and decides against ranching, but he marries a Latino woman. While Jett is finding his courage in the bottle prior to his big inaugural banquet, Jordan's wife tries to have her hair done

Jett's low social standing and his love for Leslie seem to be his cross to bear.

in Jett's new hotel. She is refused, and Jordan becomes enraged. He picks a fight with Jett, but loses. Later, because of the fight, Bick leads a defection from the grand gathering at the airport celebration. Dad has not only come to accept a small role in the family, but he comes to appreciate those whom he had formerly thought of as beneath notice. Driving home, when he notices Mexicans being refused service at a diner, he enters into a brawl with the diner's owner. Although he does not win this altercation either, he is redeemed in the eyes of his son, and makes Leslie proud of being his wife. It is perhaps not too much of a stretch to say that at the end of *Giant*, the resolution of the question of masculinity is that wise use of power, compassion, care for the powerless, and even a little aggression are a good mixture.

Peyton Place

Peyton Place is the most conspicuous place in popular American film where the disconnect between love, sex, and marriage became apparent. This is a film which has at its center the issues of illegitimacy, incest, abortion, and rape. If the movies were going to do something different than TV, here it was: not spectacle itself, but spectacular squalor.

Although the real focus of this film is on its female characters, it is the appearance of Michael Rossi (Lee Phillips) in the small New England town as a candidate for the principalship of the high school which provokes most of the action in the film. Rossi is an idealistic teacher who expresses his honest feelings to his students, unlike any of the students' parents. "Peyton Place" has become a synonym for hypocrisy, and the fun of this soap opera is discovering the secrets beneath every adult character.

As Rossi enters the town during the films' opening credits, he passes first the Crosses' derelict cabin, then drives over the railroad tracks and comes into manicured Peyton Place proper. There are secrets on both sides of the tracks. Those on the wrong side are more sensational than those on the right side. But they both involve Sex, with a capital letter.

The film focuses on the graduating class of Peyton Place High just before the outbreak of World War II. The kids are planning their prom, and most who have not lost their virginity, seem to feel the prom might be as good a time as any to do so.[1] But the adults want to make sure there is none of that. There are three intertwined plots. Most conspicuously is the conflict between Allison MacKenzie (Diane Varsi), an aspiring novelist, and her mother, Constance (Lana Turner), a local entrepreneur. Allison kisses the picture of her deceased father good-bye every morning before school, irritating her mother who thinks all men are swine. Rossi likes Constance and attempts a relationship, but his views on sex education get in the way. ("Let them learn it *after* they're married," Constance tells him, emphatically.) Mother sees libido under every one of Allison's acts, and even accuses her of skinny-dipping with Norman Page (Russ Tamblyn). Norman is no Lothario. He is sheepish around women, and Allison has practically to demand that he kiss her. Constance becomes so enraged when Allison protests her innocence about the nude swim that she inadvertently tells Allison that she is illegitimate. There is no dead father, just a married one. Hypocrite number one is revealed.

The second plot centers around the attempts of a "low class" girl to trap the town's richest kid, Rodney Harrington, into marriage. She traps him, and he's cut off by his father. When he is killed in action, his father begins a bond with his daughter-in-law, straight out of *Going My Way.*

The most sensational plot concerns the rape of Selena Cross (Hope Lange) by her drunken stepfather (Arthur Kennedy). When Selena becomes pregnant, she goes to the town's doctor to have him "force a miscarriage." The good doctor scares stepdad out of town, but when he comes back later and tries it again with Selena, she bludgeons him to death and hides the body. She is prosecuted for murder, and things look bleak until the doc breaks medical ethics and reveals all.

If *Giant* portrayed the family as a kind of circus with the father as an ineffectual ringmaster, *Peyton Place* construes the "good" family as a place where parents try by very unnatural means to prevent their children from repeating their own very natural mistakes, and bad families are very bad places. We are on the brink of the sexual revolution here: Rossi believes sex should be discussed, and it appears that everyone is doing it, in and out of marriage. But the film ends almost happily. Allison reaches a rapprochement with her mother. Mother starts dating Rossi. Selena is found not guilty, and nobody even thinks about prosecuting the doctor for anything.

Rossi represents the best of the men in this film, despite the leaden performance by Lee Phillips. He is frank and expressive verbally. He is not hypocritical. He likes women and respects them. He is a competent professional. Doc Swain shares these characteristics. Mr. Cross is their evil reverse: incompetent, cowardly, and violent. The young men in the town are really dopes, reminiscent of the fellows in *Meet Me in St. Louis.* They are easily manipulated by women, fearful of sexuality, and clueless to what's going on around them. But they are brave and patriotic. When Pearl Harbor is bombed, they all volunteer. It would be too much of a stretch to say that this movie is about men and masculinity. Because the focus is the emotional travails of women, much like the weepies of the 1940s, the male characters tend to be flat. But the film does advance our examination of the increasingly dysfunctional family a notch with the sordidness in the Cross home and the basic hypocrisy of every other one.

Cat on a Hot Tin Roof

Cat on a Hot Tin Roof is a sanitized version of Tennessee Williams's play about sex and alcoholism, set in the contemporary South. The film begins with Brick (Paul Newman), the 30-year-old favored son of a self-made planter, drunkenly trying to relive a moment of glory on his high school track field at three in the morning. He has set the hurdles, and downing a last drink from a pint bottle and imagining the cheers of the crowd, he clears several hurdles before he falls and breaks his ankle.

The next afternoon, Brick is still drinking, hobbling around a second-story bedroom in his family's plantation home. His father, Big Daddy (Burl Ives), is arriving home after a six week stay in a clinic to determine whether he has cancer. It is Big Daddy's 65th birthday, and family and friends are convened to celebrate the event as well as to welcome Big Daddy home. But they are also there to engage in much more unpleasant business. If the news is bad about Big Daddy's health, there is a ten million dollar estate and 28,000 acres of land to fight over. The main contender for the estate is Brick's elder brother Gooper (Jack Carson) and his pregnant wife Mae, whom Brick's wife Maggie (Elizabeth Taylor) refers to as "a monster of fertility." Mae has arranged for her five obnoxious children to sing, dance, and parade in Big Daddy's honor, primarily to remind him that Brick and Maggie's union has produced no heirs and is not likely to: Brick's drinking began at the same moment he stopped having "relations" with his wife. We learn about most of this situation from the conversation between Brick and Maggie, as she undresses and dresses to greet Big Daddy at the airport. Maggie is frustrated at her husband's indifference — hence the image of a "cat on a hot tin roof." Brick suggests that the best thing for such a cat to do is to jump off. Maggie suggests that the best thing for the cat to do is to endure it. Maggie makes attempt after attempt to rouse some sort of amorous response from Brick, but fails — there are several times in this scene when Brick *does* respond momentarily, but he always checks himself. Clearly there is something we need to know. The upstairs scene is interrupted while the family goes to the airport to meet Big Daddy. There, flanked by his physician, Big Daddy announces that he merely has a spastic colon. Gooper's brats play "Dixie." Gooper makes disparaging comments about Brick. Big Daddy escapes with Maggie and returns home.

Much of the three act structure of the play remains evident in the film, despite attempts to open it up cinematically. Each act moves deeper into the home, from the second floor bedroom, to the first floor living room, to the climactic scenes in the cellar. These changes in location reflect levels of psychoanalytic therapy: one attempts to move from external symptoms (Brick's alcoholism and his lack of sexual interest in Maggie), to precipitating causes (the suicide of his best friend Skipper), to the unconscious problems within the family (his relationship with his father). One of the unfortunate problems in viewing much of Tennessee Williams' work today is his reliance on such Freudian conceits.

Once returned from the airport, the remainder of the first act unfolds. Brick has continued to drink and refuses to attend the dinner for Big Daddy. Brick learns that Big Daddy *does* have cancer after all, and Maggie cajoles him to make some effort to stay in contention for the inheritance. But all Brick wants is to go back home to New Orleans, to get out of this mess.

One of the aspects of the play which did not find its way into the film was the homoerotic nature of the relationship between Brick and his best friend Skipper, which is the content of the play's second act. Brick and Maggie come down to the first floor and confront each other in the closed off living room, with Big Daddy serving as their referee. There are in fact several very different versions of the play in which this theme is explored either indirectly or in rather specific terms for the time. But if this is a theme in the film, the viewer must bring it into the film by knowing something about the play.[2] The play recontextualizes the "problem" with Brick and Skipper's friendship as a problem with facing adulthood. Brick and Skipper were a combination on the athletic field from high school through college, and into professional football. An injury to Brick put Skipper on the field without Brick for the first time, and he failed miserably. Skipper had gone into an alcoholic frenzy in his hotel room, and Maggie had been called in to see whether she could calm him. Skipper kissed her, and for a moment she wondered whether she should encourage a more serious pass, so she could wrench her husband away from his boyhood friend. But, she tells us in the scene in the downstairs living room, she realized that such a ploy might also lose her Brick altogether, depending on whom he would see as the aggressor, and so she left. Shortly thereafter Skipper dived from his hotel room onto the pavement below.

We see none of this in the film: this is a film about people talking about past events, not really reliving them for the camera's eye. Brick has been railing about "mendacity": he drinks, he tells us because the world is full of liars. Like a mean-spirited analyst, Big Daddy forces Brick to go deeper into his relationship with Skipper. Brick knew that Maggie was with Skipper shortly before his suicide, and he blames her for his death. But he has also never allowed her to tell him what happened. Knowing now that Maggie could not be responsible for Skipper's death, Brick must face facts: after Maggie left, Skipper had called him. Skipper was scared and incoherent and Brick had hung up on him and then refused to answer the phone when it rang again and again in his hospital room. Brick now understands that he could have helped his friend, and his lack of help was what drove Skipper over the edge, literally. And, presumably, his unconscious realization of this is what makes him drink.

But in this psychoanalytic fable, this is not enough. We need to know why Brick was unable to reach out to his friend in his moment of crisis. Brick tries to escape back to New Orleans, but he bogs his car down in the mud. Big Daddy comes out into the rain, and in the argument that follows, Brick blurts out the truth about Big Daddy's cancer. Big Daddy is stunned, and, drenched, he goes into the junk-filled basement of the house. The junk is the stuff of memory, and we are now in the subconscious. Brick calls Big Daddy "Pa" when he enters the basement. Big Daddy notices this and wants to know why he doesn't call him "Big Daddy." The reason is, of course, that Big Daddy gave him things, but no love. Brick couldn't love Skipper in a time of weakness because Big Daddy could not express his love for him. Now Brick understand his problem, and he can go upstairs and join in with Maggie's lie that she's pregnant, because he knows that he will be able to father a child with her.

While *Cat on a Hot Tin Roof* continues to be shown on cable stations regularly, it is a film which lacks credible character motivation from our current perspective. As has been apparent elsewhere in this book, like most American psychologists, we are unimpressed by Freudian psychology, and it takes a Freudian to make much sense out of this plot. But the movie is certainly worth a look for several reasons. First, it reminds us of the Freudian craze during the late 1940s and 1950s in American films. Second, Newman and Taylor never looked better, and their performances are fine. In fact, Taylor's drop-dead-gorgeousness in her slip and stockings is essential in developing the tension: how could any red-blooded male resist that? we wonder. And the reason for her attraction to the lean, gray-eyed Newman is obvious, despite his drinking and angst-driven verbosity. And the moments when he lets his guard down and looks at her are moments of nearly embarrassing intimacy.

Finally, this is a prescient film in terms of expressing the theme of the emptiness of the Provider role between fathers and sons, which will become more conspicuous in later films and which has given rise to Robert Bly's (1989) mythopoetic Men's Movement. Providing is not sufficient. Joe Starrett knew this, but Big Daddy and many daddies to come didn't. Big Daddy's psychology is presented in a more comprehensible, less psychoanalytic fashion. His father was a hobo, who died when he was a child, leaving him nothing, he thinks, but an empty suitcase, which he finds in the accumulated junk of the basement. This scene is probably a deliberate visual parallel to the childhood sled found among the accumulated junk at the end of *Citizen Kane,* and serves much the same purpose. Cut off from the love of an impoverished parent at an early age, both Kane and Big Daddy compensate by a drive to become wealthy and powerful and to give things to their family members rather than love. But Brick finally makes it clear to Big Daddy that things are less important than memories of loving interaction. Big Daddy has only a suitcase, but a mind full of rich memories: Brick has much stuff, but no such suitcase of memories. Big Daddy, now wracked with pain, and Brick, still hobbling on one good ankle, make their way up out of the basement/subconscious. We can hope that in the little time they have left, some repair can be done to this imbalance.

Psycho

Other than the minor character of the elderly justice of the peace and his wife and the secretary (Patricia Hitchcock) who had to take tranquilizers on her wedding night, no one is married in *Psycho*. Families are remnants: sisters, sons and mothers, ex-husbands and wives. *Psycho* dissects these left-over family relations and finds them all sinister.

In the opening scene we see secretary Marion Crane (Janet Leigh) and her lover Sam (John Gavin) in a downtown hotel room in Phoenix soon after a mid-day sexual rendezvous. As they dress, we discover that Sam lives in a nearby town and that he is financially encumbered by alimony. They want to be together, but he cannot ask her to live with him in a room behind the hardware store where he works. She wants to end the secretiveness of their affair and have dinner with her mother and sister. They part not altogether sure that they will meet again.

When Marion returns to work, she is entrusted with a $40,000 deposit on a home that a client of the real estate firm where she works has put down as a wedding present for his daughter (another father buying the love of a child?). The client would like to have a few drinks and flirt with Marion, but she leaves early to put the money in the bank before it closes. On the way to the bank she realizes that the money would solve her problems with Sam, and rather than going to the bank, she skips town. On the way out of town she sees her boss and the client. She drives through the night; buys a new car; falls asleep on the side of the road to be awakened by a policeman; finally she stops in a run-down motel where she is the only guest, because a new highway has cut off access to the motel. The owner of the motel is young and handsome Norman Bates (Anthony Perkins) who becomes friendly with her and brings her a meal from the Victorian mansion next door where he allegedly lives with his incapacitated and difficult mother. Norman's hobby is taxidermy, and the room in which they talk is filled with stuffed birds. When Marion suggests that he might be happier if he leaves, he takes offense — "A boy's best friend is his mother," he protests — and she goes to her room and prepares for a shower.

Up until this moment we have been watching a film about sexually motivated greed. Marion Crane is the main character, and the film is about her impulsive decision to steal. Marion sits down and calculates how much she has spent, and we are confident that she has decided to return to Phoenix through her conversation with shy, introverted Norman. She has learned that life on the run is not suited to her style.

Then, suddenly, we are in a completely different film.

Norman watches her through a hole in the wall between the office and her room. Once in the shower, she is savagely attacked by what appears to be a matronly woman. Marion is stabbed repeatedly and lies in the tub surrounded by her blood which spirals down the drain. Norman runs down from the house, discovers what mother has done, and then cleans up the mess and disposes of the body and the car in a nearby swamp.

The revolutionary plot now is sometimes discussed primarily by the fact that the main female star is dispatched in the famous shower scene halfway through the film, but that was not what was so startling about *Psycho* in 1960. The thriller is formulaic, and for 50 minutes one formula is pursued: the ordinary person seduced by an opportunity. This was the stuff of *film noir*. Then without a moment's notice, we are in another formula: the slasher film — if such a formula existed outside of drive-in movies at the time. Although Hitchcock had been toying with mid-film changes in the structure of his films, particularly by the mid-way revelations in *Vertigo* (1958), audiences were disoriented by the change in direction in *Psycho*.[3] Then the film becomes a film of detection, but there are three people searching for Marion. Her sister Lila (Vera Miles) is trying to restore her family's honor; Sam is looking for his girlfriend; and private detective Arbogast (Martin Balsam) is trying to recover the money. None are looking for justice. Of course, the solution is complex. Norman actually killed Marion while dressed as his mother. He did this because ... well, that remains something of a mystery. He apparently killed his mother and her lover years before, and then went out into the cemetery and dug up mom and keeps her in the house and has long, angry conversations with her, playing both roles.

The film is very pared down: it is shot in black and white, and the orchestra score consists entirely of strings. It is not shot in CinemaScope. In his famous interview with François Truffaut, Hitchcock comments on the film:

> ...People will say, "It was a terrible film to make. The subject was horrible, the people were small, there were no characters in it." I know all this, but I also know that the construction of the story and the way in which it was told caused audiences all over the world to react and become emotional.
>
> ...I don't care whether it looked like a small or large picture. I didn't start off to make an important picture. I thought I could have fun with the subject and this situation. The picture cost eight hundred thousand dollars. It was an experiment in this sense: Could I make a feature film under the same conditions as a television show [Truffaut, 1984, p. 283]?

So, by *Psycho*, films were not trying to compete with television in terms of spectacle. Whereas *Peyton Place* gave us squalor, *Psycho* gives us "psychopathology," of a particularly gruesome and sexual nature. Hitchcock tells Truffaut that he was trying to make a film for younger audiences who had grown up on television, and he capitalizes on the many similarities between film and television to set up expectations in the audience, which he shatters violently and suddenly.[4]

Who's Afraid of Virginia Woolf?

For anyone who saw *Who's Afraid of Virginia Woolf?* on its release, this was a film that changed Hollywood movies in many fundamental ways. Certainly it changed what could be said in movies, even though the language was toned down from the original Edward Albee play on which it was based and is far removed from the incessant vulgarity of many films of the 1990s. It was a film in which a major, glamorous star could be seen as unglamorous. It was a film in which the American family was exposed as a violent, sexual turmoil. None of this is apparent in the opening of the film, one of the most beautiful in all American movies. Over the beautiful contrapuntal score by Alex North, two small figures are seen crossing a beautiful college campus late at night, talking and laughing. Light bathes the campus through the trees and a light fog.

George and Martha are a senior faculty couple. They have been drinking at a faculty party at the president's house, and Martha has invited a new faculty couple over for drinks and a good flirt. Martha (Elizabeth Taylor) is the daughter of the president. George (Richard Burton) is a stalled history professor. Their guests are a new biology professor, Nick (George Segal), and his very drunk wife, Honey (Sandy Dennis). There are dark secrets in both of these marriages (shades of *Peyton Place* and *Cat on a Hot Tin Roof*), and the film shows how alcohol and relentless goading by George manage to get these secrets revealed. There are parallels between the two marriages: both of the secrets involve the absence of children. Nick and Honey's premarital sex lead Honey, the daughter of a media preacher, to develop an hysterical pregnancy. Once married, the pregnancy of course went away, leaving Nick feeling trapped in a marriage he is not sure he wants. George and Martha have been unable to have children, so they have invented an imaginary son.

Although such late night drinking bouts seem to be a way that the older couple initiates all younger faculty members, two things go awry: first, when Honey passes out, Nick responds positively to Martha's sexual advances (although because of the prodigious amount of booze everyone consumes, Nick is unable to perform sexually—or maybe he does). Second, Martha mentions the imaginary son to Nick. This was a fantasy between George and Martha, and when another person is let in on the tale, the agreement is that the son must die.

George's main game is called "Get the Guests." He reveals much about himself to Nick, none of it very flattering. He talks about embarrassing moments from his adolescence and tells, in several different versions, about an automobile accident where he may have killed someone. Or this may have been an episode in a semi-autobiographical novel. There is much ambiguity about George's stories. (Late in the film, Martha asks him, "Truth or illusion,

George. Do you know the difference?" "No," he answers, "but we must carry on as if we did.") One revelation deserves another, and Nick tells stories about his relationship with Honey. The purpose for gathering this information is to throw it back to Honey, and when George reveals what Nick has told him, Honey goes into the bathroom and curls up on the floor in fetal position.

At the end of the film, as the sun rises on the campus, Nick and Honey finally having left, George and Martha are reduced to speaking to each other in one word sentences. What we have come to realize through this rough night of psychodramatics is that George and Martha fundamentally love each other. But their love may not be enough to sustain them. They drink too much; George's career stalled; they live poorly; they have no children. In the enigmatic ending, George recalls a clever witticism from the faculty party, and he asks Martha: "Who's afraid of Virginia Woolf?" and she responds: "I am, George. I am."

Who's Afraid of Virginia Woolf? continues and perhaps climaxes a custom in serious fiction, theater, and films in the 1950s and 1960s: what might be called the story of "subconscious detection." Characters' overt actions are interesting enough, but the real point is to discover "what really drives them." Often, what really drives them is some failure with their parents. Martha's father looms large over George's inability to become a successful academic. He is described as a "big rat." Martha is clearly awed by him, but gets no emotional support from him. George was dispatched from his family to boarding school. Because they cannot connect with their parents and because they have no children, George and Martha are a modern (post-modern?) couple — because they are stunted emotionally by their remote parents, they may not be up to the job of sustaining a lasting relationship, because they cannot feel enough for each other or communicate well enough with each other.

Love Story

Love Story is one of the most vilified films of all times. Watching it thirty years later, it is difficult to imagine what all the fuss was about — both why it was so immensely popular and why it was so hated by the critical community. It is a small, sentimental, manipulative movie about young love, with fine performances and an interesting commentary on social class and privilege in America.

The film was based on the wildly popular book by Yale classics professor Erich Segal (which apparently originated as a screenplay). When the book was first released, it got good reviews in places like the *New Yorker*. Early reviews focused on the interesting portrayal of the culture clashes in the Ivy League schools, brought about by the more conspicuous representation of bright, working class students there. These highly motivated and highly talented students disdained the more traditional students of the Ivy League, children of the upper echelons of society who were there to meet and mingle with their peers and get Cs. And the disdain was mutual.

Oliver Barrett IV (Ryan O'Neal) is at Harvard for two reasons: it is expected of him and he wants to play Ivy League ice hockey. Jenny Cavilleri (Ali MacGraw) is a Roman Catholic scholarship student from Rhode Island attending Radcliffe. She's there to break out of poverty and get an education. (Ironically, Ali MacGraw was a graduate of one of the Seven Sisters colleges, Wellesley, while O'Neal was a television star — of *Peyton Place* — with a prison record.) They meet; they fight; they fall in love. In the initial scenes of the movie, one fascinating aspect of Jenny is her ability to balance her attraction for Oliver and her absolute contempt for everything she thinks he stands for.

Since Oliver IV was expected to meet and mingle with his peers, Oliver III (Ray Milland) is violently opposed to a marriage between his son and Jenny. He threatens to cut him off without a penny, and when that doesn't work, he cuts him off without a penny. Of course, a Harvard education has its advantages, and Oliver marries Jenny, moves to New York, and lands a good job. Jenny decides to abandon her aspirations in music to become a homemaker, and when repeated attempts to have children result in nothing, she consults a physician. Not only is she not going to make babies, she finds out she's not going to live much longer. And doesn't.

So, then, why was this film so popular?

For one thing, the cast was attractive, and there was a good on-screen chemistry between MacGraw and O'Neal. These characters did interesting things. This film contributed to the popularity of hockey and the custom of making snow angels. And it let audiences in on the life of people at one of the most honored institutions in America, Harvard.

For another, this film contained a message about social class which seems to be popular. The message in this film is that social class in America, although real, can be broached. Always it is the younger generation which sees that social class barriers are artificial, and the previous generation which tries to reinforce those barriers. We saw this same message in *Going My Way* and in *Peyton Place,* and will see it again in *Titanic* (1998) and *Shakespeare in Love* (1999). The casting of Ryan O'Neal reinforced this theme, because he had played the character of Rodney Harrington in the *Peyton Place* TV series.

Then we must ask, why was this film so vilified?

Certainly, there is a cloying sentimentality about this film which seems out of date. The "romantic" films of the previous few years which had attained blockbuster status were *The Graduate* (1967), in which Benjamin Braddock can neither make up his mind about a career nor make a romantic decision between his girlfriend or her mother; *Guess Who's Coming to Dinner* (1967), where race complicates true love; Zeffirelli's beautiful *Romeo and Juliet* (1968), another story about love doomed by parental manipulation; and the three buddy films of 1969, *Butch Cassidy and the Sundance Kid, Midnight Cowboy,* and *Easy Rider,* each of which seemed to suggest that male friendship was purer and less complicated than romantic heterosexuality.

Moreover, 1970 was the moment in which the Women's Movement emerged as a potent political and social force, and Jenny's decision to give up her music for marriage and family seemed wrong. Jenny does not seek a compromise between her own career and family: she simply gives up her music. In a poignant scene in the hospital at the end of the film, Oliver awkwardly crawls into Jenny's hospital bed, after she has told him that she has totally forgotten the classification system for the works of Mozart. He has no idea what this revelation means, but to a musician, this would be the equivalent of a lawyer forgetting the Rule Against Perpetuities. It's basic information in a career.

As Oliver leaves the hospital after Jenny has died, he encounters his father. *What can I do?* asks the father. *Nothing. It's too late.* A bad sequel aside, at the end of *Love Story,* we do not expect a reconciliation between Oliver III and Oliver IV. Young Oliver is hardened against his father, and we have no hope that there will be even a momentary expressive meeting between them in the future, as we expect at the end *Cat on a Hot Tin Roof.* This relationship is not fixable. Oliver IV will remain a *victim* of his father's callousness, seeing no reason to attempt to repair their relationship.

The Godfather

One way of viewing Francis Ford Coppola's 1972 masterpiece is as the end of the heterosexual family in film for nearly 25 years (Yates, 1975). The main story — another movie script quickly turned into a runaway bestseller — is about how an educated, sympathetic character, Michael Corleone (Al Pacino) is gradually seduced away from civilized society into the wild, untamed world of the unfettered male, his family's crime business.[5]

We have two meanings of the word *family* in this picture. One family is represented in the courtship scenes between Michael and Kay Adams (Diane Keaton); the other is the crime family, a place were women are not wanted and violence rules. We have essentially the same plot as 1939's *Jesse James,* except that the "moral" of the film is exactly reversed: Michael becomes something of a hero by rejecting the domestic world of Kay and by descending (ascending?) into the hierarchy of crime. He becomes, step by step, his father.

Michael is the youngest son of Vito Corleone (Marlon Brando). He has been educated to make the crime business legitimate, and has been shielded

Behind this wedding photograph in The Godfather *is the death of the functional family in popular American film for many decades.*

from all of it. His oldest brother Sonny (James Caan) will inherit the crime business. Sonny is a high testosterone male who believes his position gives him the right to skewer women on his prodigious penis and inflict violence on any man who personally affronts him. Old Vito has more codified conduct, but as Vito approaches the age when he needs to relinquish control, other crime families become worried about Sonny's stability and Vito's reluctance to get into the heroin trade with whites, so Sonny is viciously gunned down. Michael volunteers to avenge his brother's death (as Jesse becomes an outlaw to avenge his mother's death). Afterwards, Michael goes to Sicily and gets a good indoctrination about crime, and returns to New York when his father is hospitalized. Sonny marries Kay, marginalizes her, and sets about a ruthless demonstration of his willingness to use violence to protect his "family," even if it means killing his sister's husband.

This is a slick, beautiful, thoroughly amoral film. With the exception of Kay, women are portrayed as hysterical and simple, and men as calculating and violent. Relationships between men are the standard of this film. There is no morally "right" position: the police are as corrupted as the Corleone family, and the Corleone occasionally make decisions where there is some attempt at justice, although an odd one. We are seduced by the narrative to accept the code of the Corleone as "a truth," and having done this, we usually side with them in their conflicts with others worse than they are.

Conclusion

As we have looked at the handful of films produced between the mid-1950s and the early 1970s which focused on the contemporary family, we have seen a gradual erosion of a "happily-ever-after" mentality. Increasingly, we see a view emerging in which it is the family which is the source of problems. In *Giant* we see the end of the strong father. In *Peyton Place* we see the family as a hypocritical social engine for passing on fake values (and potentially a place of violence); in *Cat on a Hot Tin Roof* we see that a family legacy can be emotional distance and lies; in *Psycho,* we have a fable about how families can cause insanity; in *Who's Afraid of Virginia Woolf?* we find a family that fears the future because the present somehow didn't measure up to expectations and where love is not enough; *Love Story* reminds us that love is not forever, but emotional coldness might be; while in *The Godfather,* we have a message that the man's place is in the workplace, not in the home.

The films present us with a whole host of domineering, distant fathers (Bick Benedict, Mr. Harrington, Big Daddy Pollack, Martha's father, Oliver Barrett III, Vito Corleone) and absent fathers (Mr. Rink, Mr. MacKenzie, Mr. Bates), and a lot of damaged sons (Jordan Benedict, Jett Rick, Norman Page, Gooper and Brick Pollack, Norman Bates, George, Oliver Barrett IV, and all three Corleone brothers), all damaged in one way or another by their distant or absent fathers.

What we may need is a hero who seems to transcends his family of origin; who is a complete company man; who avoids romantic entanglements; and who has a lifestyle which transcends becoming a victim or a psychotic. What, in short, we need, is James Bond.

Ten — Bond: Stirred, Not Shaken

Beginning with the publication of *Casino Royale* in 1953, James Bond has had a nearly 50 year run as an important icon of masculinity in American popular culture. Bond is an icon to which we pay considerable attention: critics have from the first complained that his view of women contribute to their objectification (Hibbin, 1962) and contribute to the glamorization of violence (Johnson, 1958). At specific points in time, some have ventured the opinion that these films have impeded establishing a popular consensus toward a new political world order (Richler, 1972). What is of particular interest to us is that we are talking about comments by serious critics, not merely big city newspaper reviewers. Important writers such as Mordecai Richler, Umberto Eco, and Kingsley Amis have taken time to write extensively on these books and films, which are fundamentally pulp fiction and escapist movies. Boyd (1967) has even written on the Ian Fleming books as religious allegories. James Chapman's (2000) recent book *License to Thrill: A Cultural History of the James Bond Films* is a fascinating attempt to balance these divergent views. Chapman, however, provides a British context for the films which is very different from the American context we are examining. For example he places the Bond books and films in the declining global importance of Britain and as a reaction to the "Kitchen Sink" realism of the British films of the early 1960s.

As we began the research on this book several years ago, the popular press was full of speculation about whom Albert Broccoli would select as the newest actor to play the Cold War's most famous soldier, and when Pierce Brosnan was selected, it was news — not entertainment page news, but first section news. This fictional spy commands our attention and emotional responses far more than other fictional heroes of recent times.

The Bond films *are* about sex and violence (and politics). Whether these films significantly influence our cultural attitudes about these important issues can be debated. It might be easier to show that these films have had a profound effect on smaller aspects of our popular culture: the rise of casino gambling, an interest in French cuisine (certainly no one who has seen *From Russia with Love* would ever again order red Chianti with fish), and an interest in travel, among them. One of us remembers that there was a sudden run on white dinner jackets for the junior prom in 1963, because Sean Connery had worn one in *Dr. No.*

We believe that the Bond novels and films, however, index significant changes in public attitudes about sex, violence, and politics. Certainly the Broccoli-Saltzman organization (and later the Broccoli organization) has striven to produce palatable films, beginning with the *Daily Mirror* preference poll which was used in 1961 in the decision to cast Sean Connery in *Dr. No.* The Bond films have not been attempts to present landscapes of what society ought to be; rather, they have been attempts to capture as wide a paying audience as possible to tell stories about a sometimes earnest and sometimes comic actor in the arena of sexual and real politics.

This chapter will look at modulations in the presentation of the character and behavior of James Bond over the last four and a half decades, looking for significant changes in the portrayal of sexuality and violence which were associated with box office success. We will pay less attention to the issue of politics, because Price (1992) has done a convincing job in that area. Not all of the 19 Bond films (20 if one counts the comedy version of *Casino Royale*) have been successes. But in 1964, both *From Russia with Love* and *Goldfinger* were among the top five films of the year with domestic rentals of $10,000,000 and $23,000,000 respectively. The following year *Thunderball* earned over $28,000,000, and in 1971 *Diamonds Are Forever* was, for a long time, the last of the Bond films to be among the highest earning pictures of the year, coming in slightly under $20,000,000. Then for 16 years and 13 pictures, Bond percolated merrily along under blockbuster status, making a good deal of money for the producers and selling hundreds of millions of tickets. Chapman (2000) estimates that between a quarter and half of the people now living on earth have seen at least one Bond film. The recent Pierce Brosnan films have regained major box office status for the series. Sales of the novels have also been various. While plans are underway to release all of the Fleming book in an inexpensive hardback series, as of this writing, four are out of print. This chapter will not only describe how Bond has changed since his introduction, but relate the modifications of his sex-role behavior to the popularity of individual films. We will not have time to consider each film, but will consider the first outings, the three blockbusters, and then a representative film or two from each of the actors who portrayed Bond.

Introductions

The novel *Casino Royale*

In the Bond canon, *Casino Royale* holds an unusual position. As the first of Fleming's novels, it is here that we find his character exposition of James Bond. Due to complicated legal arrangements, this book has never truly been brought to the screen, although it was made into a hour-long live television drama in 1957 starring Barry Nelson, as an American secret agent. A decade later, a parody film of it was released starring David Niven as an aging, virginal James and Woody Allen as the "new," amoral, and libidinous Jimmy Bond, directed by a host of co-directors including John Huston, and containing, at most, 15 minutes of material based on the literary source — Orson Welles as the villain Le Chiffre is compelling onscreen but nothing at all like the original.

The novel concerns itself with Bond's attempts to win and keep money from Le Chiffre, a Soviet operative, who has spent the funds of a French Communist labor union on a chain of brothels, presumably to indulge his own sadomasochism — a recurring characteristic of the fictional and filmic villains (and similar to the equation in the biblical epics of heterosexual = good; not heterosexual = bad, except Bond leaves out the fidelity of the earlier film equations). Unfortunately, this investment occurred only months before new pandering laws have shut down his operation. Le Chiffre now must earn back the money at baccarat so that he can replace it before SMERSH, a unit of Soviet intelligence charged with eliminating traitors, can eliminate him. If Bond can win at the tables, SMERSH will kill Le Chiffre, and the labor union, which is suspected of being a potential "fifth column" should the Cold War heat up, will be bankrupted.

In addition to a tightly formulated plot, the book is filled with information about the details of high stakes European gambling games, *haute cuisine*, and *haute couture*. It is here that we meet Bond, and get our first picture of his physical appearance, his character, and his views about sex and violence. It is here that we meet the first "Bond girl," his assistant Vesper Lynd, and the first of many villains.

Fleming cleverly is short on details about Bond's physical appearance. James Bond has gray eyes, a scar on his face, and an unruly lock of black hair that falls over his eyes, not unlike Superman. The first real description is in bed as he falls asleep with his hand around his .38 Colt: "Then he slept, and with the warmth and humor of his eyes extinguished his features relapsed into a taciturn mask, ironical, brutal, and cold" (p. 17). His female assistant describes him later: "He is very good-looking. He reminds me rather of Hoagy Carmichael, but there is something cold and ruthless..." (p. 49).

In this novel, Bond is portrayed as smart and logical. He is described as having a slow pulse and a sanguine personality (p. 56). He is something of a loner: "Bond would have preferred to work alone, but one didn't argue with M" (p. 33). He is devoted to his work: "Bond's car was his only personal hobby" (p. 44). He describes himself to Vesper:

> You must forgive me.... I take a ridiculous pleasure in what I eat and drink. It comes partly from being a bachelor, but mostly from a habit of taking a lot of trouble over details. It's very pernickety and old-maidish, really... [p. 71].

From what fork to use, what wine to drink, and what clothes are appropriate for any occasion to who deserves to be killed and who deserves merely to be rendered unconscious, Bond views the world along simple correct/incorrect lines. This has lead to the catch phrase to describe both the novels and the early films "snobbery with violence." Bond is also a company man, a phrase he often uses to describe himself, although a nonconformist one. He initiates action to accomplish his goals, but his goals are set for him by M.

Bond's attitudes toward women do not warm feminists' hearts, as the following four quotations indicate:

> Bond was not amused. "What the hell do they want to send me a woman for?" he said bitterly. "Do they think this is a bloody picnic?" [p. 39, in response to being assigned Vesper Lynd as his assistant on the case].

> Women were for recreation. On a job, they got in the way and fogged things up with sex and hurt feelings and all the emotional baggage they carried around. One had to look out for them and take care of them [p. 41].

> He was quite honest to himself about the hypocrisy of his attitude toward her. As a woman, he wanted to sleep with her, but only when the job had been done [p. 49].

> Bond saw luck as a woman, to be softly wooed or brutally ravaged, never pandered to or pursued. But he was honest enough to admit that he had never yet been made to suffer by cards or by women [p. 57].

Violence is casual in the Bond of *Casino Royale.* Over dinner with Vesper he comments, "It's not difficult to get a Double O number if you're prepared to kill people. That's all the meaning it has.... It's a confusing business, but if it's one's profession, one does what one's told" (p. 76).

Bond's violence in *Casino Royale* is a realistic response to a desperate and sadistic villain. Bond of course wins at baccarat, and he hides his winnings in his hotel room. Le Chiffre's torture of him is lurid, if not pornographic. There are Bulgarian bombers and ruthless Russians in this mix as well.

Vesper Lynd is a rarity as a Bond girl for a number of reasons. First, Bond falls in love with her and seriously contemplates marriage, despite his initial aversion to her as a colleague. She is helpful and resourceful, and seems to fall in love with him, but at the end of the novel, she commits suicide, revealing that she is a double agent, leaving Bond conveniently unattached for further exploits, and embittering and numbed toward the espionage game. Only once again will Bond surrender himself emotionally to a woman, in both the film and book, *On Her Majesty's Secret Service*.

Le Chiffre is a smarmy villain. He is a sadist and a drug addict and a panderer and a compulsive gambler. His attraction to Communism is explained by his unheroic concentration camp experience during World War II. Bad politics, non–British extraction (Le Chiffre is an Eastern European Jew), and atypical sexuality are common among Bond's opponents. He only lacks some sort of physical abnormality to fit in with the pack of other Fleming villains. Le Chiffre clearly delights in the severe physical, genital torture he inflicts on Bond's naked body tied to a bottomless chair that takes place over several chapters in the novel. Bond's sexual appetites may seem insatiable, but they are never quirky and always heterosexual.

Film Introduction: *Dr. No* (1962)

President Kennedy told *Life* that to relax he read Ian Fleming's James Bond novels (Sidey, 1961), setting off a national craze for the British spy's adventures. *Dr. No*, the first of the Bond films, was released in 1962, starring Sean Connery as Bond.

When we see James Bond for the first time, we approach him from the back, playing chemin de fer. (Card playing is a typical activity for Bond in the early films: later in this film we see him playing solitaire.) The camera work in the introduction is dramatic, emphasizing Bond's ease at the table and his impeccable appearance. There are probably intentional references to our introduction to Rick Blaine in *Casablanca* in the location, dress, and camera work, although the director, Terence Young, has said that he copied the introduction of Paul Muni in *Juarez* (1939).

In this film, Bond faces the "Chinese" villain, Dr. No, who, supported by Asian and Black henchmen, is disrupting the American space program for SPECTRE from his base on Crab Key, somewhere off the coast of Jamaica. SPECTRE was a nonpolitical criminal organization intent on world domination, which Fleming had invented only the year before in the novel *Thunderball*. The Cold War was heating up, and the use of a real political adversary perhaps gave the heroics of Bond too much gravity after the Bay of Pigs. But by a few minor changes, the filmmakers could take advantage of several recent misfires in the U.S. missile program to create some believability to the situation.

The first "Bond girl" was Ursula Andress as Honey Ryder, a self-taught marine biologist, who collects shells on the forbidden Crab Key for her living, after her real marine biologist father was killed, probably by Dr. No.

Honey's entrance, stepping out of the surf wearing a white bikini with a conspicuous knife in the waistband is an iconic image of the early 1960s female sexuality. Honey admits to Bond that she has murdered a rapist landlord with a Black Widow spider. When she asks him if he has difficulty with this, Bond suggests it "shouldn't become a habit."

This film establishes Bond's approach to women. Bond seduces a woman from the casino, and he allows himself to be seduced by a Chinese SPEC-TRE agent twice, all of which are additions to the Fleming text. Typically, Bond is seduced by two women early in the films, one of whom is often an adversary and the other a professional or amateur accomplice. Often these women are quickly murdered by his opponents. In these early affairs Bond is typically the one who is seduced: only rarely does he make any real effort. Bond's libido is enhanced in the films, compared to the Fleming novels. In the novels, Bond's sexual thoughts are exposed to the reader, but his gentleman's code usually prohibits him from acting on those thoughts. His mutual kissing with Moneypenny, and a female car rental agent who blatantly checks out his rear end, also portray him as the recipient of unprovoked female attention.

Invariably, Bond has reason to behave "as a gentleman" toward the costarring female. He defines Honey as someone who needs his professional protection and, in this case, someone who is vulnerable to sexual advances (and is perhaps dangerous if sexually approached). Honey has "ties to nature," typical of the Bond girl (Rosenberg & Stewart, 1989). By working together in mutual support, there is usually a "romance" that develops between Bond and the principal actress. When the villain is vanquished and there is time to relax, the romance is brought to its inevitable conclusion, which is more often represented as cozy than blatantly sexual. In this respect, Bond behaves like the very good middle class civil servant that he is: he can be quickly and easily seduced "for king and country" (as he will later say in *Thunderball*), but real romance must be when he is off the job, as he suggested in *Casino Royale*. In this film he reinforces this civil servant mentality when he responds to M's query of when he sleeps by saying, "Not on the firm's time." There is an adolescent romantic quality to the plot of the most popular Bond films that is not apparent in most of the Fleming novels.

As in all of the most successful Bond films, throughout *Dr. No* there is a real sinister adversarial presence. Throughout the course of this movie there are a number of attempts on Bond's life: he is shot at three times (and almost a fourth time), once with a machine gun on the beach; the vodka in his hotel room is poisoned; he has a tarantula put in his bed; he is set upon by dogs; and there is an attempt to run his car off the road. He is beaten, drugged, and handcuffed. Additionally, a British bureaucrat and his secretary are shot and his native guide incinerated. In keeping with the typical portrayal of the enemy, there is an element of the sadistic: Honey Ryder is put into bondage which Bond rescues her from toward the end of the picture. Earlier, Dr. No's sexuality is brought into question when he lifts the covers off a drugged Bond and seems to enjoy a peek at his body.

Bond reacts to this level of threat by being violent himself. He shoots a wayward professor, stabs one guard and strangles another, and he beats Dr. No into a nuclear reactor when his artificial hands cannot grasp the structural support. There are two exciting fistfights and general mayhem which he incites at the end of the film. Bond saves the space program, and incurs the abiding wrath of SPECTRE.

The Connery Legacy

After *Dr. No,* Sean Connery starred in six more Bond films, the string of *From Russia with Love* (1963), *Goldfinger* (1964), *Thunderball* (1965) and *You Only Live Twice* (1967). In 1969 the string was broken when George Lazenby appeared as 007 in *On Her Majesty's Secret Service,* but Connery reappeared in 1971 in *Diamonds Are Forever.* After six Roger Moore outings, Connery reappeared in *Never Say Never Again* in 1983, for his last appearance as Bond.

For the one of us who is a baby boomer fan, Connery *is* Bond, and Lazenby, Roger Moore, Timothy Dalton, and Pierce Brosnan are imperfect Jimmy-come-latelies. For the other of us, it is Roger Moore who is the real Bond. But as students of popular culture and the representation of men in popular culture, we must suspend our fandom and look at how the characterization of Bond and his world has changed since 1962.

From Russia with Love

Again, the political context of the film *From Russia with Love* is changed from the Fleming novel by the substitution of SPECTRE for the Soviet secret service. SPECTRE wants to blackmail the Russians by stealing their newest decoder, and they arrange for James Bond to do the stealing, by setting an obvious trap for him, involving a beautiful girl. Englishmen, they reason, cannot resist an obvious trap, and apparently they cannot. The point of involving Bond is to kill him after he has the decoder, in revenge for his nasty treatment of Dr. No. Of course, Bond gets the decoder, eludes the SPECTRE agents, and convinces the girl, a low level operative, that life in the free world is better than life in the Soviet Union.

From Russia with Love introduces the "teaser" to the Bond film structure, an initial episode fraught with danger and often containing special effects, which may or may not be related to the rest of the film. In this teaser, the

Cold, sophisticated, and deadly, for many fans Connery is the best of the Bonds. Conversely, the image has been seen as sex, snobbery, and sadism by a legion of detractors.

assassin Grant (Robert Shaw) stalks and kills another SPECTRE agent dressed
as Bond, establishing the total indifference of the villains for life. (Later when
she views the practice area, the evil lesbian Klebb [Lotte Lenya] nods in
approval about the use of "live targets.") *From Russia with Love* also establishes the travelogue nature of subsequent Bond films. The film begins and
ends in Venice, and in between moves from Istanbul to Belgrade and Zagreb.

The character of Bond evolves only slightly in this film from its prede-
cessor, but in directions which will eventually take over his character. He
begins his series of one-liners and puns, and he also comes to rely on gad-
getry provided by Q Branch: he evolves from a serious-minded, patriotic
bureaucrat to a witty and often facetious technocrat.

Goldfinger

In *Goldfinger*, James Bond encounters the ruthless financier, Auric
Goldfinger, who is the world's foremost gold smuggler and hoarder. Goldfinger
is out to deplete the gold reserves of England and the United States to enhance
the worth of his own holdings and attempts nothing less than an invasion of
Fort Knox. Despite these enormous global ambitions, Goldfinger is petty: he
cheats at cards.

Goldfinger may be the best of the series, although it dates in some places.
Bond in this film appears too condescending toward women, and his sexual
encounter with the lesbian Pussy Galore (Honor Blackman) not only reforms
her sexual orientation, but changes her political affiliation. (Again we must
remind ourselves that this is a comic book romp, not a serious essay on international politics or the true nature of sexuality.) What makes this film watch-
able, perhaps even again and again, is that the plot is convincing and full of
detours: we begin believing that Goldfinger is trying to smuggle gold, and
then realize that he has a very inventive scheme: to enter Fort Knox not to
rob it, but to irradiate the gold reserves, thereby driving up the worth of his
own hoards of gold. (In the novel, Goldfinger did intend to steal the gold.
Critics of the novel pointed out how laughably impossible this would be. In
the film, Bond himself echoes the critics when he estimates that it would take
60 men 12 days to load the gold onto 120 waiting trucks.)

Goldfinger is a new villain: he is changed from a Soviet to Chinese agent
(Price [1992] quotes Fleming as saying, "I have always liked the Russians as
people, and I enjoyed myself when I worked in Moscow.... I could not see
any point in doing on digging at them, especially when the coexistence thing
seems to be bearing some fruit.") He has wonderful new toys of violence
including a laser with which he threatens to cut Bond in half from the groin
up, a wonderful car compressor, and an atomic bomb which resembles an airline beverage cart. He is even powerful enough to wipe out the entire Ameri-

can Mafia in one afternoon, and can delight in murder, such as when he paints a woman over with gold so that her skin will not breathe.

Thunderball

Thunderball begins with a teaser mingled with the opening credits. In this sequence, Bond, no longer having any reservations about working with female agents, observes the funeral in Paris of a SPECTRE agent. The agent's initials are also J.B. Bond invades the home of the agent and attacks the agent's widow, who is, of course, the agent in drag. He strangles him with an andiron and escapes with a jet backpack to the protection of his Oriental female coagent.

Because of the beating that he received in this incident, Bond is sent to recuperate at a spa, where he accidentally discovers the next SPECTRE plot, the theft of two nuclear NATO bombs, to be held for ransom against the destruction of a major American city (Miami).

The SPECTRE operatives are vicious in this film. They kill innocent pilots and NATO officials, and they are harsh in dealing with their own who fail in their assignments — one is blown up at a SPECTRE meeting, one is fed to sharks, one has his car bombed, and one is denied oxygen underwater. Sexually, they are perverted: Largo is a sexual sadist, his female henchwoman seems to enjoy bondage, and their main enforcer is asexual, perhaps the worst of all sexual perversions in the world of Bond.

Atypically, Bond makes real efforts to seduce a woman in this film, a physical therapist at the spa, first coming on to her before she straps him into a spine stretching machine, which a SPECTRE agent tries to make a rack of death, and then using sexual blackmail to seduce her in the steam room and later in his room.

Once again, the principal Bond girl has ties to nature. Bond meets Domino underwater, where she is swimming with a giant turtle. He rescues her when she gets caught in the rocks. Domino proves not only to be the mistress of the villain, Largo, but the sister of the SPECTRE agent who stole the plane and was killed by Largo.

This is a particularly violent Bond film, although not a particularly graphic one. Bond himself commits at least 17 murders, including a strangulation, a stabbing underwater in a pool of sharks, a shooting, moving a female agent into the line of fire, a surface harpooning, a stabbing with a flare gun, and 11 clear murders in the final underwater mayhem.

Bond is still sex-role stereotypical: he tells Domino she "swims like a man," and later he says that Largo's rifle "is for a woman." These sex-role ideas form the basis for most of his *bon mots*:

BOND: "I'm not what you'd call a passionate man."

FIONA, the SPECTRE agent (after taking Bond for a high speed drive): "Some men don't like to be driven."
BOND: "No, some men just don't like to be taken for a ride."

Lazenby: *On Her Majesty's Secret Service*

This 1969 production has the general reputation of being the least popular of the Bond films, although Leonard Maltin (1995) gives it 3½ stars and reports "some 007 fans consider this the best of the series" (p. 958). There are many things about this film to like, including great skiing and driving action sequences and Diana Rigg as the Bond girl, Tracy. It is perhaps the most faithful to the original material, the 1963 novel about Blofeld's (Telly Savalas) plot to use hypnotized allergy patients to infect British livestock for SPECTRE's advantage. This is a quintessential end-of-the-'60s film, reflecting many contemporary concerns about male role behavior. Perhaps the mirror that this film presented was too accurate for it to be very popular. There were too many warts reflected back.

The poor reception of this film is usually ascribed to the replacement of Sean Connery with Australian model George Lazenby, but there are other aspects of the film that tended to distance the film from its audience. Even in the opening credits, there is a montage of clips from previous films, accompanied by samples of the individual movie themes. Lazenby rescues Rigg from attacks while she is apparently trying to drown herself and then turns to the camera and says, "This wouldn't have happened to the other guy." This kind of Brechtian artifice was in vogue at the time, in films from *Poor Cow* (1967) to *Little Murders* (1971) and *Carnal Knowledge* (1971), but it is too off-putting for the action genre.

More importantly, Bond's character is put into a sex role quagmire in this film. He falls in love with Tracy early in the film, proposes to her, and near the end of the film, marries her. But between the time he commits to her and their marriage, he poses as a homosexual genealogist sent to legitimatize Blofeld's claims on a baronet. He allows the beautiful inmates of the allergy clinic to "cure" him, in order to gain information, which reflects a notion about homosexuality current at the time: Pussy Galore was presumably "cured" of her lesbianism by Bond's roguery in *Goldfinger*. In effect, however, Bond's promiscuity diminishes his commitment to Tracy. Even during this highwater year in the sexual revolution, marriage was seen as something distinct from rampant cocksmanship.

Tracy's father is not only an Italian noble, he is also Mafioso, which emphasizes the amorality of the plot, even though, like many film Mafiosi, the father is trying to go legit. Watching this film, one wonders what kinds of compromises this proposed union will make in Bond's career, and there are hints that he realizes that he will have to find another job.

What is finally lethal to this film as popular entertainment is its ending. Bond has always stood for something, even if we have reservations about those things. He is the ultimate *Playboy* playboy; he is the final outpost of British colonialism; he is the capitalist in struggle with socialist totalitarianism; he is sophistication rampant against primitivism; he is heterosexuality fighting against perversion. In this film he gives into domestication, Mediterraneanism, terrorism, and quirky sex.

And then, finally, after all the compromises, Tracy is shot down by Blofeld's henchwoman in a drive-by killing moments after the wedding. Bond has not vanquished his traditional enemies: he has been utterly undone by them. He has gotten neither the villain nor the girl. The antidote to antiheroics has become an antihero.

It is perhaps important to remember the events of 1969. This was not only the year of Woodstock, sex, drugs, and rock 'n' roll, but the year of the beginning of the National Organization of Women, an indication that women were dissatisfied with their share of the sexual revolution, and the year of the Stonewall riots, in which gays demanded that they no longer be thought of as "sick." Bond, that '50s Cold Warrior, is left holding "Emma Peel," a bullet delivered in her brain by an environmental thug and his androgynous harpie sidekick, weeping, denying to a gendarme that there is anything wrong. Straight, WASP, patriotic, hormonal males have had a hard time since then.

Roger Moore

Even though audiences have always known that James Bond is something of a comic book character, Ian Fleming did not completely share that view. He tended to see things in very clearcut terms: us against them, traditional values versus all sorts of new fangled ideas, such as women's liberation, anticolonialism, and socialism. Many changes occurred in the series after August 12, 1964, when Fleming died. Fleming had retained control over the material, and tied up the use of the unfilmed novels in his will. Gadgets and puns began to overcome the "serious" political messages, and Connery exited partially because he did not like some of these new directions, and partially because of other film opportunities. Roger Moore seemed an obvious replacement. He had had a long run in the television series *The Saint*, as a much more light comedian spy, but this approach seemed much more acceptable for the hedonistic and frivolous 1970s. Moore made seven Bond films, from *Diamonds Are Forever* in 1971 to *A View to a Kill* in 1985. We will look at an early and a late film in the Moore series.

The Man with the Golden Gun (1974)

The teaser for *The Man with the Golden Gun* introduces Bond's main antagonist, Scaramanga (Christopher Lee), a hired assassin with three nipples.

An American hit man arrives on Scaramanga's island retreat and is paid half of his contract to kill Scaramanga by the diminutive butler Nick Nack (Hervé Villechaize). Scaramanga plays a lethal game of hide-and-seek with the hit man in his carnival funhouse-like maze, until he shoots him squarely in the forehead. As in *From Russia with Love*, the teaser establishes the ruthlessness of the villain: he, too, uses live targets to practice assassination on; he is a person who kills others for sport.

The main narrative opens with Bond entering M's office. There is no preliminary banter with Moneypenny. Bond is taken off a case of a renegade solar technocrat because Scaramanga has sent his trademark golden bullet with a 007 etched on it. Apparently he needs more live target practice. Again, the British agent cannot resist an obvious trap. Bond provides Scaramanga's background: He was the son of Cuban circus people, a trick shot by age of ten, recruited by the KGB, now a million-dollar-a-hit hit man. He is unphotographed. Bond exits M's office. Bond asks Moneypenny about 002, an agent believed to have been killed by Scaramanga. Moneypenny fills him in that the confirmatory bullet was never found. When he tries to flirt with her, she tells him that she is tired of mere flirting, and disappears into her office.

The tightness of these introductory scenes promises a thrilling ride, but then the film fizzles. It is often regarded as the worst of the films (Rubin, 1995), and the novel, unrevised upon Fleming's death, is the least popular of his books: there is little tension in the film as the plot rambles from exotic location to other exotic locations, and Bond encounters characters with cute, offensive names (Nick Nack, Chew Me, Hip, and Hai Fat). Bond goes to Istanbul and quickly finds the bullet that killed 002, now a lucky charm in the belly button of a belly dancer. While kissing the belly button to get the bullet, Bond dispatches three operatives, to which the dancer whines: "I've lost my charm."

An analysis of the bullet suggests it was made by a craftsman in Macao, so Bond goes to Macao; eventually he shoots at the gun maker. Bond follows him to a casino; then follows Scaramanga's accomplice, Andrea Anders (Maud Adams) to Hong Kong. There he confirms Scaramanga will be at the Bottoms Up (a nudie bar). Bond waits outside. Nick Nack is around. Instead of Bond being targeted, it turns out that the target is the scientist Bond was investigating originally, and by the time they check the corpse, his device has been taken away by Nick Nack. Then off to Bangkok where Bond impersonates Scaramanga and gains access to Hai Fat's enclave. Scaramanga, however is already there and apparently in cahoots with Hai Fat. When Bond returns that evening he is taken to a martial arts school where he fights two challengers, and then escapes. He makes his getaway abetted by a Chinese agent and his karate-kicking nieces in schoolgirl uniforms (but inexplicably, they leave Bond behind, and he escapes in a river boat.)

Halfway through the movie Bond is still kill-less and has made no sexual conquests. He has not even received kisses from Moneypenny. When he suggests to his klutzy liaison Mary Goodnight (Britt Ekland) that they kill time by fooling around, she walks off indignantly. While Bond is still libidinal, women seem to have gotten the right to say "no." But there is really no such message because almost immediately thereafter Bond finds Goodnight in his hotel room dressed in a babydoll nightie. "What made you change your mind?" he asks. "I'm weak," she answers. Just as they begin, Andrea Anders arrives and Mary must hide. Andrea tells him that Scaramanga is after him; she hates him, and it was she who sent the golden bullet to London, because she knows from Scaramanga that Bond is the only person he fears. They begin to kiss (Goodnight is still in the bed, covered by sheets — Bond has told Anders that she is a three pillow decoy), and Bond asks about the solar device (he being the good company man).

If this plot seems confusing, this is not half of it. There is even a reappearance of J. W. Pepper, the redneck sheriff from *Diamonds Are Forever,* as a tourist in Thailand. Eventually Bond arrives on Scaramanga's island retreat and dispatches him in the maze. This seems inevitable, and Christopher Lee's performance seems to make it inevitable: all Bond's racing around is a manic and irrelevant prelude to a fatalistic encounter between moody Evil and high-spirited Good. Scaramanga is too likable, too tragic, and Bond is just too bubbly and frenetic.

Moreover, the film is really two different stories that have been irrationally fused together. On the one hand, there is an almost Western-style plot of the showdown between adversaries derived from the Fleming material, and then there is the plot about harnessing solar power. The film was made during the OPEC oil crisis, so this may have created some contemporary interest and suspense, but viewed 25 year later, this addition merely makes a chaotic plot more chaotic.

But the sets and the locations are great: the maze; the secret service headquarters in Hong Kong in the half sunken *Queen Mary*; Bangkok; Macao, the Chinese Islands where Scaramanga's hideout is located.

A View to a Kill (1985)

A View to a Kill may not be the best of the later Bond films, but it has many qualities of them that make it as useful one to compare to earlier films. This was Roger Moore's final outing as 007, and it is essentially a remake of *Goldfinger.* (*A View to a Kill* has no relation to the short story from which it derives its name. That story puts 007 in the role of detective, trying to discover who is killing NATO couriers.)

The plot of this film pits Bond against a complicated villain, Zorin, played by Christopher Walken, occasionally in his best frenetic acting. Zorin's henchwoman, May Day, is portrayed by disco diva Grace Jones, in revealing thong outfits and bat-ear hairdos. May Day combines qualities of both Odd Job (she is Zorin's chief assassin, a martial arts expert, and a minority) and Pussy Galore (she expresses ambiguity toward heterosexuality and saves the day at the end by a defection from the villain's camp). Zorin has many parallels to Auric Goldfinger. His plan is to corner the market in a precious commodity (microchips) in one desperate action (flooding Silicon Valley) that will create global economic chaos. He is wealthy. He cheats at games (horse racing rather than gin rummy). He possesses the latest technology.

Yet there are significant differences. Goldfinger was an industrialist who veered away from the straight and narrow and made allegiances with the Chinese. Zorin is the result of genetic experiments by a Nazi scientist. This experiment renders him a genius but psychotic. He has been raised as a KGB agent, but he has defected to become a renegade entrepreneur. An opponent with Fascist origins, Marxist upbringing, and unfettered Capitalist tendencies, with pretension to aristocratic life, makes him the ultimate 1985 villain: he is to anyone, irrespective of politics, a worse nightmare scenario. He represents extremism of every and all varieties, even acting.

This is a very "green" film. Zorin's legitimate business is oil, and his purpose is to rape the environment. To accomplish his goals he has compromised individuals and government officials who are charged with protecting the environment. He has killed all the crabs in San Francisco Bay. He will cause a massive earthquake, like the bad guys in the 1978 *Superman*. He abuses animals. If his political credentials do not turn off the audience, then his environmental record certainly will.

Rather than being the Cambridge graduate/broadly competent amateur that Sean Connery's Bond represented, Moore's Bond is by now a complete technocrat. In *A View to a Kill,* Bond has complex knowledge of microchips, nuclear physics, elevators, telephone systems, racehorse bloodlines and race handicapping, genetics, and steroids. He is an expert hot dog skier and extreme snowboarder; he can operate a snowmobile professionally in mountainous terrain; and he can drive a fire engine through San Francisco traffic. Oddly, however, although he can read a geological map, he has absolutely no knowledge of earthquake geology and must rely on Stacey Sutton (Tonya Roberts) to provide that expertise.

As a film, *A View to a Kill* has many features which are fundamentally unsatisfying. There are six major action sequences, three of which are played for comedy — the opening skiing sequence, nonsense around the Eiffel Tower, and the fire engine chase through San Francisco — and three of which are played almost straight — the steeplechase, the assault on Stacey's home, and the dizzying final fight on the Golden Gate Bridge. Bond makes just too many puns. The nature of the film is never fully defined, like the exact nature of the villain: the film never resolves itself between comic strip or serious spy story, a characteristic of many of the Roger Moore films.

Also, in this film, Bond is not a lethal weapon. He perhaps blows up two KGB agents at the beginning of the film in a helicopter, but otherwise he is closer to the journalist, James Stock, he pretends to be than the secret agent he actually is. This is unsatisfying because of the contrast to Zorin who is one of the most lethal of the Bond opponents. Early in the film May Day kills M. Aubergine with a poisoned butterfly, then strangles a British agent and a Chinese-American CIA agent. Zorin chops up a KGB agent in an oil intake valve. Zorin machine-guns dozens of his own workers. His plan will involve "millions of deaths." Bond's most lethal moment is when he shoots four of Zorin's men in their assault on Stacey's home, only to discover that his gun is loaded with rock salt.

Some critics, including Chapman, have found the character of May Day problematic. She is lethal, female, and African American. These qualities would seem to set her up for more than what happens: she discovers that Zorin does not love her when he leaves her and many of his men behind to be killed by the earthquake, and she quickly changes sides. She, in fact, is responsible for removing the detonator, but she is blown to bits by it once she has brought it above ground.

Bond, however, has his sexual way with three beautiful women: a fellow agent in a submarine in the opening sequence, an even more beautiful Russian agent (who tells him "Détente can be beautiful"), and finally Stacey at the end of the film.

In fact, the political climate of détente may be what confuses this film. While Reagan was ranting against the "evil empire," it was becoming clear to most Americans that Russia was no more a threat to them in 1985 than current Fascism or Reagan economics (or conversely that Reagan economics was just as threatening as real Nazism and Stalinism). Coming in from stage left was the specter of global ecological disaster (equal in threat to SPECTRE). Was Bond the right hero for this moment?

Dalton and Brosnan

The last of the Roger Moore films did not do particularly well box-officewise, and it was suspected that Bond was dead. But producers tried two different approaches: one approach was, in the two outings by Timothy Dalton, to de-emphasize the espionage angle and to make Bond an action hero. When this approach was less successful than hoped, the other, more outrageous approach, was to resuscitate the original Bond character in the films starring Pierce Brosnan. Both approaches abandoned any use of Fleming's original material.

Licence to Kill (1989)

Licence to Kill attempted to update the Bond film into the mold of its action/adventure competition by focusing on a contemporary plot (*Batman, Indiana Jones and the Last Crusade,* and *Lethal Weapon 2* were the number 1, 2, and 3 hits of 1989, respectively). Timothy Dalton's Bond in that film is divorced from politics, pursuing a vicious, modern day drug lord who killed his friend Felix's wife after their wedding and partially fed Felix to sharks. The plot is about a personal vendetta, driven by a friendship, hard to imagine in earlier incarnations of Bond. Bond, from Fleming through each of his screen personae, is a "company man," the quintessential bureaucrat. This personally motivated Bond is only hinted at in the last Fleming work, the novella *Octopussy,* where Bond wants to revenge the killing of his mentor, but is prevented from doing so by unforeseen circumstances. The film's title refers to the fact that Bond's license to kill is revoked because of his renegade actions. Later, we begin to suspect that M may be secretly supporting Bond's actions when Q shows up not only with gadgets but prepared to join in the fun.

Leonard Maltin's review captures *Licence to Kill* well when he says:

> Dazzling stunts, high adventure, and a sexy companion for Bond ... make this one of the best of the series since Sean Connery's departure (if still lacking that old-time panache).

Licence to Kill is also a film which makes us note some of the things that have been absent from the previous films: graphic representations of violence and four-letter words. The presence of these elements in this film make it fit very well into the contemporary film scene, but they seem somehow out of place in a Bond film. Bond doesn't need to splatter brains around or cuss.

Bond's confrontation with M is an interesting point in this film. Bond is without family, and M has always seemed a surrogate father. Here, a year before the publication of Robert Bly's (1990) *Iron John,* we find Bond anxiously dealing with the estrangement from his father figure, a father figure who is giving him bad advice.

GoldenEye (1995)

GoldenEye reclaimed the James Bond niche by focusing on the Bond character and the "old-time panache." Focusing of the character of Bond was perhaps unavoidable when the decision was made to cast Pierce Brosnan as the new Bond. Brosnan had exhibited a talent for light comedy, not only in the *Remington Steele* TV series, but in a number of film roles, such as Robin Williams's competition in *Mrs. Doubtfire* (1993). It would have been easy for him to fall into the "glib punster" portrayal of Bond, as with the increasingly disappointing Roger Moore films, without a script that was character-driven.

While many of the original Bond accessories are back in *GoldenEye* — baccarat, tuxedo, expensive champagne, fast cars — he is seriously recontextualized for present day consumption. Many critics had predicted yet again the demise of Bond after *Licence to Kill's* modest box office showing: Bond is, after all, they claimed, too sexist and violent for our times, and essentially useless after the fall of the Soviet Union. What may have surprised those critics was that the "new" Bond is sexist, violent, and fighting Russians for the first time since *From Russia with Love* in 1963. True to the new order, he is not fighting Soviets, but a Russian Mafioso (Robbie Coltrane), A Cossack nationalist (Sean Bean), a gorgeous, gleeful Georgian sadist (Famke Janssen), and a Russian computer nerd (Alan Cumming) who is after internet supremacy and hard British currency. What would also surprise those critics was that the film had a better run in the box office than any recent Bond film and has done particularly well in video rentals. After some hesitation after *Licence to Kill,* the Broccoli organization announced after the performance of *GoldenEye,* the Bond series is back for the foreseeable future.

The film's opening sequence occurs sometime during the end of the Cold War. Bond joins 006 (Sean Bean) to disarm a Soviet biological weapon research station, but things go wrong, and 006 is presumably killed by a vicious spy who readily kills his own men if they disobey his orders. Bond escapes in another stunning (and thoroughly unbelievable) freefall stunt. Unlike many of the opening episodes of earlier films, however, this one is an integral part of the film, although it is not immediately clear that it is.

When we see Bond in the present, he is zipping along the Mediterranean coast with a sexy female psychologist who has been sent by Intelligence to determine his soundness. A woman in a red sports car, Ms. Onatopp, challenges him to a race. The psychologist insists that he stop his childish competitiveness, which he does, but Bond understands there is something more sinister going on. He meets Ms. Onatopp later at the baccarat table, but she leaves with an American admiral, whom she squeezes to death with her thigh-mastered thighs while having rough sex in her yacht. She takes the admiral's security pass and gains access to a preview of a new stealth helicopter which she steals with General Ourumov (Gottfried John), after killing the pilots. Within the first 25 minutes of the film, we have established that Onatopp and Ourumov are ruthless and violent villains.

Convinced of the "new world order," the British intelligence community seems little concerned about the theft of the helicopter until surveillance discovers that a *Star Wars*–type satellite has detonated over an area in Russia and that a small intelligence station in Siberia has been blown up, killing all but one person. In fact, Onatopp and Ourumov have gone to Siberia to unleash GoldenEye (in joke: GoldenEye was the name of Fleming's Caribbean home), a nuclear device which fundamentally fries all electronic circuits within a large target area. The point of the first detonation is to disguise the fact that there is a second GoldenEye satellite which will be trained on London. After electronically transferring huge amounts of money from the Bank of England, the second GoldenEye will fuse all of London's electronic equipment (home appliances, radios, televisions, watches, computers, trains, cars, and weapons), disguising the theft and sending Britain "into the stone age."

Among Bond's problems in finding a solution to this problem is that he has a legacy of Cold War baggage to deal with. To get access to the mastermind of this plot, he must gain the help of the head of the Russian Mafia, a former KGB agent whom he had crippled. The mastermind turns out to be 006, who defected when he found out that his Cossack parents had been betrayed by British Intelligence to the Stalinists. Bond's quick exit in the opening sequence left 006 severely burned, and 006 is severely pissed.

Bond, of course, overcomes these problems, because, unlike the bureaucrats in London, he understands all these lingering animosities, and because he still has the lethal instincts of the Cold War warrior.

Bond's relationships with women are utterly redefined in this film. The Bond of Fleming's *Casino Royale*, who chafes under the yoke of having a female assistant, would be helpless in the highly feminized world of *Golden-Eye*. Brosnan's treatment of women is much like Connery's, but the reaction of the women around him is completely different. A female psychologist will determine his fitness to remain in the service, and she considers his interest in fast cars and fast women "symptoms." Young Miss Moneypenny warns him about sexual harassment when he flirts with her — she has been on a date, not waiting at home on the off-chance that James will give her a ring, as her mother had done. M is now a woman (Judi Dench), who considers Bond a "sexist ... dinosaur." She not only is a new kind of woman but a new kind of spy — she tells Bond that she suspects that he considers her "an accountant ... a bean counter," and she admits that she is. She is, if anything, more cold and more calculating than he is. The code name "M" stood for mother, but this female M has little nurturance about her. She tells him she will not hesitate to send him off to his death, although as he leaves, she admits she hopes he comes back alive. The women in this film are very mathematical (calculating?) and technocratic, while many of the men show a discomfort with numbers and computers.

In addition, in contrast to earlier films, Bond has a single conquest in this film, with Simonova (Izabella Scorupco), the one person who escaped the Siberian assault and the only person able to implicate Ourumov, who is now pursuing political power in the new Russia. Bond protects her, not only because she is a woman and because she is a potential sexual partner, but because he needs her testimony. She also has computer expertise that he lacks.

Like the sexual persona of the early Connery films, Brosnan's Bond is as pursued as pursuing. The psychologist eventually could be seduced if Bond did not sense urgency elsewhere, and Onatopp is anxious to get her clenching Georgian thighs around him. He recognizes Onatopp's thoroughly driven nature, and is never considerate of her "feminine status": he treats her only as a lethal adversary.

There is an interesting scene in this film prior to the final conflict in Cuba, when Simonova approaches a contemplative Bond on the beach, who ignores her physical advances. She understands that he is torn between his friendship for 006 and "the mission." He explains that his unemotional focus prepares him for what he has to do. She responds that such preparation is what makes him "alone." In contrast to a whole host of films from the 1970s and 1980s, in which a strong man "alone" would be viewed as noble and strong, in the logic of this picture, we want Bond and Simonova to connect. Perhaps the knee-jerk feminism of the New Miss Moneypenny will give way to a rapprochement between the old-style Bond and the new woman.

The depiction of violence in this film is less graphic than in *License to Kill,* but somewhat more realistic than in previous Bond films. Violence has consequences, no more than when Bond lets go of his former friend 006. Violence in this film occurs in a moral universe where death occurs to real people about whom someone cares.

Politically, this film is the most sobering of the Bond films. SPECTRE always seemed the stuff of comic books, and Bond's Chinese and Russian enemies were stereotypical and often dim-witted; but a chaotic former Soviet Union with its leftover arsenal of weapons of mass destruction and corruption and leftover hatreds seems a genuine threat to our everyday way of life.

* * *

We chose as the subtitle for this chapter the infamous blooper from *You Only Live Twice* (1967) when Henderson gets the formula for the Bond martini wrong. We think it an apt title though, because Bond's image gets stirred up somewhat in the course of 20 films, but his fundamental character is never shaken. He is smart, efficient, cold, patriotic, sexual, and "the ultimate company man." He is a loner, which sometimes means self-sufficient, but most recently, lonely. He is a workaholic. He has a single friend, Felix, but he either wasn't invited to his wedding or couldn't make it. And whatever he does to make the world safe for — whatever it is that he's fighting for — there's always the next sequel reminding him he has, in some way, failed.

Bond films are always set in the present, and the present changes more than Bond. Sometimes this means that the Cold Warrior is out of his element politically. The films have modulated in their genres: *On Her Majesty's Secret Service* was something of a 1960s sex romp; he could throw in martial arts when those films were popular; and *Moonraker* turned the series into sci-fi on the coattails of *Star Wars* (1977). He tried to be less violent, but a Bond shooting rock salt was just too silly. His cavalier treatment of women begins to fail in the early 1970s when women begin to be more secure and can say "no," and it is frowned upon in the most recent films: but he only partially learns to keep his libido in check. He still thinks in terms of "us and them," but he has attempted to define "them" a little less on racial lines, although nearly every film has provoked commentaries about the racial stereotypes. He remains snobbish even when what he feels snobbish about changes (we note that at some point he stopped smoking his two and a half packs of custom cigarettes a day). With Timothy Dalton, he got a bit more relaxed in his dress code, but with Brosnan he is back in suits and tuxes, fighting Russians, and drinking that martini, shaken, not stirred. Bond's masculinity is about style, work, and self.

PART IV

Superheroes and Dolts

It is probably a mistake to use decades as markers, but our historical stereotypes seem to involve decades. The general stereotypes dominating our perceptions of the 1970s, 1980s, and 1990s are that they were very self-absorbed decades. In the typical scenario, the 1970s were the first hedonic manifestation of the "me" generation. It was a time of individual excess after the collapse of the social excess of the Woodstock generation: recreational drug use, disco, singer-songwriters. The 1980s gave us "greed is good" Reaganomics, where success was measured not by which clubs one could get into on a Saturday night, but by which brand of pricey imported car one drove. Perhaps we are too close to the 1990s to get much of a sense of how they will be stereotyped but they have given us cultural relativism raised to the nth degree in the form of identity politics and social constructivism.

Certainly, the last thirty years was a time where the notion of the family changed. Divorce rates have hovered at around 50 percent. We talk about sexual, physical, and emotional abuse as if they were inherent in the fabric of family life. Romance must tread a very thin line between interest and harassment. It has been a time when portraying family life and courtship positively has become increasingly difficult.

But we have found thus far that our stereotypes of the 1940s, 1950s, and 1960s are inaccurate when we begin to look at the representation of men in popular films of those decades. Perhaps we will find these stereotypes equally wrong as we examine the films of these last three decades.

In this last section of this book, we will look at four manifestations of movie masculinity. In chapter eleven we will look at the *Star Wars* output, films which we believe changed the basic expectations about what movies could and should be and either reflected or altered some ideas about masculinity. In chapter twelve, we will look at the portrayal of men and boys in films designed for children, concentrating on the revival of Disney animated films in the late 1980s and 1990s. In chapter thirteen we will examine a whole spate of films in which men are portrayed as idiots (thus explaining part of this section's title). Finally, we will examine two recent films, *Titanic* and *Shakespeare in Love,* in which romance seems to be making something of a comeback, but in a redefined way.

The "Superheroes" portion of this section's title was chosen not necessarily because the majority of the films we will examine would fall into this subgenre of action films, but because superhero films dominated the box office during this period. Some of these superheroes come directly from comic books, such as the *Superman* and *Batman* series. Some are science fiction monsters who evolved from the nuclear war horror films of the 1950s, such as the *Terminator* series. Some are chauvinistic inflations of our national ego, as in the *Rambo* films. Clearly we were tired of the antihero, but not yet ready for a return to human-sized men in contemporary dramas.

Eleven — Star Wars

For many of today's student generation, *Star Wars* was the telling moment of their cinematic lives.[1] For them, *Star Wars* defined what the movies not only could be but should be: action, adventure, and special effects; appealing young men thrust into galactic problems well beyond their means to understand, let alone successfully deal with, but through a kind of new age magic and the mentoring of various father figures, they do deal with them.

If there was a cinematic phenomenon in the 1970s prior to *Star Wars,* it was the "disaster film." *Airport* (1970), *The Poseidon Adventure* (1972), *The Towering Inferno* (1974), and *Earthquake* (1974) represented a new form of entertainment, where special effects took precedent over human action. In fact, these films seem to be man *against* special effects. The fun of these flicks was not only in the dazzle, but in trying to figure out who would survive and who would not. More often than not, the "hero" was a person who had realized that there was something too arrogant in the enterprise to begin with. Like the biblical epics of the 1950s, these films placed ordinary, morally good men in competition with events far beyond their capabilities. In the biblical epics, it was faith which provided the resources to overcome overwhelming adversity. In the disaster films, it was technological expertise. In that way, the heroes of the disaster films had much in common with James Bond. We have in the Star Wars films a melding of both traditions: Obi-Wan, Vader, Luke, and Han are not only experts, but they possess spiritual abilities which make them capable of heroics, even though at first they appear very ordinary.

By 1977, science fiction had begun to emerge from marginal status to mainstream cinema. *2001: A Space Odyssey* was the film that replaced *The Sound of Music* in the big downtown theaters in 1968, and in 1975, of all things, a drag sci-fi musical, *The Rocky Horror Picture Show,* had become a hit. So *Star Wars* was not the film which brought respectability to the science fiction movie or even ushered in the craze. In addition to *Star Wars,* in 1977 *Close Encounters of the Third Kind* was a huge commercial success.

But *Close Encounters* was a very different kind of sci-fi film than *Star Wars.* There is little action and adventure. There is, of course, some similarity between the telepathic calling of the people in *Close Encounters* to "the Force." But *Close Encounters* is part of the "man from Mars" subgenre of sci-fi flick, and it dealt with the contemporary obsession about whether we are alone in the galaxy. *Star Wars,* within science fiction films, was something quite different, although in science fiction literature there are many books which attempted to merge spirituality and adventure.

For the decade beginning in 1977, sci-fi films dominated the screen: in addition to *Star Wars* and *Close Encounters,* 12 other science fiction films were among the 50 most popular films of the period: *Superman* (1978), *Star Trek: The Motion Picture* (1979), *Alien,* (1979), *The Empire Strikes Back* (1980), *Superman II* (1981), *E.T. the Extra-Terrestrial* (1982), *The Return of the Jedi* (1983), *War Games* (1983), *Superman III* (1983), *Gremlins* (1984), *Back to the Future* (1985), and *Star Trek IV: The Voyage Home* (1986). This was certainly a significant trend. And it was a trend with legs: sci-fi films continue to be box office hits, although not all do so — just as not all biblical epics did boffo business.

George Lucas

Pye and Miles (1979) refer to a cluster of younger filmmakers of the 1970s as "the movie brats," by which they mean a generation of directors and writers such as Martin Scorsese, Steven Spielberg, Francis Ford Coppola, Brian De Palma, and George Lucas who grew up on the visual images of film and television. The films of the directors are far more based on this visual method of storytelling than previous generations of filmmakers who learned storytelling from prose fiction. Some have come out as having learning disabilities. Mostly, these directors were graduates of film schools, and embedded in their movies were specific references to a wide variety of films, from Saturday matinee serials to serious European and Japanese films. It is perhaps no wonder that the films of these directors speak with such resonance to the visually literate (and less text literate) members of the current student generation.

George Lucas had made two feature films before *Star Wars.* His first directorial outing was the 1971 sci-fi film *THX 1138,* a grim, moody story about a man, THX 1138 (Robert Duvall), living in a grim and nearly colorless subterranean future. Sex and romance and even will have been abolished —

everyone just takes tranquilizers and watches television. THX and his room-mate LUH (Maggie McOmie) forget to take their tranquilizers, discover sex, and when their deviance is found out, THX is accused of "drug evasion" and goes on the run from an army of robot policemen. At the end, THX reaches the surface of the earth and his pursuit is called off for lack of funds. *THX 1138* was an enigma to the studio heads at Warners and reedited before its release. It was not a commercial success, either in its first release or in 1978 when the original cut was released "by the makers of *Star Wars,*" but it found a following among college students and film buffs.

It was his second film, *American Graffiti* (1973), which gave Lucas the clout to go ahead with his ambitious *Star Wars* project. *American Graffiti* was the third most popular film of the year, behind the macabre *Exorcist,* and the buddy romp, *The Sting.* The film recreates one night in 1962 as a group of high school students roam the streets of Northern California, looking for friendship and companionship. The film was an oddity for its time, partic-ularly in the use of a virtually unknown young ensemble cast (including Har-rison Ford) and its rock 'n' roll soundtrack. The aimlessness of the individual students is guided by the voice of Wolfman Jack, a radio disc jockey, who like a benign Big Brother gives advice to the weary adolescents. But *American Graffiti* was also a problem to the studio heads, and it was recut before its release, as well.

Lucas decided that his next movie would be a commercial hit. Pye and Miles (1979) quote Lucas from one of their interviews: "I researched kid's movies, and how they work and how myths work: and I looked very care-fully at the elements of films within that fairy tale genre which made them successful" (p. 133). These authors contend that T-shirts, dolls, and record spin-offs were in the forefront of his plan, and that Lucas projected a 16 mil-lion dollar domestic gross. In that last regard, he was quite off the mark. The film made 15 times that amount in first release.

Star Wars (1977)

After a brief introduction to the world of Star Wars on the preliminary crawl, we are dropped into a battle between the Rebellion and the Empire. Princess Leia (Carrie Fisher) is on board with Imperial plans. Knowing that her capture is eminent, she puts the plans inside trusty droid R2-D2. She instructs him (?) to seek Obi-Wan Kenobi and deliver the plans to him. The robot servant and his companion, C-3PO, escape in a pod and land on the planet Tatooine. Leia confronts the enormous figure of Darth Vader, breath-ing consumptively in his shiny black get-up. Leia is identified as the leader of the Rebel Forces: she has shot a few Imperial soldiers prior to her capture.[2]

On Tatooine the droids continue their comic banter in which they establish their separate identities — C-3PO is neurotic. Everything is always going wrong, and he is entirely concerned with his own well-being. R2, who speaks in only electronic squeaks and buzzes, is more focused on the total situation. He is from the first likable and heroic, despite looking like a large silver and blue popcorn popper. Eventually they fall into the custody of Luke Skywalker (Mark Hamill). Luke is an orphan living on a farm on this very dreary planet with his work-absorbed uncle and an aunt who is more sympathetic to his isolation. The Skywalker family is a kind of fantasized version of the Starretts: three people in a wild and unfriendly frontier, scratching out a hard existence. Instead of horses and cows there are droids and racers; instead of marauding deer and Ryker's men there are Sand People and Imperial soldiers. Luke hopes to escape the drudgery of farm life to study at the Academy. While cleaning R2-D2 he discovers the holographic message left by the Princess for Obi-Wan. He wonders whether Obi-Wan and Ben Kenobi know each other. He's smitten by the image of the Princess.

R2 is a droid with a mission, and when Luke returns after dinner, where he learns that Obi-Wan and his father knew each other, he discovers that R2 has set off to fulfill his mission. The next morning Luke and C-3PO set out to find him. On the way, Luke is attacked by Sand People, who Ben/Obi-Wan (Alec Guinness) chases away. Perhaps the first several times we watch this scene we may fail to note that Obi-Wan, who is rather old, has little problem scattering the ferocious Sand People.

Back at Obi-Wan's home, Luke learns something about his father (he was killed by Obi-Wan's pupil Darth Vader) and we (and Luke) begin our educations about the tradition of the Jedi knights. Obi-Wan gives Luke his father's light saber ("A more elegant weapon for more civilized times"), and he describes the Force as "what give a Jedi his power" and as "an energy field … that binds all living things together." Obi-Wan assumes that Luke will accompany him on his quest, but like a good American hero at the beginning of a movie Luke says, "I can't get involved. I have work to do...."

But the evil forces of the Empire have been following the droids and when Luke returns to the farm, they have savaged his family. This is a truly gruesome sight, with the burned corpses of his relatives caught in desperate flight. Luke returns to Obi-Wan.

Luke and Obi-Wan head to a nearby Space Post to find transportation. This is a place where multiculturalism could get a bad name (Obi-Wan refers to it as "a wretched hive of scum and villainy"). All sorts of intergalactic species are around, and none of them have any redeeming qualities. But as the duo makes their way deeper and deeper into the innards of this cesspool, we discover that Obi-Wan has a gift. "The Force" renders him mysteriously capable of influencing others with a wave of his hand and a calm suggestion.[3] While Obi-Wan finds a pilot with a vehicle capable of making their journey,

Luke has every college freshman's first bad adventure in a bar, as two toughs approach him and try to pick a fight. Only Obi-Wan's intervention avoids catastrophe.

The pilot Obi-Wan has found is Han Solo (Harrison Ford), and his ship is the Millennium Falcon. Solo has his own reasons for wanting to exit quickly: he was running contraband for Jabba the Hutt when approached by Imperial troopers. Han dumped the cargo. He has not repaid Jabba, and Han dispatches one of Jabba's henchthings who was sent to kill him in the bar.[4] As Jabba's "men" and Imperial troopers try to prevent them from leaving, Han, Luke, Obi-Wan, and the droids, joined by Han's sidekick, a nine-foot-tall canine named Chewbacca, a Wookie, manage to escape in the rather beaten up Millennium Falcon.

As they speed toward their destination, Luke gets preliminary instruction from Obi-Wan about the Force. Some of the Jedi philosophy seems to come from '60s drug culture ("Let go of your conscious self..." "act on instinct"); some of it seems straight out of Plato ("Eyes can deceive you — don't trust them"), and some of it seems based on the Human Potential movement ("Stretch out with your feelings..."). All of this with a good deal of martial arts thrown in for good measure.

The rest of the film falls into two grand action sequences. In the first, the Millennium Falcon is sucked into the interior of the Empire's ultimate weapon of destruction, the Death Star. The Death Star has just smashed to smithereens the Princess' home planet, just to put fear into the Rebel forces. (The Emperor has no hesitation about how to answer Machiavelli's question of whether it is better for a ruler to be loved or feared.) The rest of the sequence involves getting out of the Death Star. As Obi-Wan goes off to turn off a tractor beam which is holding the Millennium Falcon in place, Luke discovers that the Princess is on board, and without a plan, he, a very reluctant Han, and Chewbacca go off to rescue her. Leia is extremely annoyed that her rescuers have no plan, and she takes charge, leading them into a huge trash compactor and onto a bridge with no extension. But the droids save the day on several occasions with necessary information, and the team returns to the Millennium Falcon. Sparks fly between the Princess and Han, and as they argue and call each other names, we know there will be an inevitable romance.

As the Princess and the fellas have been shooting it up with Imperial Storm Troopers, Obi-Wan has found his nemesis, Darth Vader. They are engaged in light saber fencing as the rest of the band reaches their destination. Vader tells Obi-Wan that he must kill him, and Obi-Wan retorts: "If you strike me down, I'll become more powerful than you can imagine." And then Obi-Wan turns off his light saber and allows himself to be killed. This is an enigmatic act, one which may have had less to do with the intentions of the filmmakers than the desire of the actor. In the *USA Today* (August 7,

2000) obituary of Alec Guinness, the actor is quoted as having encouraged George Lucas to kill off Obi-Wan. "I just couldn't go on speaking those bloody awful, banal lines. I'd had enough of the mumbo jumbo." But Obi-Wan's presence will guide Luke in the next two sequels. Apparently Sir Alec could be talked into returning for a day or two of shooting for each of the following films. Luke is despondent over the sudden loss of another father figure.

The second sequence is the attack of the Rebel forces on the Death Star. The plans of the Death Star which R2 has been concealing point to a weakness, and the engine of mass destruction is attacked in a spectacular display of special effects. Luke is the pilot who makes the fatal strike, but only after he remembers the messages that Obi-Wan gave him: don't trust your eyes (or you navigational equipment), stretch out with your feelings, and trust your instincts. The conclusion of the film is a heroic reception for the pilots, and we would be happy, except that we know that Vader escaped the Death Star and the Emperor is still alive. A sequel will be necessary.

Although we have described *Star Wars* thus far as a science fiction film, it is actually a compilation of genres. One of the more conspicuous forms it follows is the "buddy picture." The buddy picture evolved out of the western genre, most conspicuously in *Butch Cassidy and the Sundance Kid*. The buddy picture came to prominence, we believe, as a response to the difficulty of representing romance on screen, which had really been the theme of most successful films up until the mid-1960s. Films about falling in love are essentially films about two people finding out about each other and about themselves. Buddies in buddy pictures often know very little about each other (late in the film Butch and Sundance discover they don't know each other's real names or where they are from). Usually there's a smart one and a reckless one. Usually there is a romantic involvement somewhere on the sidelines (some feminist critics would say this is a cover for the essential homoerotic nature of buddy pictures, but we think this is incorrect), but it is more of an irritant between the boys than a point of genuine conflict.

It is hard to impose this formula completely on *Star Wars*. At times, Luke is the reckless one (as when he decides to go save the Princess), but Han is more often the emblem of the active life, as when he chafes about waiting in the control room of the Death Star before Luke discovers that the Princess is on board. But they do bicker, and there is a little bit of competition between them for the attention of the Princess.

Power is an essential masculine trait, and in the *Star Wars* world, personal power comes from "the Force." But, we propose, that the Force is essentially feminine. Defining what was meant by masculinity and femininity was a major concern of social scientists in the 1970s. Within psychology, until this time, femininity and masculinity were conceived of as polar opposites. In 1974, Sandra Bem proposed that rather than being opposite traits, they were independent of each other. Bem suggested that masculinity in contemporary American culture consisted of *agency,* or an interest in getting things done. For her, masculinity consisted of competitiveness, force, leadership, and task-orientation. Femininity consisted of emotional expressiveness, caring, concern, and nurturing. By extension, masculinity is logical, while femininity is intuitive. Bem proposed that individuals could be traditionally masculine, traditionally feminine, or a combination of the two, which she called *androgynous*—a person who was both task oriented and expressive and nurturing. In the spirit of the time, androgyny was considered superior to either traditional masculinity or traditional femininity. In pop psychology books, men were encouraged to "get in touch with their feminine side," just as Luke is encouraged to get in touch with the Force. The Jedi is a conspicuous symbol of psychological androgyny: he is agentive in his mission, personally responsible, a leader (masculine), while using the methods of feeling, intuition, and caring.

The most traditionally masculine character in the film is the Princess. Androgyny theory would not be surprised to find a woman traditionally masculine sex-typed, nor a man traditionally feminine. She is sarcastic and wisecracking. She's a take-charge kind of gal, who, when the guys are flummoxed about what to do, is likely to grab a weapon and use it. She's also far more knowledgeable about the total situation than any of the male characters. She's the only one who understands the political significance of what is going on. In this outing, there is nothing nurturing or emotionally expressive (except in the expression of contempt) about her.

Bem also proposes a fourth type — which she calls *undifferentiated.* These individuals are neither take charge nor nurturing. Vader is such a creature. He is utterly submissive to the Emperor, and he appears utterly without nurture — he can hack down Obi-Wan and is seemingly willing to obey the Emperor's command to pursue Luke, who we will discover in the next installment is his son. (Oh, yes, but he has temporized about killing the Princess, who in two sequels away we will find out is his daughter, and he does suggest to the Emperor that it might be worth considering trying to get Luke to defect to the "Dark Side" of the Force. This little glimmer of nurturance confirms the idea that the Force, even its Dark Side, is essentially feminine.)

The Empire Strikes Back (1980)

For many fans, *The Empire Strikes Back* is the best of the four Star Wars films to date. It is the only one of the three sequels that breaks the winning formula of the original film (embroilment with Jabba the Hutt, then blow up a Death Star).[5] There is a darker edge to this film, particularly in the opening sequence in the ice world of the planet Hoth and in the scenes of Luke's education, in part because there are fewer comic touches. This is a more adult film than the others, and it is the only film where the relationship between Han and Leia heats up at all. ("You like me because I'm a scoundrel," he tells her. "I like nice men," she counters, with no conviction.) Finally, there is no heroic climax. At the end of the film, Han is immobilized, Luke has had his hand cut off by his father, and Leia is under the protection of the untrustworthy Lando Calrissian (Billy Dee Williams). If this were a stand-alone film, we might suspect we had slipped back into the realm of antiheroes, but because by the time of its release, viewers knew that this was to be the fifth of nine films, one suspected that there would be further triumphs. Anyway, even in the most heroic film, the triumph must be limited, or there would be no need for sequels.

The film opens shortly after the end of the original. Han, Luke, Chewbacca, and Leia are now in an even more godforsaken place than Tatooine, Hoth. Early on, Han and Luke are on patrol, as an Imperial spy droid drops from the sky. Thinking it is a meteor, Luke goes to investigate, but he is attacked by a snow monster who hangs him upside down in his cave, while eating his mount.

Inside the Rebel fortress, Han tells Leia that he must leave to pay off Jabba. Leia is impatient that Han has not caught Rebel Fever yet. They flirt. But Han is not only worried about getting the bounty off his head, he now must worry that Luke has not come back. Humans cannot survive a night outside in Hoth (as C-3PO calculates, the odds are 735 to 1). Luke uses his incipient Force skills to free himself from the nasty snowman, but Han must save him from freezing by putting him into the entrails of his own mount (a zany cross between kangaroo and camel). Everyone is grateful to Han, but as his flirting with Leia intensifies, she responds that she would "rather kiss a Wookie," and kisses Luke instead. Little Luke is confused, and because it takes a damsel in distress or a damsel in love to connect a Han Solo (solo, get it?) with the political universe, he readies to go. But an attack by Imperial forces alters everyone's plans.

The attack also divides the group in two for most of the film. Luke goes off with R2 to find someone named Yoda (Frank Oz), recommended as his trainer by the ghostly Obi-Wan while he was lying delirious in the snow. Han, Leia, Chewbacca, and C-3PO take off in the Millennium Falcon. This group seems not to have a destination, initially hiding within the Imperial war ship when the Millennium Falcon fails to go into light speed and then escaping with the trash. They think they have eluded the Imperial forces by this ruse, but Vader is about, and he knows where everyone is. Han decides to visit his "friend" Lando Calrissian in the city in the clouds. Lando, it seems, was the Falcon's original owner, and there is tension between him and Han because of the loss of the Falcon in a card game. When they arrive, Vader has proceeded them, and Calrissian has compromised them in exchange for keeping his own people free of the Imperial yoke. Vader tortures them all: Chewey with sounds, and Han with drugs; but he seems disinterested in prying information from them. He is merely torturing them to create a disturbance in the Force which will lure Luke from his training.

Luke has landed his spacecraft in a swamp on a remote planet, and when he encounters his new master for the first time he is a pest, looking for food and rummaging through the ship. Initially, Yoda is a loony, miniature premonition of Mr. Miyagi. He is very reluctant to take on a new pupil. Luke is too old: he has been too contaminated by experience. Yoda repeats most of the Force slogans we have heard before: "Keep your eye on the present, not on the future." "Never attack; always defend." "Try not. Do or do not." He cautions Luke against recklessness and a search for adventure.

Luke's training is typical martial arts: repetition and concentration, although much of it is focused on telekinesis. Luke can move stones around, but he fails at big issues like being able to unstick his ship from the swamp. Before his training is over, he feels his friends' suffering, and he insists on leaving, despite dire warnings from Yoda and the ghostly Obi-Wan. He leaves before his skills are well developed, and he leaves because of fear for his friends (and as we all know, *fear leads to hate, and hate leads to the Dark Side.*)

Luke arrives in the city in the clouds, mixes it up mightily with Vader, who announces his paternity right before whacking Luke's hand off, but Vader is too strong and Luke just about slips out of the bottom of the floating city. But he is rescued by Leia, Calrissian (not really a bad guy), and Chewey. Han has been frozen in carbon and shipped off to Jabba. Things look bad.

The Return of the Jedi (1983)

After a short scene in which Vader arrives on the new Death Star to see what's holding things up, the first episode begins in earnest, again with the droids C-3PO and R2-D2, who gain entrance to Jabba's enclave. They have a message for Jabba from Luke: release Han. The droids will remain with Jabba as a gift if he does so. Jabba responds in a subtitle that he will not give up his favorite decoration, and the camera reveals the carbonized Han hanging flat against the wall. Jabba sends the droids off to a droid torture chamber, but this was apparently part of Luke's plan. Eventually the whole Force force reassembles: Chewbacca is brought in as a prisoner; Lando has insinuated himself into Jabba's throne room as a guard; Leia sneaks in and decarbonizes Han, although she is captured and becomes some sort of slave to Jabba.

And then Luke arrives. He is older than when we last saw him and has a mature and confident presence about him. He is dressed similarly to Obi-Wan, but he is entirely in black, a fashion choice which is unsettling, since it also makes him appear much like his father and the Emperor (Kasdan &

Lucas, 1997). He uses the force to get through the guards. But his spell does not work on Jabba — who refers to it as an "old Jedi mind trick," and he is dropped into a pit, where he must fight off the rancor, a very nasty monster with a mouth like a sphincter. Luke dispatches the rancor, but everyone is still Jabba's prisoner.

Shortly everyone is off on a kind of sultanic picnic, where the climax will be dropping the good guys into a Sarlac, another sphincter-like monster which will digest its victims gruesomely over a period of a thousand years. Throughout the ordeal, Luke has been very confident. Suddenly, there is a fight. While the boys are off saving each other, Leia takes her chain and strangles Jabba. Again Leia, although dressed out in a very revealing cabaret costume, is the most take-charge of the team.

This time, the destruction of the Death Star takes more than the assembled team, it will require the help of a merry band of Wagnerian teddy bears. In the original episode, the destruction of the Death Star is an end in itself, but in this episode, the destruction of the Death Star becomes a personal contest for the souls of Luke and Darth Vader, and thus for the endurance of the Jedi tradition. Yoda has told Luke that he must confront his father as his last step in becoming a Jedi (wasn't he the one who just a few days before told him he wasn't ready to confront Vader?). Luke seems to understand this charge to mean killing the person who was once his father, but he rejects this idea and feels that what he must do is to reconnect his father with the good side of the force. This is of course a dangerous plan, like most of Luke's plans. Luke believes that the feelings his father has for him will reconnect him with the good side, but feelings are the things which make one vulnerable to the "Dark Side of the Force."

At the end of the film the Emperor grinds Luke into near death, but Vader responds to the good side of the force and kills the Emperor. Absent fatherhood is a corrupting thing; real fatherhood is good.[6]

Pauline Kael (1983) chastises the filmmakers in her review of *Jedi*, "There is no blood in the killings in 'Jedi,'" but is killing without blood really preferable? The picture is indecently affectless: it ends with the triumph of the good guys and the grand celebration of a bloodless nuclear explosion — with no worry, no aftermath, no fallout." Other writers echo her concerns (e.g., Palmer, 1993).

The Phantom Menace (1999)

We knew shortly after the success of *Star Wars* in 1977 that George Lucas had planned three trilogies, and that the first film was the introduction to the central trilogy. Exactly when the whole nine (or now, maybe just six) films were planned is a matter of great conjecture to Force cultists, but it took quite a while for the filmmakers to get around to the first of the series. George Lucas was back behind the camera (he had farmed out directorial duties in *Empire* and *Jedi*), and the special effects were very special indeed.

In many respects, *The Phantom Menace* is a very 1990s film, which may help us understand its critical and popular reception. Of course it made piles of money, but older fans and critics felt there was something missing. Younger audiences saw it repeatedly and bought huge amounts of spin-off stuff. Many of the older generation of fans and critics felt it was far more of a children's film than the previous three films. One reason for this feeling is that, for the first time, a child was a central character in the film (Anakin Skywalker, a.k.a. Darth Vader), and partially because of a loopy central character, Jar Jar Binks, who either greatly delighted or greatly annoyed audience members.

Jar Jar can be thought of as part of the most significant trend in the films of the 1990s — the representation of men as nitwits, discussed in chapter 13. Jar Jar is clumsy and excitable, and anything but heroic. But as a computer generated version of Forrest Gump, his silly actions often result in a heroic outcome (at one time in an incompetent attempt to retreat, he unleashes a series of bombs against the Imperial droid army, with effective results). He is what we will later describe as a "lucky fool."

Like a good 1990s film, the cast is ethnically diverse, at least verbally, with weirdly Chinese accents given to some of the villains, and Jamaican accents given to Jar Jar and his fellow-countrymen (someone we know refers to Jar Jar's most conspicuous physical features as his "dread-ears"). The queen and her decoy share Cher's fashion obsession.

The film also has many specific references to *Ben-Hur,* which may create a kind of spiritual resonance for some. We have here a subtheme about slavery, and the central speeder race seems to come directly from the climactic chariot race from that 1959 film. And of course there is the business about little Ani being the "chosen one," the result of a virgin birth....

But then, we also have the return of Yoda, a hint about the origins of C-3PO, Obi-Wan (Ewan MacGregor) as an apprentice Jedi, and a real martial arts master mixing it up with Liam Neeson. It's a pretty good romp. One feature which separates this from the previous three films in the series is motherhood. When Anakin is brought before the Jedi council, the flaw that they detect is his fear at being separated from his mother (he has no father). They decided that this fear is too much of a danger, and initially reject his training as a Jedi. If nothing else, this makes us wonder why Luke, so obsessed with discovering who his father was, never seems to have considered his mother. Will the many planned sequels tell us why?

Twelve — Disney's Men and Boys

The most popular films for most of the last six decades have been children's films. The numbers of individuals who have watched *Bambi, 101 Dalmatians, The Wizard of Oz,* and *E.T. the Extra-Terrestrial* make the number for all other films, with the exception of *Gone with the Wind* and *Titanic,* pale by comparison. Seven of the ten all-time video rentals and five of the ten all-time video sales are children's films. In the 45 years between 1939 and 1984, ten children's films were the number one annual box office hits, including *Pinocchio* (1940), *Bambi* (1942), *Song of the South* (1946), *Cinderella* (1950), *Peter Pan* (1953), *Lady and the Tramp* (1955), *Swiss Family Robinson* (1960), *101 Dalmatians* (1961), *Mary Poppins* (1964), and *E.T. the Extra-Terrestrial* (1982). During that same time seven children's films were the number two annual box office hits, including *The Wizard of Oz* (1939), *Fantasia* (1940), *Alice in Wonderland* (1951), *20,000 Leagues Under the Sea* (1954), *Sleeping Beauty* (1959), *The Jungle Book* (1967), and *The Love Bug* (1969). Since this time, *The Little Mermaid* (1991), *Beauty and the Beast* (1992), *Aladdin* (1992), *The Lion King* (1994), *Toy Story* (1995), *Pocahontas* (1995), *Tarzan* (1999), and *Toy Story 2* (2000) have become blockbusters. Any analysis of popular films must clearly attend to films for children. Most haven't.

In our previous analyses of male role behavior in popular films intended for adult audiences, we have employed rather straightforward analytic techniques. For our historical analyses we have used box office to determine which films were the most popular and compared male role behavior portrayed in those films over time.

Children's films present other difficulties. First of all, children are not free agents in the film marketplace. Most children under the age of 16 must

178

get permission from their parents to see particular films and get the money to see them. Thus, for a children's film to become popular, parents must approve of the film, or at least determine that the film is not harmful for their children. Film reviews and studio track records clearly influence these decisions.

Second, the social uses of film have changed radically over the past 60 years. In the 1930s and 1940s, children's films were aimed at family audiences. Mothers, fathers, adolescents, and children went to see such films as *The Wizard of Oz, Song of the South,* and *Old Yeller,* and these films included interest for all audience groups. Beginning in the late 1950s and early 1960s, children's films served the same baby-sitting function for parents as television. Children's films were more designed for audiences composed primarily of children, and the more modest revenues from films during the 1960s, 1970s, and 1980s may reflect this change in market segment. In the last decade, concerns about the safety of children and questions about the content of films, even those from the major children's studios, have led children's films to once again become family films, reintroducing the two-level nature of these films (one level for adults, one for children). Films such as *The Lion King* and *Aladdin* have had late night showings in most markets which have attracted large adolescent and adult audiences.

Third, a film must appeal to children to become popular, but children attend films differently from adults. Just as children demand to hear the same bedtime story over and over to the frustration of their parents, children want to view films which they like again and again. Within two weeks of the release of *The Lion King* one of us encountered a friend who had taken her two primary school aged children to see the film three times. Multiple viewings of films and the broad range of appeal account for the enormous box office of the most popular children's films.

In this presentation we will give a reading of six of the most popular children's films from the last six decades, *Snow White and the Seven Dwarfs, Bambi, Pinocchio, Old Yeller, Beauty and the Beast,* and *The Lion King,* specifically examining the portrayal of male role behavior. It is difficult not to notice that these are all Disney products. There have been few blockbuster children's films which have come from other studios. The two most notable exceptions are *The Wizard of Oz,* which we have already discussed, and *E.T. the Extra-Terrestrial,* if this can really be called a children's film. We have three of the early classic animations, one live action film from the 1950s, and two recent animations, to give the flavor of how the Disney studio has evolved in its depiction of men and boys. Of particular interest will be to contrast *Bambi* with *The Lion King,* since the latter may be regarded as a remake of the former, in the same way that *A View to a Kill* was essentially a remake of *Goldfinger.*

Snow White and the Seven Dwarfs

Snow White and the Seven Dwarfs was the first feature-length animated film from the Disney studio. The film is slight on characterization but long on drawing and music. The film stays relatively close to its Grimm Brothers source materials. A wicked queen sends her stepdaughter into the forest to be slaughtered by a woodsman because she is jealous of the child's beauty. The woodsman cannot bring himself to kill her, so he allows Snow White to escape and brings the queen a heart of a wild animal as proof of the deed. (In the Grimm story [Grimm & Grimm, 1945] the Queen eats what she thinks are Snow White's heart and the lungs.) Snow White spends a harrowing time in the woods but eventually finds a home with seven dwarfs who work as miners. The magic mirror tells the queen that Snow White is still alive. She disguises herself as a peddler and entices her stepdaughter to eat a poisoned apple. The dwarfs mourn the loss of Snow White, but she is rescued by love's first kiss.

Snow White is a young woman at the beginning of the film, not the seven-year-old of the fairy tale. Therefore, prior to her adventures in the woods, the Prince and Snow White have briefly met and fallen in love. This helps get around the creepiness in the Grimm story that the prince arrives only after Snow White is in her glass coffin and so falls in love with her after she is a corpse.

In the fairy tale, the dwarfs have no individual identities and unlike their depiction in the Disney film, they are neat and tidy (Alan, 1988). They suggest to her: "If you will take care of our house, cook, make the beds, wash, sew, and knit, and if you will keep neat and clean, you can stay with us…" (Grimm & Grimm, 1945, p. 252). In contrast, Disney's dwarfs live in squalor and are apparently unfamiliar with the custom of bathing. Their interaction with her domesticates them. This domestication of the "wild male" by contact with women was a major male theme in many of the contemporary films we examined in earlier chapters, such as *The Sheik, Jesse James,* and *Since You Went Away.* This is a theme we no longer encounter in our discussions of more recent films.

It may be worth noting differences in the critical reception of this film when it was originally released in 1938, when it was rereleased in 1958, and at its second rerelease in 1993. In a *New York Times* review in 1938, Frank Nugent has little to say about Snow White herself, but he devotes a paragraph to Dopey: "Dopey is the youngest of the seven dwarfs. He is beardless, with a buttony nose, a wide mouth, Gable ears, cross-purpose eyes and the most winning, helpless, puppy-dog expression that creature ever had." Nugent then suggests his origins, including several long-gone characters from the comics, and "Pluto of the Mickey Mouse Plutos. There may, too, be a dash of Harpo Marx. But he's all Dopey, forever out of step in the dwarfs' processions, doomed to carry the red taillight when they go to their jewel mines, and speechless." As Doc explains, "he never tried to talk." Nugent calls the film a classic "as important cinematically as *The Birth of a Nation* or the birth of Mickey Mouse. Bosley Crowther in 1958 said "*Snow White* is one of those several pictures that, like *The Gold Rush* and *Gone with the Wind*, are special to our motion picture culture…"

These glowing appreciations are in distinct contrast to the film's reception in 1993. *Fortune* reprinted a review from the *St. Petersburg Times*: "Talk about sexist trash! This is it…" Perhaps the most inflammatory part of this review is the section that says, "The worst part came when Snow White discovered the dwarfs' filthy woodland cottage. Did she say, 'You fellows need to clean up this pigsty?' No… she went and did all the dirty work.…"

Of course, this is simply not the case: Snow White mostly oversees the work that the woodland animals do, and the dwarfs/pigs are not at home when she breaks into their cottage/pigsty. Since Snow White is trespassing, she is not merely taking on the role of homemaker, she is bargaining for a roof over her head. The end of this review the reviewer suggests that parents "…forget *Snow White* and *Cinderella*, and tell their children about *Thelma and Louise*." This review was not atypical of reviews at the time.

We agreed as we set out to write this book to avoid terms like "racist" and "sexist" for a number of reasons. First, as psychologists, we were uncomfortable with these terms, which are sociological in nature. Sociologists tend to use the word "sexism" to refer to social structures which prevent women attaining power and prestige. Thus a law that prevents married women from inheriting property would be sexist, as would be a regulation — depending on the hairstyles of the times — which bars employment to persons with long hair. The popular usage of the term is more technically covered by "sexual prejudice." Technically, an individual cannot be sexist, but can exhibit sexual prejudice. Second, we know that what is labeled "sexist" by one period or culture may not be so labeled by another. Sexism is a social construction, and what one society at one time will construct as sexism may be another period's feminism. For example, in contrast to American feminists, Japanese feminists have lobbied for the right of a married woman to keep her husband's name after his death: the lack of keeping a family name implied no right to his property, including their children. What we now regard as sexually enlightened will no doubt at some time be regarded as sexism.

A decade ago *Snow White* and *Cinderella* may have appeared sexist, but now it is those claims which appear odd, just as *Thelma and Louise* (1991) now appears less feminist than many writers thought when it was first released — why do they have to die at the end? But charges of racism and sexism are constant whenever a Disney film is released, even when Disney has gone to great lengths, as it did before the release of *Pocahontas,* to develop a script that would not be offensive to Native Americans.

The main thrust of many pieces written in 1993, was that by suggesting that Snow White requires a Prince Charming to live happily ever after, young girls were provided with models which limited their becoming whatever they wanted to be. Of course, in the magical logic of the film, Snow White's only other option is to be dead. Yet that is not the full message of "happily ever after" endings of movies, because it leaves men out of the equation. Here, the Prince has been searching for Snow White, because he knows that a similar connection is what he requires. We have no particular reason to believe that he is looking for a stay-at-home wife.

Pinocchio

Pinocchio represents a major step forward in characterization in the animated feature, due in part to the richness of the literary source, a book length moral tale for boys. The film deviates from its source material significantly, and there is a cottage industry of criticism which furiously documents these deviations. Geppetto, an old and lonely toy maker, offhandedly wishes that his newest creation, a puppet, could become a real boy. During the night the Blue Fairy — significantly, the only female character in the film — grants him part of his wish. Pinocchio comes to life, but he is an animated puppet, not a "real boy." The rest of the film concerns itself with Pinocchio learning what it will take for him to be "real."

Geppetto is the first of a long line of Disney fathers. Like most that follow, he wants to be nurturing, but fathers in Disneyland not natural parents. The are uncomfortable in the role. Fortunately, Pinocchio has the far more articulate Jiminy Cricket, who will be there to guide and interpret the world for him. (The cricket gets squashed pretty early in Collodi's novel.) Geppetto can only follow conventional roles: he sends Pinocchio off to school. But like most Romantic visions of development, Pinocchio does not need book learning, he needs emotional growth. In the most popular children's films centering on male characters, in addition to boys learning to be real boys, there is a countertext about men learning to be real fathers. Geppetto will learn that fatherhood consists of more than wishing for a son and sending him off to school for others to train.

On his way to school, Pinocchio is seduced by bad companions who want to exploit him. First he is sold to a traveling circus where he is a sensation because he is a puppet who "has no strings on him." But he tires of the attention and wants to return home, only to find himself an isolated prisoner. This connection with home is the first, and most fundamental, of the three lessons that Pinocchio must learn in his quest for "real boyhood."

It is important to note that Disney films, and other popular films for children, often create genuinely frightening images of children imprisoned and cut off from their families, in films as different as *Snow White, Dumbo* (1941), *The Rescuers* (1977), *The Rescuers Down Under* (1990), *101 Dalmatians, Beauty and the Beast* and *The Lion King.* Dorothy is both imprisoned and cut off from her family in *The Wizard of Oz,* and the Extra-Terrestrial, imprisoned in Elliott's toy closet, wants nothing more than to reconnect with home. The themes of imprisonment and loss of family seem to be almost essential features of children's films. Children seem to enjoy being frightened, and there are probably no other situations as frightening as these to them.

The second lesson that Pinocchio must learn is to be less selfish. His second seduction from school is to the Island of Bad Boys where play and hedonism, including drinking and smoking, lead to a partial, frighteningly convulsive transformation into a donkey. Unlike the other boys who are completely transformed and sold off to be draft animals, Pinocchio escapes. His renunciation leaves him free, but stigmatized by the ears and tail of an ass. Like the characters in a Hawthorne tale, he bears the mark of his sin.

Finally, Pinnochio must be brave in the final confrontation with Monstro the Whale. He become resourceful in deciding to build a fire which will cause the huge creature to sneeze Geppetto and himself out, and he shows his bravery as he helps Geppetto escape from the wrath of the violated Monstro. He is nearly killed.

Here, too, the theme of man versus nature, a theme hinted at in *Snow White* in her flight from the woodman into the forest, is recapitulated. This is a characteristic of the Romantic vision of Disney films. Man is embedded in nature, but nature is violent and dangerous, something to be enjoyed for its beauty, but to be enjoyed warily. Pinocchio may swim in a school of tropic fish, but around the corner is the lethal Monstro.

But because Pinocchio has learned, like Dorothy Gale, that there is "no place like home," to be unselfish, and to be brave, he is granted his and Geppetto's wish for him to be a real boy.

Bambi

Bambi was the fourth of the Disney animated features. Like *Dumbo*, its focus was the development of a young male anthropomorphized animal. Like the recent *The Lion King,* with which there are many parallels, Bambi becomes strong and independent by dealing with the loss of a parent. Perhaps the reason that *Bambi* resonated so with war-time audiences (*Bambi* made twice as much money as *Casablanca, Going My Way, Yankee Doodle Dandy, For Whom the Bell Tolls,* and *Thirty Seconds Over Tokyo* combined) was the theme of the violent disruption of a family by an outside force, this time by "man in the forest," hunters who kill Bambi's mother. Children in 1943 were not losing their mothers, but the loss of a father may have been too close to home to represent on the screen.[1]

Bambi begins with a long shot through the dark forest, over which plays the opening song, whose lyrics emphasize the "cycle of life" theme of the movie, conspicuous in its portrayal of the seasons. The shot ends in the thicket where newly born Bambi, the "new prince," is visited by a host of animals. The child rabbit Thumper is inquisitive and watches him try to stand, and pronounces the new Prince "wobbly." Thumper's mother asks what his father told him, and Thumper recalls, "If you can't say something nice, don't say nothing at all." The animals retire and the "camera" pans to a crag above the forest, where, like a 1940s father, dad, the Prince of the Forest, is proudly waiting at a distance. The Old Prince is an absent father, off at work.

Bambi explores his world. His main difficulty seems to be coordinating his four limbs. He makes friends with two other male characters, Thumper and the skunk, Flower. While we are in a period of overreading the social significance of film, it is perhaps worth noting that Bambi forms a strong bond with a black skunk, whom he mistakes for a flower. He does not negatively stereotype this smelly neighbor. War films of the 1940s dealt with the issue of ethnic tolerance in films as diverse as *Flying Tigers* and *Destination Tokyo*. These films were not quite ready to deal with African Americans, but perhaps *Bambi* was leading the way.

Bambi is a prince, but he is immature, and his friends teach him to speak, to walk, and to hop over logs, while his mother helps him explore his environment more meaningfully. Particularly she takes him out into the meadow, but she cautions that the meadow is a dangerous place because they can be seen. Bambi meets his love interest, Faline, in a reflection in a brook. He is frightened of her, but she pursues him and licks him. Although he has gotten his legs, meeting her turns him back into a jelly-legged infant. In the meadow he encounters his father for the first time. The Prince does not speak to him, but he looks at him for a long time. His mother explains that he is the leader because he is old: "He's very brave and very wise." Man comes into the meadow and Bambi is separated from his mother. The Prince comes and leads him to safety.

Autumn comes and then winter. At first winter is exciting; Bambi runs through the snow, and Thumper tries to teach him to ice skate, but he becomes "wobbly" again. Winter is a hard time. There is nothing to eat but tree bark, and eventually the deer have stripped all the trees as far as they can reach. Then grass begins to come up through the snow, and they venture into the meadow — but this time when Man arrives, Bambi's mother is killed. Her last advice to him: "Don't look back. Keep running. Keep running." Pathetically, he wanders through the forest calling for his mother (were the writers in *Shane* referring to this scene when Joey runs pathetically across the valley calling after his lost surrogate father?). The Prince arrives and takes him under hoof.

With spring, Bambi now has a modest set of antlers and has lost his spots. He starts off with his two buddies, but first Flower and then Thumper are seduced by flirtatious women. Faline reappears in his life, and the old problem with his legs reappears: women in 1940s' films tend to make men act childishly. Another young male appears, and they fight in an exquisitely animated sequence. After Bambi wins, he and Faline walk together through the forest, until Bambi smells the fires of the hunters and hears the buzzards. There are many men in the forest. The Prince appears and tries to lead them to safety. Bambi and Faline are separated, and she is attacked by dogs. He rescues Faline, but he has been mauled by the dogs and wounded. Only a gruff admonition by his father gives him the wherewithal to get to safety on an island in the lake. He reunites with Faline, and they watch the forest burn.

Finally spring completely returns, and it is Faline's turn to give birth. The animals return to see the new fawns, this time a pair. Bambi is on the crag with his dad, but dad retires, leaving Bambi to oversee his new kingdom.

Bambi is as beautifully drawn as any animated film, and despite a few quirks, such as the Owl's explanation of love as becoming "Twitterpated," every scene in the film can be enjoyed by almost anyone. Children are often very emotional while watching the film, but they return to it again and again. The sex role message is clear and the same as in *Pinocchio*: be brave, be selfless, and connect with your family. Entwined in this is the message, so common in Disney films, to become part of the natural world, even though nature can be dangerous.

Old Yeller

Old Yeller was the first of the successful human action Disney features. It was one of the films that came out of the Disney studio's corporate strategy of expanding beyond cartoons into television and theme parks. It starred the perennial Disney boy of the 1950s and early 1960s, Tommy Kirk, who must navigate the choppy waters of a temporarily single parent household on the Texas frontier of 1859. Kirk's father must take livestock to market, leaving him the man in the family. While Kirk deals successfully with some of these obligations, he is far less successful in others, primarily his relation with his younger brother. The younger boy seems wildly attached to animals of all kinds, and Kirk is clearly strained when he must get his younger brother out of seriously dangerous scrapes. Kirk, on the cusp of adolescence, however, finds just spending time with his preschool-aged brother nearly unbearable. It is the role of surrogate father that he cannot fill very well. Again we have the theme that child-rearing is somehow contrary to male nature. The mother (Dorothy McGuire) must enforce these parental duties if they are to be carried out at all. This theme is reinforced in a subplot in which a scheming neighbor essentially abandons his daughter on the farm.

The younger boy wants a dog, and providentially a yellow hunting dog wanders into the farmyard. The younger boy is delighted, but sibling rivalry rears its ugly head, and Kirk is close to abusive to Old Yeller. Why should the younger brother get a dog before him? The dog, however, has enough social skills to become a counselor and gradually wins Kirk over, essentially becoming Kirk's dog. Old Yeller is a man's hunting dog and while tolerating the childish attentions of the younger boy, he chooses Kirk as his companion. Old Yeller knows how to treat boys and young men, even if humans don't.

This film continues the Disney Romantic vision of nature, something both infinitely beautiful and infinitely dangerous. The boys are nearly killed by a herd of wild pigs, and they are rescued, after serious gorings, by Old Yeller. Insidiously, the pigs or some of the other wild animals that must be fought bring rabies onto the farm. Old Yeller is infected. He is restrained in a corn crib, but the crisis does not pass. In the climactic act of courage and compassion, Kirk takes the rifle away from his mother and shoots Old Yeller. Again the themes of family connection, selflessness, and bravery are highlighted, as well as the theme of nature as both important and dark.

It is perhaps of some note to remember that this vision of male adolescence and a boy's relationship to his family was one which captured viewers' attention in 1957. Patrons enjoyed this film about a stressed but loving family the same year many adults spent their dollars to see the seriously dysfunctional families of *Peyton Place*. This may indicate that adults were beginning to view the family more negatively than previously, and to allow their children to see a family in crisis. This film was released shortly after the original teenpics, *The Wild One* (1954) and *Rebel Without a Cause* (1955), had failed to find a major audience. Those visions of teen *angst* and families in turmoil were not yet acceptable.

Beauty and the Beast

Theme parks and television required less investment and quicker and more assured profits for Disney from the 1960s through the 1980s. Disney continued to produce animated features during this time, but the emphasis was on less expensive products. From 1960 to 1990, the only animated features which cracked the five most profitable films of the year were *101 Dalmatians*, *The Sword in the Stone* (1963), *The Jungle Book* (1967), *The Aristocats* (1970), and the adult-oriented *Who Framed Roger Rabbit?* (1988). But computer animation made feature length cartoons less expensive, and Disney hit the market with them with a vengeance.

There are three principal male characters in *Beauty and the Beast*: the Beast, Belle's father Maurice, and Gaston, the local muscle-bulging good-old-boy whom all the women love except Belle. There are several minor male characters including a candlestick lothario, an officious clock, a cute cup named Chip, and Gaston's dumb-as-a-log friend, but we will concentrate on the three principals.

Gaston's first action in the film is to shoot a bird, aligning him with such other Disney villains as "man in the forest" in *Bambi* and Cruella De Vil in *101 Dalmatians*. The iconography of killing animals for sport is clear: Gaston will be the villain. (He later sings that he uses antlers in all his decorating.)

At first his portrayal is comic. Gaston fights, drinks beer, and spits, which gains him the admiration of the men in the local bar. They sing about the thickness of his neck. He tells Belle he can't read her book because it has no pictures. But his behavior becomes more sinister as he resorts to any means of getting Belle to marry him. Even his reasons for wanting to marry her are perverse by contemporary standards: she is beautiful and they will have beautiful children (boys). Her intellect is something that can be overcome, he suggests, reinforcing the theme of the film and its literary source of the paradox between inner and outer beauty. His secondary motivation for wanting to marry her is that when she has said no to his proposal, he must have her to regain face. "No one says 'No' to Gaston," he says.

After failing to press her into marrying him while her father is away, he resorts to very sinister tactics. First, he attempts to blackmail her into marriage by threatening to have her father committed to an asylum. When this fails, and realizing that Belle "has feelings for" the Beast, he leads the villagers on an assault on the Beast's castle. In general the assault is comic, as the villagers are met with an army of animated furniture and cutlery. But when Gaston comes face to face with a demoralized Beast, the film becomes genuinely frightening. Gaston has repeatedly said that his purpose is to kill the Beast, and his assault is fierce. He shoots the Beast with an arrow, referring back to his opening action. They battle on the rooftop of the castle. When the Beast is finally roused to action by Belle's return, Gaston becomes cowardly. When the Beast forgives him and lets him go, Gaston sneaks up and stabs him in the back, just as Belle and the Beast clasp hands. (When we have seen this film in theaters, the audiences' reaction is one of shock.) Gaston then falls from the roof to his death.

Maurice is typical of many fathers in Disney films. He is enormously kind and sympathetic, but he is also a great bumbler, in the mold of Geppetto and the *Absent-Minded Professor*. He is an inventor whose inventions never quite work. His wood-chopping machine is a menace. He is unable to navigate his way through the woods, and getting lost and seeking refuge from an attack of wolves in the Beast's castle sets the plot in motion. Yet he is willing to sacrifice his life for Belle's, as she is willing to sacrifice hers for his.

The Beast is a prince who has been put under a spell for being "spoiled, selfish, and unkind," and his transformation from the boy who had no love in his heart to the hero willing to sacrifice all for Belle's happiness is the story, along with the parallel of Belle learning to see through external ugliness. The Beast's transformation is more critical because had he not changed, there would have been no inner beauty for Belle to find.

When we first see the Beast, he paces on all fours. He is enormous. Despite his menacing presence, he is ashamed of what he has become. He has shredded an old portrait, and the mirrors in his shadowy, demolished West Wing are shattered, and when he encounters Maurice for the first time he asks: "You've come to stare at the beast?" Even the Beast cowers under the "male gaze."

The first hint of his humanity comes when Belle offers to take her father's place. His words are beastly: he insists on a permanent replacement, but the animation has him pause and express admiration for her act. For a while he must be cued on what to do by his servants. He moves her from the dungeon to a bedroom. He invites and then insists on her having dinner with him. The candlestick and teapot reduce his task to a very simple child-oriented maxim: he must learn to control his temper.

When Belle, like Eve before her, breaks his one rule — not to go into the West Wing — he rages against her, and she runs away. She, too, is harassed by the wolves, and the Beast comes to her rescue. The wolves run away, but not before they have savaged him. Belle takes him home and nurses him, despite his bluster, and he repays her kindness by giving her access to his enormous library. Unlike Gaston, who said that it was not right for a woman to read because it leads them to have ideas, the Beast has no such fears. The Beast cleans himself up, learns table manners, and even feeds birds by hand for her. Finally, he makes the ultimate gesture and releases her from her promise so that she can find her father, even though he knows that unless she says that she loves him before his 21st birthday, he will remain a beast forever.

The juxtaposition of Gaston and the Beast leaves a child audience with unambiguous messages: men should be kind, not selfish; they should be brave in defense of others, not gratuitously violent; and they should treat women with respect and as their intellectual equals, not as minions. While this fable resonated enormously with both child and adult audiences in 1992, the film is not so much a new departure in the portrayal of men's roles in children's films as a more complete portrait of those roles. The princes in *Snow White* and *Sleeping Beauty,* dictated to some degree by their literary sources, were *dei ex machina* who arrived at the end to resolve the conflicts between the female heroines and villains. But in films from *Pinocchio* to *E.T.,* boys have had the virtues of bravery and selflessness modeled for them, and in films from *Swiss Family Robinson* to *The Rescuers* they have learned about the essential equality of the sexes.[2]

We would also recommend a slightly different take on this film offered in Susan Jeffords's (1994) book *Hard Bodies: Hollywood Masculinity in the Reagan Era,* in which she sees Gaston, a modern interpolation into Marie de Beaumont's story, as a repudiated image of the Reagan-Rambo "hardbody" male and the Beast a '90s guy who can deal with a feminist Belle.

The Lion King

The Lion King is in many ways a quintessential 1990s film. It is about finding one's true identity; establishing self-esteem; and becoming in harmony with nature. But as we suggested in our discussion of *Bambi,* it also has much in common with earlier Disney films.

The Lion King is the most popular of the recent Disney animated features and one of the most popular films of all times. Despite the nattering of a few commentators who had to look hard for sexism (it seemed to be expected that the lionesses would hunt and the pride was portrayed as patriarchal), homophobia (the villain spoke with a British accent) or racism (some of the hyenas — the bad guys — were portrayed by actors of color), the film was also a critical success.

The Lion King is the most post-modern of all Disney films, with references to many literary and cinematic texts, including most conspicuously *Bambi* and *Hamlet,* but also to diverse works such as Flannery O'Connor's "Revelation" ("A warthog from hell"), *Taxi Driver* (before going into a rage, the warthog repeats: "You looking at me?") and *Vertigo* (plot precipitating and concluding falls from a high place, seen from above). The film is also another Disney green film with a simple message about living in harmony with nature and the consequences of not doing so (Afield, 1990).

Like *Bambi,* the story begins with the birth of the main male protagonist, Simba, and ends with the birth of his son. Unlike Bambi, Simba's father is present at the birth, not looking on from afar, and he is present at the end. While *Bambi* is the story of the loss of a mother, *The Lion King* is the story of the loss of a father, Mufasa, hence resonating not only with the Hamlet-plot, but echoing one of the more popular works of the time, Robert Bly's *Iron John.* In *Bambi,* when his mother is killed by hunters, his father steps in and takes over his socialization. But nothing can substitute for a father's influence, so Bly would tell us, and so Simba is suffering a more difficult loss.

Bambi's loss of his mother is full of pathos, and the sadness and fear that children watching the film experience is, no doubt, meant to influence their participation in blood sport. Simba's loss comes about for other reasons — political power: his sly uncle Scar enlists the comically villainous hyenas to stampede a herd of wildebeest. Mufasa rescues his son, but while attempting to find refuge, Scar lunges at his dangling brother, who falls to his death. Scar compounds the loss of his father by telling Simba that his father's death is his fault and suggests that he leave the kingdom at once. Simba roams the savanna and desert, meeting up with a hyperactive meerkat and a jovial, if dumb and stinky, warthog. Finally, he encounters Nala, his childhood playmate and intended bride, who has come in search of a savior: Scar has proven to be a poor administrator and his league with the hyenas has lead to environmental degradation: the lions are starving and Silent Spring is about to become a reality.

Simba doubts that he can help. His socialization was interrupted too early and he is wracked with guilt about the death of his father. Nala tries to egg him in to returning, but finally she leaves in disgust. (The warthog and meerkat are happy about this because Nala threatens to break up their adolescent bond, just as Thumper and Flower vow never to become "Twitterpated.")

In a twist on a contemporary theme, Simba gets in touch with his inner adult, through the intervention of a mandrill shaman who assists him in finding his father within himself and by — quite literally — knocking some sense into him. Like Hamlet's father's ghost, the ghost of Mufasa repeats a single word to his son: *remember* (rather than *swear*), and Simba is off to fight for his kingdom.

The parallels between *The Lion King* and *Hamlet* are not exact. There is an officious advisor to the kings, Zazu, but Simba does not kill him. Ophelia/Nala does not drift off in winsome lunacy, but turns out to be a physically powerful ally (as cubs, she always pins him when they wrestle). Scar seems to have no sexual designs on Simba's mother, although he physically abuses her at the moment Simba reappears. There are no Rosencranz and Gildenstern nor acting troop. And, most importantly, Simba triumphs at the end, restoring order in the power structure just as a fire and spring rains bring the savanna back to life. Importantly, as he triumphs, those around him first identify him as Mufasa, and he learns that Scar was his father's murderer (although Mufasa's ghost is silent on this fact).

Conclusions

We have looked at a few successful children's films. Images of these films are deeply embedded in our memories and on the memories of following generations who have viewed these films in rerelease, on television, and on video.

Children's films which become popular are not squeamish. They are filled with powerful and often violent images: children in bondage, children attacked by wild beasts, murderous adults who exploit children, families in crisis: The Queen holding a box she believes contains Snow White's heart; Bambi's mother missing after a murderous attack; Dumbo able only to touch his mother's trunk through iron bars; Dorothy melting the Wicked Witch; Old Yeller being shot; Belle imprisoned by a huge, pacing Beast. But these frightening situations are resolved by film's end, with children neatly tucked back into the context of a warm family. Maybe they have had to give up the friendships of the Rescuers, the Scarecrow, or Mary Poppins, but family has been restored.

Certainly these images have influenced us in many, nearly primal ways. The anti-fur movement must have some basis in the 101 Dalmatian pups being hunted by Cruella De Vil for their hides, and the lethal stink of her yellowish smoke must provide a concrete image for those anxious about side-stream cigarette smoke. We can barely control references to *Bambi* when persons we know in our rural Virginia home go hunting, and when administrators tell us about next year's salary increases, we virtually see their noses grow.

Here we are interested in the lingering memories of what it is like to be a boy and a man that these films have taught us. Unlike adult films, there has been little change in what children's films have had to say in this regard. Simply, these films have told us that the process of moving from boyhood to manhood involves becoming embedded in family, learning to be compassionate, and then taking that compassion a step forward to become selflessly brave. After the bravery, the hard part is becoming an involved enough father to pass on these values to the next generation.

Thirteen — Gump *and* Gumper: Men as Idiots

In this chapter we will examine the phenomenon over the past two decades of portraying men as dimwits. There are perhaps three separate trends here. In serious films, there is a character who could be called "the wise-fool": a person whose intellectual capacity may be limited, but who somehow has insights into the things that are happening around him greater than those of others who are more conventionally smart. This tradition has been around at least since the wonderful 1950 comedy *Harvey,* where befuddled and perpetually inebriated Elwood P. Dowd (Jimmy Stewart) does not understand, among other things, that his eccentric behavior is hurting his niece's chance for matrimony or that he is being committed to a mental institution, but he seems capable of seeing into each character's heart. A second trend in serious films is the "lucky fool," a person who seems to have nothing particular going for him but an endless stream of lucky breaks. Earlier manifestations of this tradition are the wickedly funny *Being There* (1979), Peter Sellers's final performance as the retarded gardener Chance, who knows nothing but television and plant husbandry, but who ends up as a political insider rumored to be in line for becoming the next President; and even *Tom Jones* (1963). The third trend is men as outright idiots. This trend certainly has origins in such films as those of the Marx Brothers or the Three Stooges, but in the recent versions, these idiots are set in a real world, not the fantasy world of "Marxist" and "Stoogist" mayhem. Jim Carrey has the most distinctive oeuvre in this genre, but Pauly Shore, Ben Stiller, Adam Sandler, and Brendan Fraser (who also can deliver memorable serious performances, as in *Twilight of the Golds*

192

[1996] and *Gods and Monsters* [1999]) are not far behind. We are not so much interested in the portrayal of men as idiots as a new phenomenon in the 1980s and 1990s — which it is not — but that there have been so many such portrayals recently which have capture huge audiences

Hard Bodies of the 1980s

In her book *Hard Bodies: Hollywood Masculinity in the Reagan Era,* Susan Jeffords (1994) seems conflicted about the lack of impact social movements have had on the portrayal of male (and to some extent, female) gender-role behavior in the films of the 1980s. She expects more of a nod toward feminism and at the same time more impact as the "Reagan Revolution" mellowed during the Bush and Clinton presidencies. She concludes that Hollywood has not registered much impact from either social movement:

> They (traditional "hard body" male images) have shown their resiliency as models because they appear to critique, at times even to reject, their earlier versions, only to renarrate them in ways more complex and more intimately woven into the fabric of American culture [pp. 192–193].

Women's impact on the movies probably happened earlier than in many other forms of popular culture. While there were only a few women directors working in early Hollywood (Slide, 1988), there were many important women scriptwriters and actresses with significant enough clout to influence films in a pro-feminist way (Lawrence, 1991[1]). One needs only think about the roles of the extremely popular actresses Bette Davis, Joan Crawford, and Katharine Hepburn to note that there were many rich portrayals of independent women in the 1930s and 1940s. Moreover, Doherty (1993) has documented how, despite good market research to the contrary (Austin, 1984), Hollywood executives through the 1940s believed that women primarily decided which movies to attend. So there may have always been an emphasis on women (and women who made family decisions) in major studio productions.

Jeffords' book is actually an extensive chronicle of how gender roles have changed, although not necessarily in the way mainstream feminism would have expected. For example, in 1979's *Kramer vs. Kramer,* the idea of gender equity led filmmakers to seriously question whether either sex should have prerogatives. *Kramer vs. Kramer* questioned whether women were "naturally" the better care-provider after a divorce. After watching Dustin Hoffman's agonizingly sympathetic father reduced to short bouts of contact with his son, the audience might come to the conclusion that the answer was at least not clear. Woody Allen upped the ante on this same issue when he had his son-rearing estranged wife portrayed as a hostile lesbian in *Manhattan* that same year (and portrayed by the same actress, the virtually unknown Meryl Streep).

Men and women have found the demands of home and office too demanding to maintain both, so often the primary heterosexual bond is broken, leaving the career individuals to find time to work on parenthood. *Three Men and a Baby* (1987) is the emblematic film of this trend from the men's perspective during the 1980s. The three men who have been left an infant to care for (Tom Selleck, Steve Guttenberg, and Ted Danson) are fools when it comes to the most basic facts of child care. But when seen in theaters, when infant Mary's mother returns, the audience audibly groans at the thought that the three surrogate dads will have to give up little hyper-regular Mary. As we have described, this reconceptualization of the family probably began with the upheavals after World War II and was fully registered on the screen in the social dramas of the 1950s. This change is consonant with — although in films somewhat earlier to — Pleck and Pleck's (1980) observation of change in male sex role behavior around 1965, away from the roles of companion and provider. Writing in 1980, the Plecks anticipated gains in sex and gender equity, due to probable gains brought about by the women's movement, the gay rights movement, and the fledgling men's movement. The only fly in the ointment, which they discuss only briefly, was the conservative "Moral Majority."

Jeffords has a 12 year difference in perspective from the Plecks (and she is specifically writing about movies, not general culture). She could assume the hegemony of the New Right and see the blunting of all of the liberal gender-based social movements. And yet expecting a pinnacle of conservatism in films early in the decade giving way to more liberal values, Jeffords was disappointed. Jeffords, like many academics, probably overestimated the effects of short-term social movements, either the liberal (women's, gay, and men's movements) or conservative ones (the Moral Majority and the Reagan Revolution). Perhaps by looking at the films of the 1990s we can better understand the effects of the social movements of 15 to 20 years ago.

Part of the image of the male "hard body" is often that the size of the intellect does not necessarily match the size of the pectoral muscles. Sylvester Stallone has made a career of portraying a small mind trapped inside a hulking body, and Arnold Schwarzenegger only gradually was able to take on roles of some intellectual substance.

To some extent, the vast number of popular films centered on a dimwitted male is a response to feminism — or at least to the same social forces which gave rise to feminism. One strain of popular feminism, which emphasizes the differences between the sexes, has portrayed men as more simple to understand than women. This is characterized by such slogans as "Men have one thing on their minds," or even "All men are pigs." One way of dealing with such accusations is to take them and run with them, if for no other reason than to explore their absurdity by developing them for two hours on screen.

This very well may be the impetus for the broad comic films which do portray men as simpletons. A more measured response to feminism, particularly its sociological versions, which assume "men have all the power" is to create films about powerless men. Taking another slogan rampant in this period, "Knowledge is power," filmmakers can create a group of powerless men, men who are intellectually/knowledge challenged. By focusing on intellectually handicapped heroes, filmmakers in the wake of feminism can create interesting dynamics among their male and female characters not possible with other kinds of heroes.

The 1990s

The 1990s were a difficult decade to evaluate for trends in movies. The decade began with a blockbuster film about a nasty little boy outwitting two dimwitted thieves (*Home Alone*), followed three years later by a nearly identical sequel, together earning a quarter of a billion dollars in North American theatrical rentals. The first half of the decade witnessed the new Disney revival, with four blockbuster animated films, *Beauty and the Beast* (1991), *Aladdin* (1992), *The Lion King* (1994), and *Pocahontas* (1995), which collectively have also earned a half a billion dollars in North American theatrical rentals and as much more again in each of the international and video markets. Disney also scored big with a different retelling of the Beauty and the Beast story in 1990, this time about a beautiful prostitute who humanizes a calculating executive, *Pretty Woman*. (If one looks primarily at the character of Vivian Ward [Julia Roberts], the film is more of a mixture of *Pygmalion* and *Cinderella*, but, in any case, it is a Disney fairy tale.) The decade continued the 1980s trend of comic book characters come to life on the big screen (*Teenage Mutant Ninja Turtles* [1990], *Batman Returns* [1992], *The Flintstones* [1994], and *Batman Forever* [1995]) and terrifying superheroes in *Terminator 2: Judgment Day* (1991), but many of the special effects horror films have done disappointing business, notably the presciently titled Schwarzenegger vehicle, *Last Action Hero* (1993).

Romance made something of a return, but often with a peculiar twist: Sam Wheat (Patrick Swayze) and Molly Jensen (Demi Moore) are reunited in *Ghost* (1990), but, regrettably, Sam is dead, and their reunion lasts only a tearjerking six seconds as he fades in and out of ghostly focus. Mitch Robbins (Billy Crystal) in *City Slickers* (1991) reconnects with his wife and family by falling in love with a calf. Sam Baldwin (Tom Hanks) and Annie Reed (Meg Ryan) don't meet in *Sleepless in Seattle* (1993) until the last moments of the film. Harry and Helen Tasker (Arnold Schwarzenegger and Jamie Lee Curtis) rekindle the spark in their marriage after he makes her dance in her underwear in *True Lies* (1994) as he lurks, anonymously, in the shadows. John

Dunbar (Kevin Costner) and Stands with a Fist (Mary McDonnell) barely speak the same language in *Dances with Wolves* (1990). Forrest Gump (Tom Hanks) finally comes together with his Jenny (Robin Wright) but only after she has broken his heart, had his child without telling him, and contracted AIDS. In each of these films — all blockbusters — men and women want to come together but cannot satisfactorily. What impedes them is not so much the psychological distrust of the films of previous decades, but more socio-logical, structural problems, such as language, physical distance, and job requirements.

While heterosexual connection becomes more difficult in the 1990s, iron-ically, fatherhood seems to have become more prominent, particularly in films about the distanced father coming back into a bond with his children (*Hook* [1991]; *City Slickers* [1991], *Mrs. Doubtfire* [1993], *Sleepless in Seattle* [1993], *True Lies* [1994], *The Santa Clause* [1994], and *Liar, Liar* [1997]). In five of these films, it is an overdemanding job which takes the father away from the child; in the other two, it is the break up of a marriage, one by divorce, the other by death. We no longer have the emotionally distanced father, such as those so prominent in films of the 1950s, such as *Giant* and *Cat on a Hot Tin Roof.* These 1990s fathers want to be connected to their children, they just don't have the opportunity. In this respect, these films reflect an unpleasant reality of contemporary society: parents, both mothers and fathers, are work-ing longer hours and are spending far less time with their children. In most polls,[2] parents are not pleased with either development, and social critics are beginning to wonder what the long-term impact on children will be. At other times the absence of fathers seems to be the main driving force of a film, either when their absence is temporary, as in the *Home Alone* films and *Apollo 13* (1995), or when the father is permanently absent, as in *Forrest Gump* (1994), *The Lion King,* and *Twister* (1996).

It may be profitable to discuss two serious films at this point, *Unforgiven* (1992) and *Forrest Gump.* In *Unforgiven,* we can perhaps best see the effects of the gender social movement in high relief on this most traditional of male film forms, the western. *Forrest Gump* is worth considering because it has been the most profitable "human" film of the 1990s — only the animated *The Lion King,* discussed in the last chapter, the lizard flick *Jurassic Park* (1993), and the boat and ice film *Titanic* (1998) made more money. We will spend considerable time in the next chapter on *Titanic.*

Unforgiven

The two protagonists in *Unforgiven* are both named William, Will Munny (Clint Eastwood), the retired bounty hunter, and Little Bill (Gene Hackman), the sadistic sheriff. At some level it may be useful to see these two characters as part of the same self, two aspects of the male "will." Men have potential for both good and evil. There is a good and dark side of the Force.

The engine which begins and guides this revenge story is the mutilation of a prostitute by a cowboy after she comments negatively on the size of his penis. The law judges that reparation of two horses will provide for her welfare (since a mutilated prostitute no longer has value in her chosen profession). The "cut whore," as she is referred to throughout the film, is satisfied with this settlement, but among her colleagues are those intent on vengeance, and they refuse the offer for her. They pretend to post a bounty (in actuality they have no money) on the head of the two cowboys. (The second cowboy either helped his friend or the prostitute; the film is shot so that what he does is not clear, adding to the moral ambiguity of the film.) In order to gain sympathy for their cause, they exaggerate the extent of the mutilation. An inexperienced (and nearly blind) aspiring bounty hunter, The Schofield Kid, lures Will and his ex-partner Ned (Morgan Freeman) to help him, with the promise of money.

We first see Will Munny wallowing in the mud with his sick pigs. He has become what the ranchers in *Shane* taunt the sod-busters with being: a pig-farmer. Will had given up his wild ways — including killing and drinking — for the love of a woman. She is now dead, and he is, like a good film '90s father, strained by the conflict between work and fatherhood. He wants to give up farming and go into the dry goods business in San Francisco. Reluctantly he agrees to the task, giving into an impulse on a get-rich scheme, the frontier equivalent of junk bonds or a corporate takeover. Screw hard work, this is the '90s. But unlike some of today's financial wizards, Munny acknowledges that he is in it for the money, and that he must forget about the "morality" of the situation.

The basic situation of *Unforgiven* tells us a great deal about how far we have come in the portrayal of men in the cinema. Will Munny is old and tired, and he cannot balance fatherhood with strenuous work. He does not call up his mother-in-law and turn over the raising of his children to her. He sees his salvation not in the frontier, but in returning to the city. What he has been told about the mutilation is a two-fold lie: there is no money to back up the bounty and the mutilation has been exaggerated. But he — like every other character in this film — is wearing a gray hat. We admire his devotion to his children. We admire the fact that he is not deluded by an ends-justifies-the-means argument: he know that what he is about to do is wrong. We admire the intensity of his vengeful violence after Ned is killed and publicly mutilated by Little Bill. But still what he is doing is wrong, enormously wrong, and he deliberately descends back to the creature he was before he was redeemed by his dead wife: he drinks, he swears, he murders; he only restrains his old lifestyle by refusing the offer of "free ones" from the prostitutes. He should know better. He does know better.

This man knows better than to be doing what he is doing. Will Munny descends back to his wild man's nature to raise funds to take his children back to civilization.

The Schofield Kid is the dimwitted character in the film. He has not received much attention by critics, but his character tells us a good deal about changes in the representation of masculinity in the movies. He could be construed as one of the various forms of "men as idiots" in the films of the 1990s we are discussing. On the other hand, he is Joey Starrett grown a little older, still unmentored by an absent father. While Joey wanted to learn to shoot a gun, The Schofield Kid aspires to be a cold blooded killer in the way most children dream of becoming dentists or interior decorators. But he has failed to imagine, on either a practical or moral level, without the guidance of a father, what it means to kill someone. Killing is so much a part of the tradition of the western, that it is particularly disturbing to see so much emotion and moral discourse surrounding such a commonplace act for the genre. Munny becomes his mentor, and what he learns is not how to be a cold-blooded killer (the man Munny used to be and has temporarily resumed) but how to be a compassionate man (the man Munny really is). This is the dark side of the Force, transported into the recent American past.

Certainly, this film was influenced by feminism, but it is not the kind of film early feminist film critics envisioned. In the first place, there are no female role models here, as Molly Haskell demanded. Except for Ned's wife, all of the women are prostitutes, and not one of them is a Vivian Ward: they are not "pretty women" and there is not one heart of gold to be had among them. They are liars and cheats. Men have become no more egalitarian with respect to women than Ahmed is to Lady Diana in *The Sheik*.

This is an extremely violent film, and the violence is of a very close and personal nature (this is not Rambo prettily wasting a hundred Vietnamese soldiers with imaginary weaponry or Luke Skywalker blowing up a Death Star: these are men slowly beating each other to death, one by one, blow by ugly blow). As a critique of violence, and particularly violence against women, the film has sometimes been described as a feminist western (Howe, 1992). But it seems that it is more likely a response to or critique of feminism, particularly in the portrayal of the lead prostitute who is more interested in some sort of vengeful action which blames all men, than in seeking the real advantage of the woman involved; the exaggerations of the claims of mutilation seem to be a comment on the misandrous exaggerations of some segments of the women's movement.

Forrest Gump

Reading about *Forrest Gump* now we are reminded of the cute gump-isms ("Stupid is as stupid does"), the special effects in which Tom Hanks is seamlessly placed into historical footage, and the peculiarly American idea that you don't have to be smart or even work all that hard to become successful, just straightforward and honest.[3]

Before its popularity became clear, reviewers were less inclined to see the film as a romp through recent American history and popular culture than as a rather dark, cynical piece (Maslin, 1994). Both elements seem to be in the film, and it was probably this unresolved tension which made the film popular with audiences (you can find what you want), although less pleasing to critics. Forrest (Tom Hanks) is a handicapped child, raised by an eccentric single mother (Sally Field). Forrest develops an ability to run straight ahead without much thought, either about his goal or about his own safety. This ability makes him an excellent football player and soldier. In three of the central moments of the film, Forrest visits the White House, twice as athlete, once as war hero. In each case he would embarrass himself if he had sufficient self-awareness to be embarrassed.

What holds the narrative together, aside from Forrest's incredible streak of good luck, is Forrest's love for a woman, Jenny (Robin Wright). Jenny, like so many 1990s heroines, comes from an abusive home (Forrest later will have her old house demolished as an act of love for her) which leads her down a path of self-indulgence, and ultimately, self-destruction. Forrest just loves her in the same straightforward manner in which he runs, and he comes to understand that she cannot commit to someone like him. He is far too straightforward and straitlaced for her party-hearty life.

The last two scenes of this film, after Jenny's death, are the most significant to our discussion and perhaps the most effective. In the penultimate scene, Forrest discusses his life and his life vision with Jenny at her grave. He has perhaps grown intellectually a mite, accepting life as paradoxically planned and random — a race and a box of chocolates, if you will. With Little Forrest now in his life, one expects that he will stop running aimlessly. He weeps through the entire scene.

In the final scene, Forrest chats with his son at the bus stop before his first day in school. Little Forrest is bright, and Big Forrest's body is completely at rest now that he knows this. After the bus has taken his son away, he just sits there, as he sat in the first part of the film chatting with whomever came his way in the park in Savannah. But in the park, he was restless and going somewhere — although exactly where he didn't know. At the school bus stop, he has come to rest.

We have subtitled this chapter "men as idiots." Both of these films are serious Hollywood films, in which main characters, The Schofield Kid and Forrest Gump, are intellectually limited, and their intellectual limitations are their tragic flaws. Had the Schofield Kid been a bit more aware of the situation and about the nature of the enterprise he aims for, the horrible violence that comes in the wake of his ambition to be a killer would not take place. Likewise, Forrest cannot plan, and his intellectual limitation makes him unattractive to Jenny. So it is only a series of ironically good breaks for him hidden within others' tragedies (the deaths of Bubba and Jenny) which lead him finally to financial success and a peaceful, albeit truncated, family life. The term "idiot" is only insensitively applied to these two characters, but there appears to be a relatively recent trend in American films which feature intellectually limited heroes (e.g., *Rain Man* [1988], *Dominick and Eugene* [1988], *The Other Sister* (1999)).

Gumper

Forrest Gump may be the most acceptable representative of the most popular genre of films emerging in the 1990s, the dumb guy film. The *Home Alone* films, and a whole host of films starring Adam Sandler, Pauly Shore, and others, present men, particularly young, white, straight men, as morons. Unlike Forrest Gump, they are also insensitive, but like Forrest, they participate in their culture uncomprehendingly. There are equivalent dumb girl and dumb black guy films, but most of these films have redemptive plots — blacks and women shed their naiveté and their selfishness and are transformed

This man is clueless about what is really going on around him; but this actor, Jim Carrey, commands the highest salaries in Hollywood and knows that dumb is better.

into caring individuals on the brink of wisdom. Gays are still not really represented in popular films. Young, straight, white guys just bumble along into possible sequels, without growing intellectually or emotionally. This is a message received almost daily by this group from those older than them, women, gays, and blacks — they are dumb and insensitive (although, interestingly, many of these films are first studio outings of savvy young, white, straight male film directors, like Ben Stiller).

Jim Carrey is of course the god of this kind of film, having made five films in a five year period which topped a billion dollars in North American theatrical revenue. Perhaps the most extreme of the Jim Carrey films is *Dumb and Dumber* (1994). In this film Carrey plays Lloyd, an inept limousine driver who, along with his equally inept dog groomer roommate (Jeff Daniels), travels from Providence, Rhode Island, to Aspen, carrying a briefcase with ransom money in it. Along the way they play pranks on people, some of which kill their victims.

Trying to watch this film seriously presents the viewer with a very frightening view of an aspect of our culture: those who for some reason participate in their culture without a lick of comprehension of it. In one of the first gags of the film — and one of the few clean enough to discuss in full — Lloyd stops his limo, hops in the back seat, rolls down the window and attempts to engage a woman standing at a bus stop in conversation. (Where has he been for the last 20 years?) After she speaks in a clearly German accent, he misidentifies her as Latin American; when she corrects him by saying "Austrian," he responds knowingly by suggesting she "Throw another shrimp on the Barbee." The fact that he is a limo driver and is this ignorant of geography is almost sad. Fortunately, for the sake of Western Civilization, his bosses recognize his stupidity and fire him, allowing him the free time to go on the road with his roomie, also recently fired.

At one point in this film, Lloyd has a vision of being popular and classy. He is in Aspen, après-ski. He and a group of stylish young adults are drinking and having a good time. He is the center of attention. Step by step his behavior goes to the edge and then beyond it. Finally, to the great delight of all present, he lights a fart...

There's Something About Mary (1998)

There is something very simple about There's Something About Mary. It is based on two very straightforward assumptions from popular feminism: Women are goddesses; men are jerks (perhaps jerk-offs). But there's an interesting connection between these two premises: goddesses make men jerks (Twitterpated, as the Owl in Bambi would say). Five men in this film are completely undone because of mere exposure to Mary (Cameron Diaz). Of course she's not only a beauty, but a pro-level golfer, a volunteer with handicapped children, and a neurosurgeon. Crude as this film is, it's also very funny (Ebert, 1998). As an assault on political correctness, it is to be admired, although everyone who proclaims to be against political correctness will be appalled by at least one of its gags making fun of the intellectually handicapped, the physically handicapped, Latinos, women, and animal rights activists. It also makes considerable fun of the middle class and men. And it might also be the ultimate 1990s film, if subsequent decades are as crude as the 1990s. Each of the men in this film becomes a complete idiot because of his love for Mary. They become stalkers or failures, wear fake dentures (because she likes big teeth!) or become pretend paraplegics. The film takes the idea from the films of the 1940s that flirtation involves deception, and runs with it.

Of course, it's not Mary's fault. She's just living her life, successfully, while the men around her go careening off into disaster. Men are the idiots. Women are the calm center of the universe.

And yet, men know in this film that they cannot be as sexual as they would like to be, and so the most normal of Mary's suitors (Ben Stiller) is told that to be properly nonlibidinous on his first real, successful date with Mary, he needs first to take thing in hand....[4]

* * *

In chapter two we examined the two principal characters in *Gone with the Wind,* particularly looking at the view of masculinity implied in Clark Gable's characterization of Rhett Butler. Clark Gable fought a succession of directors on this film about his scene with the body of Bonnie. Gable thought real men didn't cry, and he had a clause in his contract to prove it. Men were strong, men were brave, men loved good women, and lusted after bad ones. We have now come to Forrest Gump. He is physically strong, as a compensation for mental infirmity. He is brave, because he is too stupid to be afraid. He loves a woman, but he cannot compete with the excitement of a liberated world.

Lesley Howard as Ashley Wilkes was the other hero of that 1939 film. It is not necessary to make many comparisons between this man of exquisite taste and manners, who really does understand the nuances of the changing times he finds himself in — who was regarded at the time as a good second choice of heroes, after Gable — and Lloyd in *Dumb and Dumber,* to see cultural changes not easily predicted. Lloyd is stupid, unmannered, and out of touch with every aspect of his historical context. Yet, unlike Ashley, Lloyd gets the girl.

In chapter five, we spent a good deal of time talking about Rick Blaine. He took time wondering how to approach Ilsa, but we certainly cannot imagine him stopping into the casino's restroom to take the edge off of his date.

Fourteen — Post-Feminist Heroes: Jack and Shakespeare

Film reviewers had little good to say about James Cameron's (1997) *Titanic* when it appeared. Many were appalled by its budget, and it was common to compare the costs of the film to the building of the ship around which the movie revolved.[1] We were in the midst of the "independent film explosion" when American audiences had seemingly rediscovered the "little film," which could both be financed by the credit cards of their auteurs and concentrate on authentically portrayed relationships. Surely the big-budget, special effects movie and the costume drama were dinosaurs from the 1980s.

And yet, despite critical warnings against the movie's creaky dialogue and often poorly motivated scenes, the film did boffo business. That is an understatement: *Titanic* became the highest grossing film in the American market of all time. Undaunted by its popular reception, the press continued to snipe at the film and its male star, Leonardo DiCaprio (Jack). In a smear not unlike the vilification of Valentino 75 years earlier, the press simultaneously questioned DiCaprio's heterosexuality and portrayed him as a hedonistic user of women, climaxing with the innuendo that the reason he moved to suppress nude photographs in *Playgirl* was that his endowment was less than titanic (*Time*, 1998). The box office of *Titanic* was snidely attributed to repeat viewings by prepubescent girls, the implication of which was that young women were too stupid to know a good film or a bad one when they saw it. Indeed, teen-age girls did make up an important segment of the movie's viewership, but they did not comprise the majority. In fact, the movie had an extremely wide audience, and most segments, with the probable exception of movie critics, liked it.

The critical situation was completely different for *Shakespeare in Love* the following year. The critics, with the exception of Christian conservatives who found its glorification of extra-marital sex disturbing, adored this film, originally niched for the American art house circuit.[2] The casting of the American actress Gwyneth Paltrow in the central role of Viola and the American hunk Ben Affleck as the actor who portrays Mercutio probably indicates that the filmmakers had higher hopes for the film. The dialogue was witty and full of references that only English majors from departments which still taught Dead White Men would get. The film was a gender-bender, with the most glamorous young female star of the day, playing an emancipated woman, impersonating the male actor who would first play Juliet. Earlier in the film, Paltrow gets to rehearse Romeo's lines in bed with the Bard, playing Juliet. Joseph Fiennes (Shakespeare) might be described as "beautiful" rather than "ruggedly handsome," but he was tricked out in scruffy facial hair, and clearly met the definition of masculine good looks a bit more traditionally than Leonardo DiCaprio. When he read Juliet's lines, we feel he is just prompting, not speaking from his feminine side.

As improbable as the script for *Shakespeare in Love* is historically, given a few willing suspensions of disbelief, it is plausibly motivated from a contemporary psychological perspective. We can imagine that an independent woman with poetic inclinations who finds herself bartered for a title might rebel by having a fling with the Bard. A poet in a dry spell, experiencing financial difficulties, might become enamored of a beautiful woman with money. Shakespeare first notices Viola in auditions when she reads a speech from one of his plays, after everyone else has auditioned by reading the same speech from Marlowe's *Dr. Faustus*. Flattery works both in our time and in Shakespeare's world. The gender-bending is of course historically correct. Juliet would have originally been played by a boy playing a woman, so the gender confusion is inherent in trying to portray Shakespeare's stage accurately.[3] The mixing of social classes is improbable, but if it would occur in Elizabethan England, the theater was a place where it might have occurred. Unlike *Titanic,* however, there are never times when we are forced to think: people don't act like this!

And yet, it is interesting to observe that both films share many similar plot points. Both films are centered on a young woman trapped in a loveless, arranged engagement, in which she is economic merchandise. Both women are headed from England to America on ill-fated ships. (*Shakespeare in Love* takes place in 1593, so the ship which she leaves at the end of the film will be destined for failure in establishing her husband's plantations in Virginia.) Both women become actresses. Both women rebel by having a sexual liaison with a pretty working class boy with artistic tendencies. Both meet this boy when he transgresses physical social barriers (Viola's party and the first class

Romance makes something of a revival in several blockbusters at the end of the century. But Shakespeare and Viola will have little more than a fling, although Shakespeare will find his muse because of it, and Viola may find enough poetry there for a life of aristocratic confinement.

deck of the *Titanic*). Both women follow the boy to his working class haunts (Viola to a London brothel, Rose to a steerage revel). Both women are transformed by this social class revelation and enter into a sexual relationship with the working class artist. These experiences allow both women to endure the hardships of the life imposed on them, Viola to her unfortunate marriage, and Rose to a hidden life in America. Likewise, both of the working class boys are empowered by their sexual relationship: Jack becomes heroic as the ship sinks, and Shakespeare overcomes his writer's block to finish *Romeo and Juliet* and then begin *Twelfth Night*.

The fiancés, the third apexes of these love triangles, also share some commonalities: they are both cads. Both are obsessed with money. Both are impervious to the arts: Wessex (Colin Firth) doesn't seem to get theater. When we first see him, he is the only member of the audience watching an early Shakespeare comedy who isn't laughing. Cal (Billy Zane) sees no merit in Rose's collection of Monets and early Picassos. They are portrayed by actors who can be described as both handsome and young. Both go ballistic when they find out about their fiancées' affairs. Lord Wessex, it turns out, is really not as violent as we are led to suspect, because for some time in the film we are led to believe that he has had Christopher Marlowe murdered. Billy Zane's Cal does go murderously haywire in the second least probable action in the film: although memoirs of people from the real *Titanic* did tell of people whose behavior became chaotic, Cal's rampage is too orderly, and if one is acting orderly, one does not risk one's own life to try to harm someone who will be dead by other means in 15 minutes. Both times we saw this film in a theater, the audience howled with laughter at his rampage scenes.

And there are similarities about the receptions of the two movies: both received Best Picture Academy Awards: Kate Winslet and Gwyneth Paltrow received Academy Award nominations as best actresses, while neither Leonardo DiCaprio nor Joseph Fiennes received much acting recognition, even though both movies hinge on a plausible attraction to their characters by the central female character.

It may be of some interest to examine the similarities of these movies as exemplars of the kinds of situations and characters which are highly appealing to contemporary audiences. Both were highly successful, but their primary audiences were very different, and so these similarities may well help us understand widely-held popular gender ideas of our period. For example, both films glorify extra-marital sex, both because they emphasize the transforming and redemptive power of erotic love for both men and women and because they view marriage as incarceration, at least for women. Both center on the attraction between a somewhat empowered and definitely headstrong woman and an artist. In neither case does this attraction last very long. Both films are strongly concentrated on the issue of social class in a way that seems very distant from the current social class situation in America. We will examine these two films in terms of feminism, marriage, social class, and masculinity.

Jack, Shakespeare, and Feminism

We suggest that both *Titanic* and *Shakespeare in Love* can be classified as Post-Feminist works. First-wave feminism of the 1970s and 1980s is clearly still strongly alive in both the political and critical realm. There are many women and men who still view gender from a structural sociological perspective through concepts such as power and victimization, often in the formula that all men have power and all women are their victims. But there is also clearly a second force in feminism which rejects the sociological perspective, favoring a more psychological one: a concentration on individuals rather than as exemplars of their sex. For want of a generally accepted term for this force, we may adopt the term Post-Feminism, not to imply that feminism is over, but to attach a similar meaning to Post-Modernism in its architectural and visual arts definitions. Post-Modern architecture accepts many of the methods and materials of Modernism, but has abandoned the proscriptions against the pre-Modern and developed alternative uses of the pre-Modern vocabulary of art and architecture, often ironic, to develop a new style. Likewise. Post-Feminism, while largely adhering to feminist goals of equality of opportunity for the sexes, rejects the sociological premises, and allows certain themes from previous decades to emerge, such as the redemptive nature of love, although love may be regarded with a certain sense of irony.

One of the most important ways in which Post-Feminism differs from first-wave feminism is in the understanding that while as a group men have more economic and political power than women, most men do not hold such power. Rose and Viola have more financial and social resources than do Jack and Shakespeare. Jack does not have the cash necessary for even a steerage ticket home to America at the beginning of the movie, and Shakespeare desperately needs 50 pounds throughout the film so that he can move from a by-the-word laborer to a middle class entrepreneur, by becoming a partner in the Admiral's Men. It is difficult to recall a successful American movie from the 1970s and 1980s with such a power inequity in favor of the female protagonist, although in the last decade films such as *Disclosure* (1994) have dealt seriously with the issues of powerful women and less powerful men. There were many pre-feminist films which dealt with this situation: *It Happened One Night* (1934), *Gone with the Wind* (1939), *I Was a Male War Bride* (1949), *Rear Window* (1954), *Giant* (1956), and even *Lady and the Tramp* (1955) come to mind.

And yet, Viola and Rose are not free operators. Wessex and Cal are more powerful than they, oppressors in the style of male characters in movies produced during first-wave feminism, such as *The Godfather* (1972), *The Way We Were* (1973), *9 to 5* (1980), and *The Color Purple* (1985). Shakespeare and Jack are not powerful, visually indicated by their statures when standing next to their leading ladies, who appear to be slightly taller than they are. Boyish as the good looks of the actors may be, both Jack and Shakespeare behave like men. They are direct. Both actors have piercing gazes, which in the context of these two films we do not interpret as invasive, if for no other reason than they are artists, and artists are granted the status of the keen observer.

Of course making a hero of Shakespeare, the most blazing icon of "Dead White Men," in itself can be viewed as a challenge to first-wave feminism. There is potentially a political agenda here in making a smart, independent woman fall in love with the Bard. We would suspect as much in the hands of another author, but co-screenwriter Tom Stoppard's career-long effort to deal with the legacy of Shakespeare suggests that his screenplay is just another stage in this attempt.

Marriage

Both *Shakespeare in Love* and *Titanic* construe marriage as a vehicle of female repression and economic dominance, something that both women and men would be best without. There is nothing like a happy marriage portrayed in either movie, just as critics have pointed out there are no happy marriages in Shakespeare (Bloom, 1998). In *Titanic,* the elderly Rose (Gloria Stewart) seems to have had a good marriage, but we are not told anything about it, while Molly Brown (Kathy Bates) momentarily recalls a happy marriage. But both women are widows and so we do not see an exemplar of a good marriage. And Rose's final act in the film seems to indicate that the relationship which meant the most to her in her life was with Jack, not her husband. Not only does her husband not survive, but the children who were the outcome of that marriage are not around, either. There is only her granddaughter, a relationship far removed from the concept of a nuclear family. Of course, her lack of children may be in the film only to convey her extreme old age, but she is unencumbered by traditional family ties. Yet, both Rose and Viola look forward to marriage — not their arranged marriage, but an ideal state vaguely in their futures. Marriage could be possible, but both will settle for a romp, however brief, with a kindred spirit.

Shakespeare in Love portrays marriage as being repressive toward women more thoroughly than *Titanic*. In *Shakespeare in Love*, Viola's marriage is arranged between Wessex and Viola's father. Viola is not consulted. Wessex's concerns are whether she can bear children and whether she is "obedient." To the latter question, her father slyly responds that she is as obedient as any mule in Christendom, which the dolt Wessex seems to construe as a "yes." Viola's mother is a very small part in this movie, but she, too, offers only a negative view on the institution of marriage. As her husband is about to conclude the final arrangements with Wessex, she complains that she will have to spend two weeks in his company in the country.

The marriage must be blessed by the Queen (Judi Dench). Elizabeth, who herself eschewed the state of marital bliss, provides wry commentary on the institution and this particular arrangement. She sees Wessex as a throwback and Viola as a force that Wessex will neither control nor even comprehend. After her second meeting with Viola, she perceives that she has been "plucked" and not by Wessex, but he seems not to comprehend what she is saying, either because he cannot imagine such a possibility or because he cannot comprehend metaphor. He is entirely focused on the financial benefits of the union. But the message eventually sinks in and he comes to the Rose

Theatre and attacks Shakespeare. He is not a wounded lover, but a man defending property rights. Shakespeare defends himself admirably: he is the wounded lover, because Viola has confirmed to him that while he will have her heart, she will marry Wessex. But he cannot vanquish his rival, because he is using a prop sword: he is in no way a match for the aristocratic Lord Wessex. In some respects, this is the climax of the film, because this is the point at which both the film and the play within the film turn from comedy to tragedy. This is the point when Shakespeare sees that his love is doomed.

We also see the institution of marriage from Shakespeare's perspective. He has been living in London for four years, having been expelled from the house of his wife. Before that he had been cut off in the marriage bed after the birth of the twins. Anne Hathaway is presented as greatly his senior in age and his superior in social class, exaggerations of the historical facts. In his discussion with his apothecary-therapist, there are mentions of at least seven affairs that he has had since his arrival in London. Writing, it seems, is dependent on such relations. Shakespeare uses the language of inspiration and muses when he describes these affairs, but the apothecary brings them down to earth by identifying them as primarily associations with prostitutes. By implication, then, marriage is seen as constraining for men as well as women. It is the act of falling in love and entering into a sexual liaison which gives Shakespeare his voice, not settling down to the marriage relationship. He was not a poet in Stratford-upon-Avon. The play he will write, *Romeo and Juliet*, is about a marriage, but one which will last a single night and result in the death of the two lovers.

Titanic's assault on the institution of marriage is less thorough-going. Jack has never been married, so we do not have his perspective on that institution. It is difficult to tell whether he would want to make an honest woman of Rose after their sexual encounter, or whether he would just like her to join in on his vagabond cruise through life. Nor do we have the groom and his father-in-law arranging the marriage. Here, it is Rose's mother who has arranged her daughter's marriage. This is again a marriage of economic necessity, but it is Rose's family who needs the money. Her mother complains that when her husband died, he did not leave them well enough provided for to maintain the extravagant lifestyle to which they had become accustomed, and they are about to run out of the funds necessary to attract a suitably well-heeled husband for Rose. Mom seems far less concerned about Rose's well-being than her own. This arrangement of forces implies both that women have economic advantages from marriage and that women can oppress other women through the institution of marriage.

Cal is a troublesome character, and the relationship between Cal and Rose is poorly defined. They are certainly not kindred spirits, which seems to be Molly Brown's prescription for a good marriage. He does not under-

Jack seems to be on top of the world at the beginning of his crossing the Atlantic. But even an on-board romance with an American socialite cannot sustain this buoyancy.

stand her interest in art, although he seems willing to support it. In the scene where he presents her with the big blue diamond, he even comes off sympathetically. His bourgeois background gets in the way of his communicating effectively with Rose — why would he suspect that she would value this icon of monarchy when she actually values the anarchy of Impressionism and Picasso? — but he admits his lack and seems to be asking her to help him understand her needs and feelings. Rose must know something about him that is never revealed to the audience, because she would rather die than marry him. Yet, after her rescue from her flamboyant suicide attempt by Jack, she seems to be, if anything, stuffier and more class conscious than Cal. Just as she cannot tell Cal why she hates him, she cannot tell Jack why he intrigues her. In trying to make sense of this film, we must recall that we are in the action/adventure mode, from a director/screenwriter who is a master of that genre. Individual scenes may make sense or at least have immediate psychological impact. It may be too much to ask for the characters and their relationships to be consistent from scene to scene, even if the film costs $200,000,000.

Like Wessex, Cal must avenge his honor when he discovers that his possession has been violated. No longer sympathetic or attempting an intellectual rapprochement, and certainly not wounded, he just goes plain nuts. It

adds a certain amount of tension to the sinking scenes to have someone shooting off a revolver, even if it doesn't make any psychological sense.

Social Class

One of the most perplexing aspect of both of these films is their strong
social class messages. Both films are minefields of social class barriers for the
heroes. There seems to be a very simple equation going on here: Jack and Shakespeare are both working class boys, and both are good; both fiancés are of a
higher class and bad. The tragedy of both films is that both heroes lack the
social standing to allow them to "get the girl" in an official, matrimonial way.

One of the problems with most American analyses of these films is that
they have taken a contemporary two class model of society: working class vs.
the bourgeoisie. Without the consideration of an upper class, these films make
no sense. Wessex is an aristocrat. Cal certainly represents more than the "middle class," as seen by his fascination with a monarchical gem. In fact, both of
these films glorify the middle class. In both films, the heroes aspire to the
middle class: Shakespeare wants to become a partner in the Admiral's men
and Jack wants to become a society portraitist. The tragedy comes from the
fact that others aspire for both women entry into the upper class, thereby
putting them completely out of range for their working class lovers.

The scenes of upper class life in both movies are glamorous but shallow.
Even in the stilted dialogue of *Titanic,* there are perceptible increases in its
stiltedness when we are entirely within the first class spaces of the ship. Jack
must study the behavior of the first class passengers, and his unrefined and
direct language is apparent, as is Molly Brown's. We identify with Molly but
she is a very wealthy woman. When we are at court in *Shakespeare in Love,*
the language becomes no more obscure, but the ironical detachment and
ridicule become evident. Onstage or offstage at the Rose, or the bedroom,
the dialogue remains Shakespearean, but there it has a direct quality to it
which contrasts to the language at court, even when it is blunt Queen Bess
who is speaking.

We know nothing of what will happen to Viola — except to speculate
whether she will survive her 1593 voyage to America. (Viola survives ship-
wreck in *Twelfth Night.*) Permanent settlement in Virginia is 15 years away.
Rose appears to have had a good life. She became an actress, married, had
children, and lived an exceptionally long life, during which she never needed
to cash in the multi-million dollar bauble Cal gave her the night before the
Titanic sank. When she arrives on the salvage ship, she shows that she is very
used to first-class service.

Earlier we alluded to the second most improbable action in *Titanic.* The
most improbable act is when the elderly Rose tosses the "Coeur de Mer" into

the ocean. This act serves one legitimate function in the film: it identifies "Old Rose" as the Rose from the manifest from the *Titanic*. It lets the audience know that her memories are real. It also serves a more questionable function: now that the explorers have given up their quest of finding a fortune in the hull of the ship, it allows her to posthumously give Jack her most precious gift — presumably her virginity or her love was not that.[4]

Yet this action makes absolutely no sense. If she disclosed the jewel to the crew, there is no reason to believe that they will knock her over the head and toss her into the icy deep. There is no threat that makes this act sensible. Moreover, there is no reason why this materialistic gift from her jealous fiancé is an appropriate offering to her dead one-night-stand from eight decades ago. As heart-wrenching as this act might at first seems, in retrospect it makes us reexamine the motives of both Rose's character and the screenwriters. If Rose's most precious gift is her most expensive and an emblem of monarchy, then she is not quite the romantic love child we may have suspected. We also wonder about her attachment to her granddaughter: wouldn't this trinket have made her life much more bearable? Rose seems to be affirming her similarity here to her own self-interested mother.

Masculinity

Of course, our major concern is to define what it is that these two films say about the nature of masculine presence and behavior onscreen at the end of the 20th century. On the positive side, Jack and Shakespeare have four things in common. Both are artists. Both are so overtaken with love that they risk life and limb. Both are sexually active. And both are out of their league.

That both characters are artists may simply be a convention of movies. Movie characters in general overrepresent artists. *Titanic* is a film about visual effects, and having the main male character a visual artist may fit the nature of the film well. James Cameron is a visual artist (he drew all of Jack's pictures for the film [Marsh, 1997]) and may merely have projected himself into the role of Jack. *Shakespeare in Love* is a film about words, and making the main character Shakespeare cannot be a mere convenience, Tom Stoppard can certainly bring to this film a wealth of knowledge about the process of writing for the stage.

But we believe that there is more to it than that. Because they are artists, both are viewed as capable of understanding women. They are soulmates of the women with whom they fall in love. It is safer to allow men who are artists understand women in a contemporary movie than it would be if the protagonist were a cowboy or a dog groomer or a Jedi knight ... or merely a middle class husband. Yet, understanding women is presented as an ideal. Men should understand women. This ability to understand women is also conveyed in the androgynous good looks of the actors. Someone who is somewhat feminine probably has a feminine side to get in touch with. Why the prospective marriages are oppressive seems primarily because their fiancés neither understand Rose or Viola, nor see much need to.

Love makes these men strong and active. This is one of the most enduring qualities of masculinity that we have seen in all of our analyses of American films. Valentino's Sheiks, Rhett Butler, the various fighting men of World War II, Joe Starrett and Shane, and perhaps even Luke Skywalker, all get their real strength from romantic involvement with women. When grounded in such love, men can become heroes. When social conventions make such involvement difficult, as we saw in the films of the 1970s and 1980s, men are either antiheroes as in the *Godfather* saga or evolve into some sort of god or monster, operating from a primordial internal violence, which can be either for ill (*Terminator*) or for good (*Terminator 2*).

Masculinity in both films is seen as involving a good measure of sex. The context of the sex act really places these films squarely as Post-Feminist works. In most of the films of the 1970s and 1980s, sex between men and women was problematical. The sexual attraction in both films is both quick (two days after the principals meet in both films) and mutual. While the marriages into the upper classes oppress both of the women in these films, neither film invites us to view the premarital affairs as oppressive to either party. On the contrary, both films construe sexuality as liberating for women and grounding for men.

What distinguishes the romantic component of these films from pre-feminist films is that there is no happy ending. In neither film does the hero live happily ever after with the heroine. In *Titanic* Jack does not even live, while Cal does. In *Shakespeare in Love,* Lord Wessex gets the girl. Oddly, though, the final resolution of both films is bittersweet, rather than tragic. In a time where most marriages end in divorce, happily ever after is just too unbelievable. They had their time, albeit short, and so that is better than never having loved at all. There were social forces that neither of these men had the resources to overcome. But we are not left with the gloom of some of the more biting commentaries from the 1950s. We are not left at the end here with an ever lonely Milton Warden in *From Here to Eternity* or drunken Jett Rink in *Giant,* mere victims of a social class structure which they can never influence. Barriers *were* overcome, if only temporarily.

In fact, one of the things we find most refreshing about both of these films is their lack of victimization. Rose will escape her arranged marriage, and while Viola will not, we have the authority of the Virgin Queen that she will control the marriage. Shakespeare writes. Cal gets reimbursed for his diamond, and Wessex gets enough money to revitalize his social standing. Only poor Jack gets nothing but an icy grave. But he is a victim of little more than a big chunk of ice, poor quality steel, and his own inability to float in water.

Chapter Notes

Introduction

1. We will use the term "box office" throughout the book. Partially this term disguises the fact that we often do not know much about the number of tickets actually sold (box office gross) until the last three decades. Strange as it may seem to us today when the movie industry is so driven by sales figures, up until the mid-1930s, the studios kept few records by individual film. From the earliest days of the American movie industry and continuing on into the 1950s, studios made the movies, distributed them, and mostly owned the chains of theaters which showed them. But by the 1930s there were enough independently owned theaters that the studios began keeping track of "rentals," which was what the theater owners paid to the distributing arms of the studios. Rentals are somewhat interesting data, but they do not reflect the actual number of paying customers: they are more equivalent to the number of screens showing films, although rentals were prorated on the size of the house. We have relied on a number of sources to determine box office, most notably the two editions of Susan Sackett's (1990; 1996) *The Hollywood Reporter Book of Box Office Hits.*

The April 29, 1994, issue of *Entertainment Weekly* provided an intriguing list that attempted to estimate from all sources (first and subsequent theatrical releases and video rentals) which movies have been viewed by the most individuals. The first five films in this list were *E.T.* (1982), *Gone with the Wind* (1939), *101 Dalmatians* (1961), *Star Wars* (1977), and *Fantasia* (1940). They make a comparison with a ranking of the top films by domestic gross, which were *E.T.* (1982), *Jurassic Park* (1993), *Star Wars* (1977), *Home Alone* (1990), *and Return of the Jedi* (1983).

2. A notable exception to this statement is the 1993 volume *Reflections in a Male Eye: The Films of John Huston,* edited by Gaylyn Studlar and David Desser.

3. Pleck and Pleck (1980) describe the period from 1860 to 1920 as the "Strenuous Life" society. During this period, both men and women were expected to be morally pure, although men were afforded recreational sex in a wide array of houses of prostitution. Life was strenuous, and the rise of institutions such as YMCAs and organized athletics gave men an alternative, outside of the home, to avoid tempta-

tions of the flesh. During this time, men bonded with other men, looking back nostalgically to the brotherhood of war. The Plecks believe that this male bonding was a reaction to the Suffrage Movement, and that men were threatened by women. It may be worth looking at silent films of the period before 1920 to see whether they conform to this idea. Certainly, the films of D. W. Griffith, such as *The Birth of a Nation* (1915) and *Broken Blossoms* (1919), portray male bonding and fear of women, respectively. But the films of Chaplin and Keaton — although life is always strenuous for these actors — seem not to involve fear of women. It would be a worthy addition to this analysis to examine the films of the period prior to 1920. We have not done so primarily because of the difficult issue of defining popularity, but also because we have more than enough material from the past 60 years.

Wars seem to be the markers in the Plecks' history. The Civil War (and the Suffrage Movement) signal the beginning of the Strenuous Life period; World War I, the beginning of the Companionate/Providing period; and the Vietnam War for what they describe as the "Contemporary Period." It seems odd to us that they do not recognize the impact of World War II.

One — Valentino, the First Star?

1. Francis X. Bushman probably deserves the real credit here. Halliwell (1980) describes him as "heavily built American leading actor of the silent era, once known as the handsomest man in the world" (p. 116). Formerly a stage actor and sculptor's model, he appeared in dozens of films annually from 1911 until 1920. His most important role was in the 1926 *Ben-Hur,* as Messala.

2. The "pink powder puff scandal" is worth mentioning in more detail. A Chicago journalist visited the men's room of a posh restaurant in the Windy City and noticed that face powder and powder puffs were being provided for customers. He drew the connection between the Valentino film and this accommodation to male fashion, and wrote a vitriolic attack on Valentino, suggesting that Valentino's personal use of make-up was corrupting male values. The article insinuated that Valentino was a homosexual. Some social historians have used this episode to suggest that Valentino's erotic film persona threatened American males, and that the only way the American male audience could deal with the Latin Lover was to queer him. Yet there is no evidence that this "scandal" affected Valentino's popularity, so there is probably little reason to attribute one journalist's anti–Valentino and anti-gay rantings to the "American male audience." Similar journalistic tactics have been levied in recent years against Tom Cruise, Richard Gere, Leonardo DiCaprio, and Kevin Spacey. A spicy account of the whole episode can be found in Kenneth Anger's (1975) *Hollywood Babylon.*

Valentino is a staple of commentary about how threatened American men are in the face of overtly expressed sexuality. But the evidence for this claim is tenuous. Women at the time clearly found him attractive, even when — or particularly when — he was playing the role of a seducer. But the typical male moviegoer also seemed to enjoy his films, as seen in the survey of high school students. That some contemporary commentators were threatened by his sexuality does not necessarily mean that most men in the audience were.

3. "Hooey" perhaps reflects our cultural imperialism. The filmmakers of 1920 were faced with the problem of translating a complex novel onto the screen, a novel in which meaning, reality, and symbol were importantly fused. Although films had been based on novels before this time, from Georges Méliès' *A Trip to the Moon* (1902) and Edwin S. Porter's *Uncle Tom's Cabin* (1903), nothing this complex had been attempted.

It is difficult now to realize how new all of these kinds of methods of story-telling were in 1920. And while the special effects may not satisfy our post–*Star Wars* view that films can represent anything, the fact that so much was attempted was a major draw to the audience of 1920.

4. Jackie Stacey's (1994) book *Star Gazing: Hollywood Cinema and Female Spectatorship* is influential in our understanding of how women might view with pleasure the scenes of abduction in *The Sheik* and its sequel. Drawing on a number of studies of romance novels and soap operas, Stacey comes to reject many of the Freudian and Lacanian analyses of similar films (she does not analyze Valentino's films themselves) by shifting from an analysis of the "text" to an analysis of the audience. Stacey's problem with most psychoanalytic readings of films is that a particular reading seems to be dogmatically decreed as the "correct" reading, without any possibility that audience members will read the film in a different way. Thus, it may be decreed that the only way of viewing this film is to suggest a rape or seduction fantasy in the male and female members of the audience. In contrast to the standard psychoanalytic-feminist view of this film, we might suspect there could be considerable interest in simply watching the physicality of Valentino's performance by both male and female audience members, as well as Agnes Ayres' strong rejection of her role as hostage. Following Stacey's logic, we suggest that the pleasure that many women could find in viewing a film such as *The Sheik* may come from the fact that Lady Diana is *not* raped and that her willful ways do not lead her to physical violation.

5. This is the plot of both versions of the film we have seen. *The American Film Institute Catalog* (Munden, 1971), however, has a distinctly different plot summary of the end: "Although he is indifferent to her, Diana nurses him back to health and declares her love for him. At last he relents, and they embark on their honeymoon." Perhaps there are alternative versions of the film, but we are unaware of them.

Two — 1939

1. In a very bawdy essay, Joe Fisher (1993) describes Gable's control over his reputation and what that reputation was, on screen, in the tabloids, and in the Hollywood rumor mill, and how that was used to advantage in the casting and publicity for *GWTW*. Fisher also suggests that the film is essentially an instructive tale about the Depression and the role of the South and of women in the "reconstruction" period of the late 1930s. Margaret Mitchell always adamantly denied that her story had anything to do with 20th century history.

2. Consider, for example Frank Nugent's (December 31, 1939) *New York Times* Ten-Best List, which included *Made for Each Other, Stagecoach, Wuthering Heights, Dark Victory, Juarez, Goodbye, Mr. Chips, The Women, Mr. Smith Goes to Washington, Ninotchka,* and *Gone with the Wind.*

3. The best work on the subject of women's appreciation of Scarlett and their reaction to this scene is found in Helen Taylor's (1993) *Scarlett's Women:* Gone with the Wind *and Its Female Fans.*

4. Like Salman Rushdie (1992), we find the black and white envelope of the film flawed. In the book, Dorothy goes to a real place called Oz and returns. The "and-then-I-woke-up-and-found-it-was-all-a-dream" finale, like the ending of every bad high school story, hurts the rest of the film. Rushdie's book may be the best piece of film criticism ever written, and it has clearly influenced our perspective here.

Three — Musicals of World War II

1. Early on in our investigation we came across Vivian C. Sobchack's (1975) brilliant essay "*The Leech Woman's* Revenge, or a Case for Equal Misrepresentation." Sobchack faces directly the issue of stereotypes in films, and she concludes that they are necessary, as they are in any other narrative medium. She draws primarily on E.M. Forster's (1927) *Aspects of the Novel*. In that essay, Forster distinguishes between "flat" and "round" characters. Most minor characters will be flat — comprised of a few broad strokes to make them memorable. In any novel or any movie, there will be many flat, stereotypical characters, and only a few round ones. One cannot spend as much time developing the character of sourpuss India Wilkes as Scarlett O'Hara.

While one does not become overly concerned about flat, minor characters in prose, there is a problem in the cinema, Sobchack points out, because the characters all appear round. Each character who appears on screen is dressed in a certain way, has mannerisms chosen by the actor or director, has certain specific facial features, appears in a specific context, in addition to his or her lines and position in the plot. We alluded to this problem when we suggested in the previous chapter that the Tin Man, the Scarecrow, and the Lion *should be* allegorical figures, but everything from their costumes and makeup to their individualistic singing and speaking voices tend to make them seem very round indeed.

Sobchack contends that an individual stereotyped performance should be of little concern. She suggests that we should be worried about stereotyping only if the same stereotype is projected in film after film. For example, regionalism is often portrayed stereotypically in the films of World War II, as part of a trope that shows how a diverse set of men unite into an *American* fighting unit, despite misgivings at first over regional differences. The Southern man is often portrayed as gregarious, loud, and ill-educated. Yet there are enough significant variations from this stereotype that any viewer who saw half a dozen films about the War would find many counterexamples.

2. And which they will still not lend out — which is why there will be no illustrations in the chapter on Disney.

Five — Casablanca

1. The film was given limited release in November 1942, but it was deemed to be primarily a film of 1943, because its national release occurred in January 1943.

2. I taught this film in a course entitled "Images of Masculinity in Popular American Films" at the American University in Bulgaria in 1998. Many of the students in this class had read Eco's essay in another class which had looked at the film. They were convinced that ugly stereotypes existed in this film. After viewing the film twice using Eco's scheme, we find no evidence for it. We are really not sure that Americans, either in 1942 or 1999, really have stereotypes for Russians (happy and stupid) or Bulgarians (sad and sexual). Most of Eco's comments seem to be both culturally-insensitive and downright wrong. They are, as mentioned in the Introduction, one of the main reasons that we decided to focus only on American films in this book. When we, as postwar Americans, look at Rossellini's (1946) *Roma, Città Aperta,* we notice, with more than a bit of skepticism, that all Italian men in this film are anti-Facist activists. The only Italian Fascist is young, female, bisexual, and drug-addicted. It is easy for us to view this film as an apologia for Fascism (it wasn't us, honest) rather than to see the film, as it should be, as a document about a large segment of the Italians in 1944.

There is an interesting aspect of the English translation of Eco's essay, an almost interchangeable use of the terms "stereotype" and "archetype." These are terms as psychologists we would like to keep separate, the former meaning an inappropriate generalization of a group characteristic to an individual (as assuming all Italians are hot-blooded lovers), and the latter a universal mythic form, such as the hero who must slay the dragon to save a group. (ADT)

3. I sat in on a course taught by my colleague John D. Wells at Mary Baldwin College on "Men in Society" in which *Casablanca* was shown. While most of the students responded positively to the film, a few indicated that they were uninterested in it because Bogart "wasn't buff" or "is ugly." One student wrote: "A story about this old guy and this pretty young girl is kind of gross, but the tension is great. I don't get why she likes either Rick or Laszlo."

Seven — Saints and Sinners: Masculinity in the Biblical Epics of the 1950s and 1960s

1. Solomon's (1978) fascinating book *The Ancient World in the Cinema* goes to great lengths to show how the filmmakers in many of these films went to elaborate, expensive efforts to get tiny details correct (e.g., exact copies of pharaonic costume) while occasionally completely missing the spirit of the times that were being depicted. But, for the most part, Solomon supports his premise that if the filmmakers went to the care of getting the details right, they also probably worked equally hard on other aspects of the storytelling.

Perhaps the most bizarre of these "authentic" details occurs when filmmakers attempted to get things right based on much later representations. For example, there is a flashback during Peter's sermon in *Quo Vadis?* when the apostles at the Last Supper assume the costumes, hairstyles, and poses of da Vinci's *Last Supper*; in a trailer to *The Ten Commandments*, director DeMille reports that his casting decision was based on the fact that Charlton Heston "looked like Moses," by which he meant Michelangelo's 16th century statue.

2. Sackett (1996) notes the strong visual comparisons between Victor Mature's look and the image Stallone uses in the Rambo films — long, curly, dark hair, sweat band, tightly bound waist with complete chest exposed, quiver, very dark skin. There are bondage scenes in *Rambo: First Blood, Part II* which seem directly copied from the slavery sequences in this film.

3. Apparently this was a theme that needed repeating to the 1950s audience three years later in *Seven Brides for Seven Brothers,* a musical based on the Roman myth of the Rape of the Sabine Women. In both of these films abduction works: Marcus will eventually have Lygia and the seven brothers get their brides. The only compensation for this view that what women really want is to be mastered is that in both cases there was mutual attraction before the abduction and that in these films no actual rape occurs: the moral of both stories might be construed to be that abduction creates more problems that necessary. This is a continued theme from the two Valentino Sheik films, and again, we see no necessity to assume a rape fantasy in the unconscious of the women in the audience who liked these films. Robert Taylor and the dancers in *Seven Brides* are interesting to look at and potentially desirable. Their actions are those of non-rapists.

4. An anonymous reviewer of an earlier version of this chapter took considerable exception to this statement. Aboard the galley, Arrius seems to be obsessed with Judah. He goes down in the galley and watches him straining at the oar. Although there is

no external documentation for the attraction, it seems obvious to us in watching the film. Others may disagree.

There is, however, external documentation for a sexual relationship between Judah and Messala. Gore Vidal (1976), who worked on the script, reports that he suggested that a previous adolescent sexual relationship which Messala wants to continue and which Judah has outgrown could possibly motivate the enormous hatred that Messala feels for Judah. That hatred must drive a very long movie, and the political motivation does seem flimsy. Vidal reports that director William Wyler agreed to the idea. Wyler neither confirmed nor denied Vidal's story. Yet there is no obvious trace of this specific back story in the film itself, although as we note, this is the one biblical epic where heterosexual love does not find a prominent place. But we want to avoid the pitfall of assuming that there must be sexuality in every screen performance, and therefore in the absence of overt heterosexuality there must be closeted homosexuality. There is no hint of it in the source material of Lew Wallace's novel, and just because Vidal suggested a homosexual relationship between the two male characters at one point in script development, this does not mean that this idea found its way into the film through subsequent script changes, decisions made by the director or editor, or the actors' interpretations. In other popular biblical epics, there are a number of examples of Roman homosexuality as one of the contrasts between the "good" heterosexual Christian and the "bad" Roman. On the other hand, there are many examples of extravagant ruthlessness on the part of Romans in trying to stamp out whatever is "non–Roman."

5. Virginia Wright Wexman's (1993) excellent book *Creating the Couple: Love, Marriage, and Hollywood Performance* has a lengthy chapter on the relationship between method acting and the portrayal of masculinity in crisis. In particular, she finds the method acting technique in films of the 1950s useful in portraying anxiety and conflict as forming a couple becomes more difficult.

Nine — Love Is Having to Say You're Sorry: Dysfunctional Families of the 1950s, 1960s and 1970s

1. This film also establishes the "prom" as a major film event. The prom in *Carrie* (1976) is certainly memorable, but there have also been a half dozen popular films over the past decade in which the prom — and its demarcation of sexuality — are central, *There's Something About Mary* (1998), *She's All That* (1998), *American Pie* (1999), *10 Things I Hate About You* (1999), among them.

2. How the film was expected to be viewed in 1958 is open to debate. There are two possible, very nuanced suggestions from Big Daddy that there was something "unmanly" about the relationship between Skipper and Brick, but we think that these would now be read by most viewers not as a suggestion of homoeroticism but as "not mature." Of course, any direct reference to homosexuality would have been forbidden by the Hayes Code and would have gotten any film which got by that censoring body in serious trouble with the Catholic Legion of Decency. Probably the film's writers and producers attempted a double meaning for the film. For most viewers, this is a film about taking on the male role: giving up boyhood chums and college sports for the real job of establishing a family. For those familiar with some versions of the Williams' play, the homoerotic theme is almost there, although in a very unspecified way. In some versions of the play Skipper *is* gay, and when he reveals his feelings to Brick, Brick severs their relationship.

3. As a publicity stunt, Hitchcock insisted that viewers not be admitted after the beginning of the film. Yet, one has to see the film from the beginning to get its full impact. This stunt reminds us that viewing films in 1960 was done differently than now. People routinely went to movies irrespective of starting times and watched through the end of the film, until "the point at which we came in." We have gotten more respectful of the narrative form in theaters — although the same method of watching films now occurs on pay-per-view channels.

4. Gus Van Sant's 1998 remake of *Psycho* is an interesting experiment. He used Hitchcock's shooting script with only a few minor changes in dialog and even camera angles. He retained the original score. The purpose, according to Van Sant, was to make the work accessible to younger audiences who had difficulty with the small, black and white format. There is a little more skin, notably Viggo Mortensen's, as Sam, and we know earlier on that Norman Bates is a loony because of Vince Vaughn's performance. Although the film received little critical acclaim and did not become a particular box office success, it is certainly worth a look by serious viewers of film to note how much decisions such as color, wide screen, and specific actors influence a film.

5. In a 1978 *Sight and Sound* review of the reedited epic for television, David Thompson makes an interesting point about the film:

> Then, in far smaller type, at the foot of the page, this grim waiver couched as solicitude: PARENTAL DISCRETION ADVISED. Has anyone adding that phrase ever wondered about the actual processes comprising parental judgment? Does anything else on TV help nourish it? Or is it simply the slick escape of the medium from the implications of offense and distress, as opposed to the reckless envy they will go out and buy? Did anyone pause to reflect how far *The Godfather* is a devout study of the efficacy of cruel parental discretion? Or is the skirting of real parental care only part of the pessimism that supports the inhumane patriarchy of *The Godfather* [p. 78]?

Eleven — Star Wars

1. In surveys I have conducted over the past several years in my undergraduate and graduate classes, one of the *Star Wars* films is the most frequently remembered first film, the most frequently listed "best" film, and the most frequently listed "favorite" film. Second place films are instructive as well. *Superman,* part of the sci-fi aftermath of *Star Wars,* is the second most remembered first film. For "best film," *Star Wars, Return of the Jedi, Forrest Gump,* and *Citizen Kane* each got about 10 percent of the vote. As for favorite film, *Titanic* was the clear second place favorite, slightly more popular among women than *Star Wars* films. (ADT)

2. The scene was originally conceived quite differently. Instead of the female character of Princess Leia, it was originally Luke's brother who put the plans in the droid. He was to lose his life in battle. Instead of a sacrificed brother, we are given his strong sister, who survives to fight. Of course, we do not know that Luke and Leia are brother and sister in this episode or even in the next sequel.

3. There are many references to popular and classic films in the *Star Wars* series, and Obi-Wan's gestures and his calm hypnosis-like effects within the unreal spaces of the renegade city seem to refer to *The Cabinet of Dr. Caligari* (1921). As Budd (1990) remarks about *Caligari,* the bizarreness of the costumes, faces, behavioral style, and incomprehensible spaces produce a very disquieting effect on the audience. Also, by

specifically referencing *Caligari*, who was anything but a benign mentor, Lucas sets up a moral ambiguity about Obi-Wan and the Force which pays off in the later films.

4. There are some problems in writing about this sequence as it was altered in the later "enhancement" of the original film. Two changes are particularly telling. The first is the inclusion of a scene between Jabba and Han, which some find successful, but many cultists dislike because Jabba is just too cute to be really menacing — for those the motivation to get out of town was more effective when Han was fighting off Jabba's lackeys and Jabba himself was an unseen menace. More importantly, the sequence of events when Han kills the assassin is altered. In the original version, sensing that he is about to be killed, Han raises his weapon and shoots. In the revised version, the assassin shoots first. Since these are our first impressions of Han, that impression is much different. In the first version, he was a pragmatic, amoral take charge individual, while the revision presents him as a more traditional hero — he kills only *in extremis*.

5. In an interview with Goldberg, Lofficier, Lofficier, and Rabkin (1995), the director, Richard Marquand, states categorically that *The Return of the Jedi* is not a sequel: "Is this a sequel? What this film does is end the third chapter of a coherent story. *Superman III* isn't the coherent end of anything; it's just a remake of the same movie. *James Bond* is merely a remake of an old movie and you just hope that this time they can remanipulate your characters and come up with something slightly different.... The actual *Star Wars* saga from chapters one through nine is a total symphony, if you like, though it's actually just a movie... I'm not making a sequel. I'm doing the third movement of a piece of music. The themes are being developed and ended here. That's why it's satisfying..." (p. 181).

Of course it *was* a sequel. And the metaphor of a symphony is inappropriate, because the themes of a symphony are different from movement to movement. That *Superman III* wasn't the coherent ending of anything (and it wasn't) is irrelevant.

6. It may be way too much to expect to make sense of all of the Force ideas here. But it may be that sympathy and empathy are good emotions to have, while anger and fear are bad ones. Much of this has to do with the Hollywood version of the martial arts (and Eastern philosophies in general), which are usually portrayed as based on enigmatic paradoxes. So righting a wrong is a good thing, but alleviating the suffering of your friends might be too personal and lead you from a sense of justice to anger.

Twelve — Disney's Men and Boys

1. As we were about to put this book to bed, a coalition of major organizations, led by the American Medical Association and the American Psychological Association, came forward with a statement that "epidemic" violence among young people was directly linked to the presentations of violence in the media. Various media spokespersons immediately suggested that the media are only reflecting the nature of present day society. This is an interesting example of our premise that movies (and by extension all media) both reflect and influence behavior.

Of course, the suggestion that we live in one of the most violent of all times is sheer exaggeration. We reside in a community of 35,000 with a murder rate of about four people per year. Rome, in the full flower of the Renaissance, was a city of about this size, with a *daily* murder rate of eight to ten.

2. Another criticism of feminists about Disney films is the overrepresentation of evil mothers and sinister women. But this seems to be a lingering tradition from children's literature of evil stepmothers and witches. There is something much more

sinister, however, about a child being imprisoned by a man than it is for a child to be held by a woman, if for no other reason than that women are less physically powerful and can sometimes be counted on to exhibit maternal instincts. Viewing the film, *The Rescuers,* and its remake *The Rescuers Down Under,* can make this point clearly. In both films, children are held captive, but in *The Rescuers Down Under,* it is a male trapper who holds the child, and it is difficult not to make some connections with child abuse. The *Rescuers Down Under* is about the only Disney animation of the 1990s which failed at the box office, we think not only because of the sinister male presence which turned off parents, but because it has a very strange ending: rather than being reunited with his distraught mother at the end of the film, the boy goes off with his animal friends.

Of course we are talking about animated women here. Glenn Close is disturbing as Cruella DeVil in the 1996 live-action *101 Dalmatians.* That film is also marred because the dogs don't talk.

Thirteen — Gump *and* Gumper: Men as Idiots

1. Lawrence's point is that Hollywood has tended to silence women's voices, but the primary examples in her book are films with central women characters, written and directed by men, based on literary works authored by men. She gives counterexamples of situations in which women's voices emerge, which are when women serve as important roles in the making of the film.

2. See, for example, the 1994 Gallup Poll on Work and Family published in *USA Today,* May, 14, 1994.

3. Elwood P. Dowd in *Harvey* says that his mother told him he either had to be "oh, so smart" or "oh, so nice" in order to be successful in life. Elwood concludes: "Nice is better." Gump owes much to Elwood. Both seem to have a philosophy of life based on maternal aphorisms. Both strike up conversations with strangers, which seems to be their principal vocation. Both are non functional in society: Forrest is borderline mentally retarded, while Elwood is an alcoholic who would be institutionalized by film's end were it not for the fact that the hospital's psychiatrist is a bigger flake than he is — just as high school coaches, college admissions officials, and army recruiters seemed to overlook Forrest's limitations.

4. Need we suggest that a whole history of the representation of masturbation in film needs to be written, from Shirley MacLaine's rousing, unapologetic performance in *Being There* (1979) and Judge Reinhold's embarrassing moment in *Fast Times at Ridgemont High* (1982), where a self-pleasure session is interrupted by a sister, to Jeremy Davies's sessions in *Spanking the Monkey* (1994) and the pie sequence in *American Pie* (1999). Self-love becomes possible to portray, when other love becomes difficult.

Fourteen — Post-Feminist Heroes: Jack and Shakespeare

1. Kenneth Turan's review in the *Los Angeles Times*, for example, begins with the question, "What does $200 million buy?" and he suggests that it could put on a presidential campaign or put a dent into poverty or sink a 90 percent scale model of the *Titanic* in a 17-million gallon tank. The rest of the review is not friendly.

2. Kenneth Turan began his review of the film with the phrase "a ray of light in a holiday film season that was starting to look as gloomy as the scowl on Ebenezer Scrooge's face." He does go on to call the film a confection, but he views it as a decidedly well crafted one, text-wise and visually.

3. While the references to *Romeo and Juliet* are more obvious, much of the film parallels the second play *Twelfth Night* in which Duke Orsino falls in love with his page, who is a shipwrecked woman protecting herself by disguising herself as a man.

4. When we presented an early version of this paper at the Popular Culture Association in New Orleans (Trice, Holland, and Wells, 2000), there were several British audience members who took issue with this analysis. Their assumption was that Rose was an Anglophile snob who actually liked all the glamour and elitism of the first class dining room and was fascinated with the meaning and price of the diamond.

Bibliography

Afield. (1990). We say "Two Paws Up" to These. *Sierra, 75* (2), 18–19.

Agee, James. (1958). *Agee on Film: Reviews and Comments.* Boston, MA: Beacon Press.

Alan, R. (1988). Fifty Years of Snow White. *Journal of Popular Film and Television, 15,* 157–159.

Amis, Kingsley. (1965). *The James Bond Dossier.* New York: New American Library.

Anger, Kenneth. (1975). *Hollywood Babylon.* New York: Dell.

Austin, Bruce A. (1984). Portrait of an Art Film Audience. *Journal of Communication, 34,* 74–87.

Beesley, Lawrence. (1912). *The Loss of the S.S.* Titanic. New York: Houghton-Mifflin.

Bem, Sandra L. (1974). The Measurement of Psychological Androgyny. *Journal of Consulting and Clinical Psychology, 42,* 155–162.

Bloom, Harold. (1998). *Shakespeare: The Invention of the Human.* New York: Riverhead Books.

Bly, Robert. (1989). *Iron John: A Book About Men.* New York: Addison-Wesley.

Boyd, Ann S. (1967). *The Devil in James Bond.* Richmond, VA: John Knox.

Budd, Mike. (1990). The Moments of *Caligari.* In Mike Budd (Ed.), *The Cabinet of Dr. Caligari: Texts, Contexts, Histories* (pp. 7–120). New Brunswick, NJ: Rutgers University Press.

Capra, Frank. (1971). *The Name Above the Title: An Autobiography.* New York: Macmillan.

Chapman, James. (2000). *License to Thrill: A Cultural History of the James Bond Films.* New York: Columbia University.

Crowther, Bosley. (June 5, 1942). [Review of *Mrs. Miniver.*] *New York Times,* 21:3.

_____. (March 2, 1959). There's Always "Snow White" and "Henry V." *New York Times,* II, 1:8.

Dick, Bernard F. (1996). *The Star-Spangled Screen: The American World War II Film.* Lexington, KY: University of Kentucky.

Doherty, Thomas. (1993). *Projections of War: Hollywood, American Culture, and World War II.* New York: Columbia University.

Ebert, Roger. (August 7, 1998). [Review of *There's Something About Mary*]. *Chicago Sun-Times. www.suntimes.com/ebert/ebert_reviews/1998/07/071501.html.*

Eco, Umberto. (1990). *Travels in Hyperreality.* New York: Harcourt Brace.

———, & del Buono, Oreste (Eds.). (1966). *The Bond Affair.* London: MacDonald.

Entertainment Weekly. (April 29, 1994). The Big Pictures. *Entertainment Weekly, #220,* 24–25, 28–30, 32–34, 36–38, 40–41.

Feuer, Jane. (1993). *The Hollywood Musical* (2nd Ed.). Bloomingdale, IN: Indiana University.

Fisher, Joe. (1993). Clark Gable's Balls: Real Men Never Lose Their Teeth. In Pat Kirkham and Janet Thumim (Eds). *You Tarzan: Masculinity, Movies and Men.* New York: St. Martin's Press.

Fleming, Ian. (1953). *Casino Royale.* London: Jonathan Cape.

Forster, E. M. (1927/1954). *Aspects of the Novel.* New York: Harvest Books.

Franson, J. Karl. (1995). From Vanity Fair to Emerald City: Baum's debt to Bunyan. *Children's Literature, 23,* 91–114.

Gilligan, Carole. (1988). *In a Different Voice.* Cambridge, MA: Harvard University Press.

Goldberg, Lee, Lofficier, Randy, Lofficer, Jean-Marc, & Rabkin, William. (1995). *Science Fiction Filmmaking in the 1980s: Interviews with Actors, Directors, Producers and Writers.* Jefferson, NC: McFarland.

Grant, Elliott Mansfield. (1945). *The Career of Victor Hugo.* Cambridge, MA: Harvard University Press.

Grey, Rudolph. (1994). *Nightmare of Ecstasy: The Life and Art of Edward D. Wood, Jr.* Portland, OR: Feral House.

Griffith, R., & Mayer, A. (1957). *The Movies.* New York: Simon and Schuster.

Grimm, Jacob, & Grimm, Wilhelm. (1945). *The Complete Grimm's Fairy Tales.* New York: Pantheon.

Halliwell, Leslie. (1980). *The Filmgoer's Companion* (6th Ed.). New York: Avon.

Harmetz, Aljean. (1992). *Round Up the Usual Suspects: The Making of* Casablanca — *Bogart, Bergman, and World War II.* New York: Hyperion.

Haskell, Molly. (1987). *From Reverence to Rape: The Treatment of Women in the Movies* (2nd Ed). Chicago, IL: University of Chicago Press.

Hibbin, Nina. (October 6, 1962). [Review of *Dr. No.*] *Daily Worker.*

Howe, Desson. (August 7, 1992). [Review of *Unforgiven.*] *Washington Post. www.washingtonpost.com/wp-srv/style/longterm/movies/videos/.*

Jacobs, Lewis. (1967). *The Rise of the American Film: A Critical History.* New York: Teachers College.

Jeffords, Susan. (1994). *Hard Bodies: Hollywood Masculinity in the Reagan Era.* New Brunswick, NJ: Rutgers University Press.

Johnson, Paul. (April 5, 1958). Sex, Snobbery, and Sadism. *New Statesman, 55,* 430–432.

Kael, Pauline. (May 30, 1983). Fun Machines. *New Yorker, 89,* 17–18.

Kalogerakis, George. (March, 1997). Mob Cat. *Premiere, 10* (7), 57–60.

Kasdan, Lawrence, & Lucas, George. (1997). *Return of the Jedi: The Illustrated Screenplay.* New York: Ballantine.

Kawin, Bruce F., & Mast, Gerald. (1992). *A Short History of the Movies* (5th Ed). New York: Macmillan.

Kirkham, Pat, & Thumim, Janet (Eds.). (1993). *You Tarzan: Masculinity, Movies and Men.* New York: St. Martin's Press.

Koszarski, Richard. (1990). *History of the American Cinema: 3. An Evening's Entertainment: The Age of the Silent Feature Picture, 1915–1928.* New York: Charles Scribner's Sons.

Lawrence, Amy. *Echo and Narcissus.* (1991). Berkeley, CA: University of California Press.

Littlefield, Henry M. (1964). *The Wizard of Oz:* Parable on Populism. *American Quarterly, 16,* 47–58.

Maltin, Leonard. (1995). *Leonard Maltin's Movie and Video Guide 1995.* New York: Signet.

Marsh, Ed W. (1997). *James Cameron's* Titanic. New York: HarperCollins.

Maslin, Janet. (July 6, 1994). [Review of *Forrest Gump.*] *New York Times.*

Mellen, Joan. (1977). *Big Bad Wolves: Masculinity in the American Film.* New York: Pantheon.

Munden, Kenneth W. (1971). *The American Film Institute Catalog of Motion Pictures Produced in the United States: Feature Films, 1921–1930.* New York: R. R. Bowker.

New York Times. (November 7, 1921). [Review of *The Wonderful Thing* and *The Sheik.*] N 7, 20:1.

Nugent, Frank S. (1938). [Review of *Snow White and the Seven Dwarfs.*] *New York Times,* January 14, 21:1.

_____. (October 20, 1939). [Review of *Mr. Smith Goes to Washington.*] *New York Times,* 27:2.

_____. (December 20, 1939). [Review of *Gone with the Wind.*] *New York Times,* 31:2.

_____. (December 31, 1939). Tradition Dictates Another "Ten-Best." *New York Times, IX,* 5:1.

_____. (January 1, 1940). [Review of *The Hunchback of Notre Dame.*] *New York Times,* 29:4.

Only in America. (1993). [Sexist stereotypes in Disney's *Snow White and the Seven Dwarfs.*] *Fortune, 128* (3), 96.

Palmer, William J. (1993). *The Films of the Eighties: A Social History.* Carbondale, IL: Southern Illinois University Press.

Pleck, Joseph H., and Pleck, E. H. (1980). *The American Man.* Englewood Cliffs, NJ: Prentice Hall.

Price, Thomas J. (1992). The Changing Image of the Soviets in the Bond Saga: From Bond-Villains to "Acceptable Role Partners. *Journal of Popular Culture, 26,* 17–37.

Pye, Michael, & Myles, Linda. (1979). *The Movie Brats: How the Film Generation Took Over Hollywood.* New York: Holt, Rinehart, and Winston.

Richler, Mordecai. (1972). *Shoveling Trouble.* Toronto: McClelland & Stewart.

Robb, Brian. J. (1996). *Johnny Depp: A Modern Rebel.* London: Plexus.

Rosenberg, Bruce A., & Stewart, Ann Harleman. (1989). *Ian Fleming.* Boston: Twayne Publishers.

Rosenstone, Robert A. (1995). *Visions of the Past: The Challenge of Film to Our Idea of History.* Cambridge, MA: Harvard University Press.

Rosenthal, Donna McCrohan. (1999). Personal communication with author.

Rottenberg, Josh. (March, 1997). Arrested Development. *Premiere* 62–68, 100.

Rubin, Steven Jay. (1995). *The Complete James Bond Movie Encyclopedia.* Chicago, IL: Contemporary Books.

Rushdie, Salman. (1992). *The Wizard of Oz.* London: BFI Books.

Sackett, Susan. (1990). *The Hollywood Reporter Book of Box Office Hits.* New York: Billboard Books.

_____. (1996). *The Hollywood Reporter Book of Box Office Hits* (2nd Ed.). New York: Billboard Books.

Sarris, Andrew. (1990). James Stewart. *Film Comment, 26* (2), 29–30.

Sidey, Hugh. (March 17, 1961). The President's Voracious Reading Habits. *Life, 50,* 55–60.

Slide, Anthony. (1986). "Rudolph Valentino." In James Vinson (Ed.). *The International Dictionary of Films and Filmmakers: III. Actors and Actresses.* Chicago, IL: St. James.

_____. (1988). *Early Women Directors.* New York: A. S. Barnes.

Slotkin, Richard. (1992). *Gunfighter Nation: The Myth of the Frontier in Twentieth-Century America.* New York: Atheneum.

Sobchack, Vivian C. (1975). *The Leech Woman's* Revenge, or a Case for Equal Misrepresentation. *Journal of Popular Film, 4,* 236–257.

Sodowsky, Alice, Sodowsky, Roland, and Witte, Stephen. (1975). The Epic World of *American Graffiti. Journal of Popular Film, 4,* 47–57.

Solomon, Jon. (1978). *The Ancient World in the Cinema.* New York: A. S. Barnes.

Stacey, Jackie. (1994). *Star Gazing: Hollywood Cinema and Female Spectatorship.* London: Routledge.

Studlar, Gaylyn, & Desser, David (Eds.). (1993). *Reflections in a Male Eye: John Huston and the American Experience.* Washington, DC: Smithsonian Institution Press.

Taylor, Helen. (1989). *Scarlett's Women:* Gone with the Wind *and Its Female Fans.* London: Virago.

Thompson, David. (1978). The Discreet Charm of the Godfather. *Sight and Sound, 47,* 76–80.

Time. (April 6, 1998). DiCaprio *au Naturel.* 79–81.

Trice, Ashton D., Holland, Samuel A., & Wells, John D. (April, 2000). *Masculinity in Recent Academy Award Winning Movies.* Paper presented at the Popular Culture Association meeting. New Orleans, LA.

Truffaut, Francois, & Scott, Helen G. (1983; 1984, English version). *Hitchcock.* New York: Touchstone Books.

Turan, Kenneth. (December 19, 1997). "Titanic" Sinks Again (Spectacularly). *Los Angeles Times.*

_____. (December 11, 1998). *Shakespeare in Love*: A Welcome Winter's Tale. *Los Angeles Times.*

USA Today. (May 14, 1994).[Gallup Poll on Work and Family.] First section, 1.

_____. (August 7, 2000). Subtly Powerful Screen Force Alec Guinness Dies at 86. Entertainment section, 1.

Vidal, Gore. (November 17, 1976). Who Makes the Movies? *New York Review of Books,* 17.

Walsh, Andrea S. (1984). *Women's Films and Female Experience.* New York: Praeger.

Wells, J. D., & Trice, A. D. (March, 1993).*Changing Images of Men in American Films: An Analysis by Genre and Decade.* Virginia Humanities Conference, Williamsburg, VA.

Wexman, Virginia Wright. (1993). *Creating the Couple: Love, Marriage, and Hollywood Performance.* Princeton, NJ: Princeton University Press.

Yates, John. (1975). *Godfather* Saga: The Death of the Family. *Journal of Popular Film, 4,* 157–168.

Index

229